FOOD&**WINE**

Wine
Guide
2016

D1316813

by the Editors of Food & Wine and Richard Nalley

FOOD & WINE WINE GUIDE 2016

Published by Time Inc. Books
1271 Avenue of the Americas, 6th floor
New York, NY 10020
Copyright © 2015 Time Inc. Books

editor in chief **DANA COWIN**
executive wine editor **RAY ISLE**
editor **SUSAN CHOUNG**

volume editor **WENDY G. RAMUNNO**
copy editor **ANN LIEN**
research chief **JANICE HUANG**
researchers **MARY KAN, ELLEN MCCURTIN, PAOLA SINGER**
digital coordinator **JOHN KERN**

cover photography **ULF SVANE**

produced for FOOD & WINE by
gonzalez defino editorial & design / gonzalezdefino.com
principals **JOSEPH GONZALEZ, PERRI DEFINO**

ISBN-10: 0-8487-4650-3
ISBN-13: 978-0-8487-4650-6

ISSN 1522-001X
Manufactured in the United States of America

FOOD&WINE
BOOKS

FOOD&WINE

Wine
Guide

2016

FRANCE
ITALY
SPAIN
PORTUGAL
GERMANY
AUSTRIA
GREECE
UNITED STATES
AUSTRALIA
NEW ZEALAND
ARGENTINA
CHILE
SOUTH AFRICA

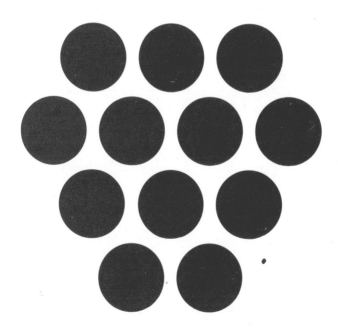

Contents

OLD WORLD

France   16

   ALSACE   19

   BORDEAUX   24

   BURGUNDY   33
   Beaujolais   43

   LOIRE VALLEY   45

   RHÔNE VALLEY   52

   SOUTHERN FRANCE   61

Italy   66

   PIEDMONT   69

   OTHER NORTHERN ITALY   76

   TUSCANY   82

   OTHER CENTRAL ITALY   93

   SOUTHERN ITALY   97

Spain   104

   RIOJA & NAVARRA   107

   GALICIA   114

   SOUTHEASTERN SPAIN   117

   CATALONIA   119

   CASTILLA Y LEÓN   121

Portugal   126

Germany   134

Austria   144

Greece   154

2016

NEW WORLD

United States	162
CALIFORNIA	165
OREGON	203
WASHINGTON STATE	210
OTHER US STATES	218
Australia	222
New Zealand	238
Argentina	248
Chile	256
South Africa	266

OLD & NEW WORLDS

Champagne & Other Sparkling Wines	274
CHAMPAGNE	275
OTHER SPARKLING WINES	282
Fortified & Dessert Wines	290
FORTIFIED WINES	291
Sherry	291
Port	294
DESSERT WINES	297

Key to Symbols	6
Foreword	7
Wine Terms	8
Buying Guide	11
Pairing Guide	302
Pairing Chart	304
Recipes	310
Index of Producers	316

KEY TO SYMBOLS

TYPE OF WINE

- ● RED
- ● ROSÉ
- ○ WHITE

PRICE

$$$$	OVER $60
$$$	$30+ TO $60
$$	$15+ TO $30
$	$15 AND UNDER

FOR MORE EXPERT WINE-BUYING ADVICE

Visit *foodandwine.com*

Follow us *@foodandwine*

Foreword

There's a big, big world of wine out there. With over 8,000 producers in America alone, it's tough to sort out the choices. Our mission at FOOD & WINE is to cut through the clutter. In our Tasting Room, we sample thousands of bottles each year, at every price. This work is the backbone of our wine articles, and helps suggest pairings for our recipes. It's also crucial for this book, our yearly guide to the world's most trustworthy producers. With these names at hand, you'll be able to pick a great bottle, no matter where you happen to be. Our goal is to simplify the process of buying wine. We hope you feel we've succeeded.

Dana Cowin
Editor in Chief
FOOD & WINE

Ray Isle
Executive Wine Editor
FOOD & WINE

Wine Terms

You won't find much fussy wine jargon in this guide, but some of the terms commonly used to describe the taste of wine might be unfamiliar or used in an unfamiliar way. References to flavors and textures other than "grape" are meant to serve as analogies: All the wines in this guide are made from grapes, but grapes have the ability to suggest the flavors of other fruits, herbs or minerals. Here's a mini glossary to help you become comfortable with the language of wine.

ACIDITY The tart, tangy or zesty sensations in wine. Ideally, acidity brightens a wine's flavors as a squeeze of lemon brightens fish. Wines lacking acidity taste "flabby."

APPELLATION An officially designated winegrowing region. The term is used mostly in France and the US. In Europe, a wine's appellation usually reflects not only where it's from but also aspects of how it's made, such as vineyard yields and aging.

BALANCE The harmony between acidity, tannin, alcohol and sweetness in a wine.

BIODYNAMICS An organic, sustainable approach to farming that takes into account a farm's total environment, including surrounding ecosystems and astronomical considerations, such as the phases of the moon.

BODY How heavy or thick a wine feels in the mouth. Full-bodied or heavy wines are often described as "big."

CORKED Wines that taste like wet cork or newspaper are said to be corked. The cause is trichloroanisole (TCA), a contaminant sometimes transmitted by cork.

CRISP A term used to describe wines that are high in acidity.

CRU In France, a grade of vineyard (such as *grand cru* or *premier cru*), winery (such as Bordeaux's *cru bourgeois*) or village (in Beaujolais). Also used unofficially in Italy's Piedmont region to refer to top Barolo vineyards.

CUVÉE A batch of wine. A cuvée can be from a single barrel or tank (*cuve* in French), or a blend of different lots of wine. A Champagne house's top bottling is called a *tête de cuvée.*

DRY A wine without perceptible sweetness. A dry wine, however, can have powerful fruit flavors. *Off-dry* describes a wine that has a touch of sweetness.

EARTHY An earthy wine evokes flavors such as mushrooms, leather, damp straw or even manure.

FILTER/FINE Processes used to remove sediment or particulates from a wine to enhance its clarity.

FINISH The length of time a wine's flavors linger on the palate. A long finish is the hallmark of a more complex wine.

FRUITY A wine with an abundance of fruit flavors is described as fruity. Such wines may give the impression of sweetness, even though they're not actually sweet.

HERBACEOUS Calling a wine herbaceous or herbal can be positive or negative. Wines that evoke herb flavors can be delicious. Wines with green pepper flavors are less than ideal, and are also referred to as "vegetal."

LEES The sediment (including dead yeast cells) left over after a wine's fermentation. Aging a wine on its lees (*sur lie* in French) gives wine nutty flavors and a creamy texture.

MINERAL Flavors that (theoretically) reflect the minerals found in the soil in which the grapes were grown. The terms *steely, flinty* and *chalky* are also used to describe these flavors.

NÉGOCIANT In wine terms, a *négociant* (French for "merchant") is someone who buys grapes, grape juice or finished wines in order to blend, bottle and sell wine under his or her own label.

NOSE How a wine smells; its bouquet or aroma.

OAKY Wines that transmit the flavors of the oak barrels in which they were aged. Some oak can impart toast flavors.

OXIDIZED Wines that have a tarnished quality due to exposure to air are said to be oxidized. When intended, as in the case of sherry (see p. 291), oxidation can add fascinating dimensions to a wine. Otherwise, it can make a wine taste unappealing.

PALATE The flavors, textures and other sensations a wine gives in the mouth. The term *mid-palate* refers to the way these characteristics evolve with time in the mouth.

POWERFUL Wine that is full of flavor, tannin and/or alcohol.

RUSTIC Wine that is a bit rough, though often charming.

TANNIN A component of grape skins, seeds and stems, tannin is most commonly found in red wines. It imparts a puckery sensation similar to oversteeped tea. Tannin also gives a wine its structure and enables some wines to age well.

TERROIR A French term that refers to the particular attributes a wine acquires from the specific environment of a vineyard—i.e., the climate, soil type, elevation and aspect.

Buying Guide

Knowing where and how to shop for wine makes discovering great wines easy and even fun, no matter where you live or what your budget. Take advantage of these tips to shop smarter.

IN SHOPS

SCOPE OUT THE SHOPS Visit local wine shops and determine which ones have the most helpful salespeople, the best selection and the lowest prices. Ask about case discounts, and whether mixing and matching a case is allowed. Expect at least a 10 percent discount; some stores will offer more. These days, many retailers are increasing their discounts and offering one-liter bottles and three-liter wine boxes that deliver more wine for the money. Finally, pay attention to store temperature: The warmer the store, the more likely the wines are to have problems.

ASK QUESTIONS Most wine-savvy salespeople are eager to share their knowledge and recommend some of their favorite wines. Let them know your likes, your budget and anything else that might help them select a wine you'll love.

BECOME A REGULAR The better the store's salespeople know you, the better they can suggest wines that will please you. Take the time to report back on wines they've suggested—it will pay off in future recommendations.

GET ON THE LIST Top wine shops often alert interested customers to special sales, hard-to-find wines or great deals in advance. Ask to get on their e-mail lists.

ONLINE

KNOW YOUR OPTIONS Take advantage of the Internet to easily find the wine you want and get the best price on it. The two most common ways to buy wine online are via online retailers or directly from wineries. Retailers may offer bulk discounts if you buy a case and/or shipping discounts if you spend a certain amount. Wineries don't often discount, but their wines can be impossible to find elsewhere. A great advantage of online shopping is price comparison: Websites like Wine-Searcher.com allow you to compare prices at retailers around the world.

BE WILLING TO ACT FAST Some of the steepest discounts on prestigious or hard-to-find wines are offered via so-called "flash sales" at sites such as WineAccess.com, WinesTilSoldOut.com and Lot18.com. Announced by e-mail, sales typically last just a day or two, and the best deals might sell out in under an hour.

KNOW THE RULES The difference between browsing for wine online and actually purchasing it has everything to do with where you live and how "liberal" your state is about interstate wine shipments. The laws governing direct-to-consumer interstate shipments differ from state to state. If you're considering buying wine from an out-of-state vendor, find out first whether it can ship to your state.

KNOW THE WEATHER If you're ordering wine online when it's hot outside, it's worth paying for express delivery: A week spent roasting in the back of a delivery truck risks turning your prized case of Pinot into plonk. Some retailers and wineries offer free storage during the summer months; they'll hold purchased wine until the weather cools and you give the OK to ship.

IN RESTAURANTS

CHECK OUT THE LIST Many restaurants post their wine list online or are happy to e-mail it upon request. Scoping out the wine menu in advance dramatically increases your odds of picking the right wine for your meal. For starters, if the selection looks poor, you can ask about the restaurant's corkage policy and perhaps bring your own bottle instead. A mediocre list might be limited in selection, have a disproportionate number of wines from one producer, fail to specify vintages or carry old vintages of wines meant to be drunk young and fresh. When faced with a bad wine list, order the least expensive bottle that you recognize as being reasonably good.

On the other hand, if the list is comprehensive, you can spend all the time you like perusing it in advance, rather than boring your dining companions while you pore over it at the table. You'll have plenty of time to spot bargains (or overpriced bottles) and to set an ordering strategy based on the list's strengths and your own preferences.

ASK QUESTIONS Treat the wine list as you would a food menu. You should ask how the Bordeaux tastes in comparison to the California Cabernet as readily as you'd ask about the difference between two fish dishes. Ask to speak to the wine director, if there is one. Then, tell that person the type of wine you're looking for—the price range, the flavor profile—as well as the dishes you will be having. If you want to indicate a price range without announcing the amount to the table, point to a bottle on the list that costs about what you want to spend and explain that you are considering something like it. And if you're unsure how to describe the flavors you're looking for, name a favorite producer who makes wine in a style you like. With this information, the wine director should be able to recommend several options.

TASTE THE WINE When the bottle arrives, make sure it's exactly what you ordered—check the vintage, the producer and the blend or variety. If it's not, speak up. You may be presented with the cork. Ignore it. Instead, sniff the wine in your glass. If it smells like sulfur, cabbage or skunk, tell your server that you think the wine might be flawed and request a second opinion from the wine director or the manager. If there's something truly wrong, they should offer you a new bottle or a new choice.

OLD WOR

16
FRANCE

66
ITALY

134
GERMANY

144
AUSTRIA

LD

France
Italy
Spain
Portugal
Germany
Austria
Greece

104
SPAIN

126
PORTUGAL

154
GREECE

France

As an old French saying has it, "Burgundy for kings, Champagne for duchesses, claret for gentlemen." But what about crisp Vouvray from the Loire? Or summery rosés from the coast of Provence, or great red Hermitage from its famed hill in the northern Rhône? (Besides, reserving Burgundy just for kings seems more than a little unfair.) No matter who's opening the bottle, France is the most significant country in the world when it comes to wine. It's the birthplace of most of the grapes we know best, and it produces more than a billion gallons of wine every year–everything from utterly nondescript bottles to the greatest wines in the world. There's no way around it: If you want to learn about wine, you have to learn about France.

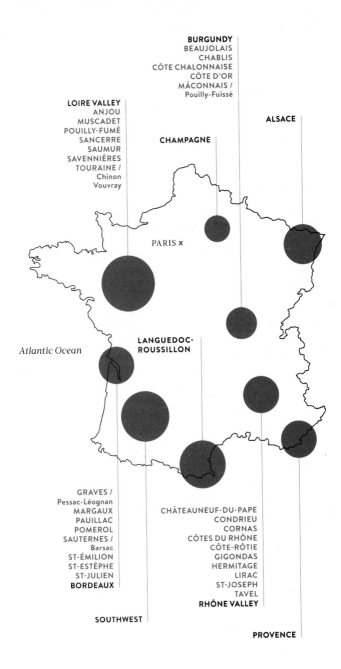

BURGUNDY
BEAUJOLAIS
CHABLIS
CÔTE CHALONNAISE
CÔTE D'OR
MÂCONNAIS /
Pouilly-Fuissé

LOIRE VALLEY
ANJOU
MUSCADET
POUILLY-FUMÉ
SANCERRE
SAUMUR
SAVENNIÈRES
TOURAINE /
Chinon
Vouvray

ALSACE

CHAMPAGNE

PARIS x

**LANGUEDOC-
ROUSSILLON**

Atlantic Ocean

GRAVES /
Pessac-Léognan
MARGAUX
PAUILLAC
POMEROL
SAUTERNES /
Barsac
ST-ÉMILION
ST-ESTÈPHE
ST-JULIEN
BORDEAUX

CHÂTEAUNEUF-DU-PAPE
CONDRIEU
CORNAS
CÔTES DU RHÔNE
CÔTE-RÔTIE
GIGONDAS
HERMITAGE
LIRAC
ST-JOSEPH
TAVEL
RHÔNE VALLEY

SOUTHWEST

PROVENCE

WINE TERMINOLOGY

France's Appellation d'Origine Contrôlée (AOC, or "controlled region of origin") regulations ensure the authenticity and local origin of everything from cheeses to lavender. The French regulations governing wine are, not surprisingly, among the most sophisticated in the world, which can also make them tricky to understand. The important point is that most French wine labels, with a few exceptions, are based on place names—called appellations—rather than grape names. To use an appellation on a label—Bordeaux, for example—a producer is required to follow rules designed to ensure that the wine reflects a certain style and quality. The regulations may cover everything from permitted grape varieties and harvest dates to aging periods and production methods. The most prestigious appellations are tiny sub-appellations within larger regions, or in some cases, single vineyards. In general, the smaller and more specific the place name, the stricter its rules.

APPELLATION D'ORIGINE CONTRÔLÉE/APPELLATION D'ORIGINE PROTÉGÉE (AOC/AOP) At the top of the quality ladder are AOC wines (the full title appears spelled out on labels: "Appellation Chablis Contrôlée," for instance). Regulations vary by appellation, but might typically specify permitted grapes, winemaking practices, minimum alcohol levels and harvest size (overly large harvests tend to yield diluted wines). A newer designation for AOC wines is AOP ("protected region of origin"), which EU regulators hope all member countries will soon employ.

VIN DE PAYS/INDICATION GÉOGRAPHIQUE PROTÉGÉE (VDP/IGP) The VdP/IGP category includes wines from six broad regional zones (such as the Pays d'Oc, which stretches from the Pyrenees to the Rhône). The category's requirements are less stringent than AOC regulations, allowing for higher yields and greater freedom in choosing grape varieties. Winemakers may also label VdP/IGP wines with the grape variety. The category is appealing to those who wish to produce large quantities of commercial wines, and to independently minded vintners who take advantage of the designation's relative freedom to put out quirky, high-quality bottlings.

VIN DE FRANCE/VIN DE TABLE The bottom of the three quality rungs, the Vin de France category was introduced in 2010 to incorporate the old Vin de Table ("table wine") designation that is gradually being phased out. Meant to attract drinkers who are more interested in grape variety and brand name than in origin, this new category allows winemakers to blend wines from different regions and still list vintage and variety information on the labels.

ALSACE

CLAIM TO FAME

Alsace produces some of the world's finest Rieslings and Gewürztraminers, two Germanic grapes that reflect the bicultural heritage of this eastern border region. Blocked from cool, wet Atlantic weather by the Vosges Mountains, the dry, relatively sunny Alsatian climate creates wines that are lusher and more powerful than the typical German versions (though the difference has diminished considerably over the past generation). Their combination of zesty acidity and minerality makes them incredibly food-friendly, while their reasonable prices offer terrific value. Alsace's wines are also refreshingly easy for Americans to identify and understand: Bottled in traditional, tapered green glass, they carry the name of their grape variety (or type of blend) on the label.

🍇 KEY GRAPES: WHITE

GEWÜRZTRAMINER Often produced in an off-dry (i.e., slightly sweet) style, the spicy Gewürztraminers of Alsace (the word *gewürz* means "spice" in German) display flamboyant lychee and floral aromas.

MUSCAT Alsace Muscat can be made from three different Muscat varieties: Muscat Blanc à Petits Grains, Rosé à Petits Grains and Ottonel. The wines tend to be delicate, lightly floral and dry, although some sweet late-harvest versions are made.

PINOT BLANC Alsace Pinot Blancs are often a blend of genetically related grapes, including the full-bodied, Chardonnay-like Auxerrois. The wines tend to be broad on the palate, sometimes spicy and smoky, with musky apple and floral tones.

PINOT GRIS Pinot Gris is the same grape as Italy's Pinot Grigio, but Alsace Pinot Gris tends to be creamier and richer than its light, crisp Italian counterparts.

RIESLING The region's most widely planted grape is also arguably its greatest, yielding medium-bodied wines whose stony flavors reflect the minerally soils. Wines range from bone-dry to sweet dessert and late-harvest styles, although most Alsace Rieslings are dry.

SYLVANER, AUXERROIS & CHASSELAS These three unexceptional grape varieties generally do not make great wines on their own—except in the hands of certain skilled vintners—but they are often key components of affordably priced, sometimes intriguing blends.

🍇 KEY GRAPES: RED

PINOT NOIR The region's only red grape makes light red and rosé wines defined by crisp berry character, as well as sparkling rosés and the relatively rare sparkling Blanc de Noirs of Crémant d'Alsace.

WINE TERMINOLOGY

ALSACE The basic Alsace designation includes nearly all of the region's still wines. The quality standards that these wines must meet include a limit on vineyard yields and minimum ripeness levels for grapes.

CRÉMANT D'ALSACE Usually based on the Pinot Blanc grape, these sparkling wines typically display lively acidity and fresh, fruity flavors.

EDELZWICKER This term is used to denote blends made from Alsace's best varieties (*edel* means "noble" in German). It's now a catchall category for white blends, typically simple, zesty wines that taste best when consumed within a year or so of release.

GENTIL Generally of a higher quality than *edelzwicker* blends (see above), *gentil* wines are made to AOC standards. These multivariety blends must contain at least 50 percent of some combination of Riesling, Gewürztraminer and Muscat.

GRAND CRU Wines from 51 vineyards may use this designation, which sets limits on vineyard yields. Some major producers have protested that not all the designated vineyards deserve inclusion in this category, and refuse to use the term on their labels.

RÉSERVE Producers use this term to indicate a higher-quality wine, though its exact meaning is not regulated.

VENDANGES TARDIVES (VT) & SÉLECTION DE GRAINS NOBLES (SGN) These terms identify sweet white wines made from late-harvested, very ripe grapes. SGN wines typically contain a portion of grapes affected by botrytis, or "noble rot" (see p. 298).

Producers/ Alsace

DOMAINE MARCEL DEISS

Iconoclastic vintner and third-generation owner Jean-Michel Deiss turned his family's estate biodynamic in the 1990s. He then planted blends of grapes in top vineyards, including *grands crus*—a practice usually reserved here for everyday wines. Deiss feels that his blends are truer to Alsace's history and reflect their vineyards more genuinely than single-grape wines. Granted official *grand cru* labeling in 2005, these multilayered and intense blends are some of Alsace's most sought-after wines.

BOTTLES TO TRY
○ Alsace / $$
○ Burg / $$$

DOMAINE MARC KREYDENWEISS

Three centuries of the Kreydenweiss family have made wine in Alsace, but today's patriarch, Marc, blazed his own trail as an early adopter of biodynamic viticulture and ardent proponent of *terroir*-based wines—even when it meant planting difficult-to-work slopes, late picking and small yields. Now under the direction of son Antoine, the 30-acre domaine continues to turn out full-flavored, complex whites that typically showcase the minerality of the Andlau Valley's schist and sandstone soils.

BOTTLES TO TRY
- Andlau Riesling / $$
- Lerchenberg Pinot Gris / $$

DOMAINE OSTERTAG

All of the vineyard work and winemaking at André Ostertag's small biodynamic domaine is very natural, including fermentations that are allowed to linger and linger (nearly all Ostertag wines are bottled dry). While most wines are steel-fermented, the Pinot Blanc and Pinot Gris ferment and partially age in small oak barrels. Ostertag groups his wines according to his own system: the young-drinking *vins de fruit* (green label, like the Les Vieilles Vignes de Sylvaner); the very ageworthy, vineyard-expressive *vins de pierre* (with vineyard names, like the Muenchberg Riesling); and the top late-harvest wines, v*ins de temps*.

BOTTLES TO TRY
- Les Vieilles Vignes de Sylvaner / $$
- Muenchberg Riesling / $$$

DOMAINE WEINBACH

This estate produces some of Alsace's most sought-after wines. The walled Clos des Capucins vineyard lies at the heart of this ancient property, already known as Weinbach ("wine creek") when the Capuchin friars arrived in 1612. The estate also draws sumptuous wines from a handful of other renowned sites, including the Schlossberg, Furstentum and Altenbourg vineyards. Grapes harvested from micro-plots of vines are turned into as many as 20 to 30 different cuvées in a single vintage, including luscious, powerful Rieslings and Gewürztraminers.

BOTTLES TO TRY
- Réserve Personnelle Riesling / $$
- Cuvée Théo Riesling / $$$

DOMAINE ZIND-HUMBRECHT

Olivier Humbrecht turned his family's relatively humble 1959 estate into one of France's most influential wineries—not by modernizing it, but by going back to radically traditional wine-making with a biodynamic flair. Working with fruit from a superb collection of vineyards assembled by his parents, Léonard and Geneviève, Humbrecht eschews fining, filtration, added yeasts and almost any kind of modern manipulation of grape juice. In recent years, the opulent, saturated wines—already among the best (and costliest) in Alsace—have shown even greater precision and purity.

BOTTLES TO TRY

○ Pinot Blanc / $$

○ Zind / $$

HUGEL ET FILS

Among the best-known and most widely distributed vintners in Alsace, the Hugel family has been making wine in the village of Riquewihr since 1639. Their extensive offerings encompass three broad tiers: the dry, food-friendly Classic line, with very worthy entry-level bottlings; the more complex Tradition line, made primarily from estate-grown fruit; and the Jubilee line, sourced entirely from the family's 62 vineyard acres, many of which are *grand cru* sites. Most coveted are the late-harvest wines.

BOTTLES TO TRY

○ Cuvée Les Amours Pinot Blanc / $

○ Jubilee Riesling / $$$

MEYER-FONNÉ

Highly esteemed importer Kermit Lynch has brought this small, family-run estate to the attention of US wine lovers. Made from naturally farmed, hand-tended grapes, Meyer-Fonné wines are vividly aromatic expressions of the vineyards' granite and limestone soils. Some bottlings, like the everyday Gentil, show off Félix Meyer's blending skills; others, like Rieslings from the great Schoenenbourg and Kaefferkopf *grands crus*, display his deft touch in creating multilayered wines from very different sites while keeping their distinctive personalities intact.

BOTTLES TO TRY

○ Gentil / $

○ Kaefferkopf Pinot Gris Grand Cru / $$$

MURÉ

Winemaker Thomas Muré is the 12th generation of his family to work this estate, most famous for the top wines it produces from its entirely owned *grand cru* vineyard, Clos St. Landelin, a steep, nearly 30-acre slope that produces a variety of wines, from dry Riesling to Pinot Noir to sparkling *cremant d'Alsace* to luscious dessert wine. The wines from the Clos, like many of Muré's other bottlings, are known for their ripeness, thanks to the vineyard's southern exposure and protected location.

BOTTLES TO TRY
- Clos Saint Landelin Pinot Gris / $$
- Clos Saint Landelin Riesling / $$$

TRIMBACH

Trimbach's bracing, traditionally styled, mineral-rich wines include some of Alsace's most reliable bargains, as well as some of its most iconic whites, such as the collectible, luxury-priced Clos Ste. Hune Riesling. Cuvées such as the Frédéric Emile Riesling and the Réserve wines deliver impressive complexity and pleasure at somewhat more approachable prices. Made since 1626 by the Trimbach family—current winemaker Pierre Trimbach represents the 12th generation—the wines are uncompromisingly dry, steely and fresh.

BOTTLES TO TRY
- Pinot Blanc / $
- Cuvée Frédéric Emile Riesling / $$$

BORDEAUX

CLAIM TO FAME

Bordeaux's stately châteaus form many wine drinkers' images of French wine culture, including, apparently, collectors in the global marketplace, who have sent prices for top producers—like Château Lafite Rothschild, Château Latour and Château Pétrus—into the stratosphere. Bordeaux has historically set the standard by which Cabernet Sauvignon– and Merlot-based reds produced around the world are judged (not to mention Sauvignon Blanc and Sémillon white blends). Fortunately, the high-priced stars are not the whole story; this vast Atlantic region also produces millions of bottles of delicious wines at more affordable prices.

Though reds make up about 90 percent of Bordeaux's output, the region's perfect combination of maritime climate (warm days, cool nights) and wine-friendly soils (gravel and clay) are suited to dry and sweet whites, too—including the famous Sauternes.

REGIONS TO KNOW

CÔTES DE BORDEAUX This new umbrella appellation groups four low-profile subregions occupying hilly slopes (*côtes*) on the right banks of the Gironde estuary and the Garonne and Dordogne Rivers, where a growing number of producers are offering high-quality, value-priced wines.

ENTRE-DEUX-MERS This sprawling area between the Dordogne and Garonne Rivers (its name means "between two seas") produces the bulk of Bordeaux's white wines. Most are crisp, affordable bottlings with straightforward citrus and herb flavors.

GRAVES South and inland of Bordeaux proper, the Graves subzone is known for three things: world-class dry whites based on Sémillon and Sauvignon Blanc; relatively light good-value reds from Merlot, Cabernet Sauvignon and Cabernet Franc; and, most famously, the prestigious sub-appellation of **Pessac-Léognan,** home to exalted châteaus such as Haut-Brion.

LEFT BANK The gravelly soils on the Gironde's left (western) bank are ideal for growing Cabernet Sauvignon, especially in the Médoc plain, which fans north and seaward from the city of Bordeaux. The left bank's most famous subregions—**Margaux, Pauillac, St-Julien** and **St-Estèphe**—produce firmly tannic, cassis- and cedar-inflected reds of impressive structure and longevity. Less famous left bank appellations, such as **Haut-Médoc, Moulis** and **Listrac,** are also worth paying attention to, as they can produce terrific values.

RIGHT BANK Clay soil mixes with gravel on the right (eastern) bank of the Gironde and its Dordogne tributary, making this Merlot and Cabernet Franc country, with plusher and less tannic wines than those from the left bank. **Pomerol** and **St-Émilion** are the right bank's most prestigious subdistricts; regions such as **Fronsac, Lussac-St-Émilion, Lalande-de-Pomerol** and **Côtes de Blaye** offer similarly styled wines at far gentler prices.

🍇 KEY GRAPES: WHITE

SAUVIGNON BLANC This grape is responsible for the hallmark citrus- and herb-driven aromas and zippy acidity in Bordeaux whites. It is usually blended with Sémillon.

SÉMILLON Rounder than Sauvignon Blanc, Sémillon is marked by its creamy, rich texture and minerally fruit, and it gives Bordeaux's best dry whites their ability to age. Traditionally blended with Sauvignon Blanc, it yields medium-bodied, citrusy wines. Sémillon is also the primary grape used to make the sweet wines of Sauternes (see Dessert Wines, p. 297).

🍇 KEY GRAPES: RED

CABERNET FRANC Generally lighter in body, with slightly earlier ripening than Cabernet Sauvignon, Cabernet Franc typically plays a supporting role in Bordeaux's reds, to which it lends its signature spicy violet, sweet tobacco and herb aromas. There are, however, a handful of very famous exceptions, such as the wines of Château Cheval Blanc and Château Ausone, in which Cabernet Franc takes center stage.

CABERNET SAUVIGNON Now grown around the world, the famed grape rose to prominence in Bordeaux—specifically, on the left bank of the Gironde, where the Médoc subzone turns out wines of peerless finesse, power and aging potential. In contrast to the majority of California Cabernets, Bordeaux examples display more austere, less fruity flavors, with herbal cassis notes and sharper acidity. Nearly all Bordeaux Cabernet gets blended with Merlot and other traditional blending grapes to soften its firm tannins and add fruitiness.

MERLOT The most widely planted grape in Bordeaux, Merlot is at its best on the right bank of the Gironde and the Dordogne River. Less sweetly ripe than bottlings from the world's warmer regions, Bordeaux versions showcase the grape's characteristically supple tannins and rich plum and black cherry, along with herb and spice notes.

PETIT VERDOT & MALBEC Thick-skinned, darkly colored and tannic, these red varieties are only small players in Bordeaux wines today, even though both grapes are native to the region.

WINE TERMINOLOGY

Bordeaux's most basic wines are labeled *Bordeaux*. Bordeaux Supérieur wines are made to slightly higher standards. Wines with district designations—such as Médoc, St-Émilion and Graves—are required to meet higher standards than those labeled *Bordeaux* or *Bordeaux Supérieur*. Within the districts are communes, such as St-Estèphe and Margaux; wines with communal designation must meet further stringent requirements.

BORDEAUX Wines in this entry-level category can be made anywhere in Bordeaux. Most of them are straightforward and ready to drink; many are whites from Entre-Deux-Mers.

BORDEAUX SUPÉRIEUR A step up from basic Bordeaux, these wines must be higher in alcohol, implying that they were made from riper grapes—historically a measure of higher quality.

CLARET Not legally defined, this primarily British term for red Bordeaux wines generally denotes a lighter, simpler version.

CRU BOURGEOIS A stamp of approval rather than a true classification, this category includes Médoc châteaus that didn't make the *cru classé* cut (see below) but are still of high quality.

CRU CLASSÉ Bordeaux's system for ranking wines, established in 1855, created a hierarchy of wineries (or châteaus) considered superior based on the prices their wines commanded. It applies only to châteaus in Médoc and Sauternes and a single château (Haut-Brion) in Graves. The ranking grouped 61 superior wineries by *cru* (growth), from first (*premier cru*) to fifth. In 1955, a similar system was set up for the St-Émilion district, using just three rankings: *grand cru, grand cru classé* and, at the top, *premier grand cru classé*. Unlike the 1855 classification, it is subject to revision every 10 years or so, most recently in 2012. The basic *grand cru* ranking applies to most estate-bottled St-Émilion wine. The now-famed red wines of Pomerol are not ranked.

MIS EN BOUTEILLE AU CHÂTEAU Only estate-bottled wines made from estate-grown grapes can use this term, meaning "bottled at the winery." Theoretically, these wines are better because of the greater control the producer has over both fruit and wine.

Producers/ Bordeaux

CHÂTEAU ANGÉLUS

In 2012, Angélus was elevated to *premier grand cru classé A*, a long-overdue recognition of its place among St-Émilion's elite. Fourth-generation owner Hubert de Boüard de Laforest brought his family's château up from also-ran status with the aid of consultant Michel Rolland. Angélus's wines, blended from Merlot and Cabernet Franc with the tiniest splash of Cabernet Sauvignon, have gained fame for their consistency of character, a combination of full-bore ripeness and supple, silky texture.

BOTTLE TO TRY

● Chateau Angélus Premier Grand Cru / $$$$

CHÂTEAU CANON LA GAFFELIÈRE

The jewel in the crown of the von Neipperg family holdings and led for a generation by Count Stephan von Neipperg, this property has ascended to a position just below St-Émilion's very top rung. Consultant Stéphane Derenoncourt took the reins in 1996 and shifted the vineyards (planted to a 55-40 mix of Merlot to Cabernet Franc) toward natural farming and a winemaking style designed to produce opulent, forceful but balanced wines.

BOTTLE TO TRY

● Château Canon la Gaffelière Grand Cru / $$$$

CHÂTEAU DE FIEUZAL

The tail—the estate's relatively small production of flavorful white wine from Sauvignon Blanc and Sémillon—has sometimes wagged the dog at this historic Pessac-Léognan estate, though the much-improved reds sell for what amount to moderate prices these days. Irish banker Lochlann Quinn bought the sleepy estate in 2001 and has infused it with a new energy, including hiring talented winemaker Stephen Carrier and seeking consulting help from Hubert de Boüard of Angélus.

BOTTLES TO TRY

○ Château de Fieuzal / $$$

● Château de Fieuzal Grand Cru / $$$

CHÂTEAU D'ISSAN

Château d'Issan's wine was served at Eleanor of Aquitaine's wedding in 1152, and the winery's exalted motto translates roughly as "For kings' tables and gods' altars." In recent history, the estate's grounds, complete with a moat-enclosed castle and gliding swans, have lived up to its fairy-tale image, even if the wines did not. But since Emmanuel Cruse took over the Margaux estate from his father in 1998, wine quality has been on a steady upward march. Look for classic Margaux refinement here, polished wines with lifted dark berry aromatics.

BOTTLES TO TRY

- Blason d'Issan / $$$
- Château d'Issan Grand Cru / $$$$

CHÂTEAU DUCRU-BEAUCAILLOU

This is one of the "super second" estates poised to join Bordeaux's first growths if—unthinkably—the 1855 Médoc reclassification were ever revised; its *grand cru* bottling typifies the St-Julien qualities of elegance, firm structure and graceful concentration. The estate's name comes from the vineyard's *beaux cailloux* ("beautiful stones"); its impressive château dates from the early 1800s. Ducru's prices are now stratospheric; price-conscious drinkers should look for the second wine, Croix de Beaucaillou, and wines from sister châteaus Lalande-Borie and Ducluzeau.

BOTTLES TO TRY

- Croix de Beaucaillou / $$$
- Ducru-Beaucaillou Grand Cru / $$$$

CHÂTEAU GRAND-PUY-LACOSTE

No one could call this admired property "underrated," except that as a fifth-growth producer surrounded by famous neighbors in Pauillac, it offers wines that are relatively gently priced for their often superb quality. This is a name to seek out for those wishing to understand what all the fuss is about in great, powerfully structured Cabernet Sauvignon–dominated Bordeaux. Part of the prominent Borie family's holdings, the winery is owned and overseen by François-Xavier Borie, whose younger brother Bruno manages Château Ducru-Beaucaillou (see above).

BOTTLES TO TRY

- Lacoste Borie / $$$
- Château Grand-Puy-Lacoste Grand Cru / $$$$

CHÂTEAU LA LAGUNE

Winemaker-proprietor Caroline Frey divides her time between La Lagune and her family's famous Rhône firm, Paul Jaboulet Aîné, and the results at La Lagune have been inspiring. (Both were purchased since the turn of the millennium; the family also owns a substantial share of Champagne Billecart-Salmon.) A third-growth producer, formerly best known for its gateway-to-the-wine-country location, La Lagune, under Frey and consultant Denis Dubourdieu, is now gaining a following for complex and concentrated wines with polish and refinement.

BOTTLE TO TRY
- Château La Lagune Grand Cru / $$$$

CHÂTEAU LILIAN LADOUYS

This sleeper winery has risen to the occasion in the most recent top Bordeaux vintages—notably 2010—and why not? Lilian Ladouys's main parcel of 40-year-old vines in St-Estèphe occupies the high-rent district, with near-neighbors like Lafite Rothschild and Cos d'Estournel. Under the ownership of the ambitious Lorenzetti family since 2008, the property seems to have put its history of financial difficulties behind it. With Emmanuel Cruse of d'Issan consulting, these are realistically priced, medium-rich, very approachable wines with a generosity of palate thanks to a 40 percent–plus Merlot component.

BOTTLE TO TRY
- Château Lilian Ladouys / $$

CHÂTEAU LYNCH-BAGES

Though classified in 1855 as a less prestigious fifth-growth producer, Lynch-Bages was fortunate to come into the possession of Bordeaux's remarkable Cazes family in 1939, who for three generations have treated the beloved property like the star it deserves to be. Having long aimed above its rank, the winery today produces some of Pauillac's top wines. Made in a powerful, firmly structured style, the wines are also reasonably priced, given their quality (thanks to the estate's unfairly low historical status). Also a smart buy is the estate's second wine, Echo de Lynch-Bages, and the third, Pauillac de Lynch-Bages.

BOTTLES TO TRY
- Echo de Lynch-Bages / $$$
- Château Lynch-Bages Grand Cru / $$$$

CHÂTEAU PALMER

Named for a British major general who acquired the estate in 1814, Palmer is one of the Margaux appellation's stars. It's now owned by the Sichel and Mähler-Besse families, who have kept the long-lived *grand vin* on a steady course while introducing a second wine, Alter Ego, which delivers plenty of class and structure at about a quarter of the price. Both wines stand out for having a higher-than-typical percentage of Merlot (sometimes even equal to or more than the Cabernet), which gives them an added generosity of texture.

BOTTLES TO TRY
- Alter Ego / $$$$
- Château Palmer / $$$$

CHÂTEAU PICHON LONGUEVILLE COMTESSE DE LALANDE

Better known by its nickname, Pichon-Lalande, this benchmark Pauillac producer owes its modern prominence to May-Eliane de Lencquesaing, who brought it to the forefront of Pauillac's great estates before selling it to Champagne Louis Roederer in 2007. Roederer has tweaked a few things, giving Cabernet an increasing role in the blend, for example, but it hasn't tinkered too much with success. These sumptuous wines are famous for their appellation-straddling character: Pauillac-like in structure and intensity, but with a pronounced St-Julien-style elegance.

BOTTLES TO TRY
- Réserve de la Comtesse / $$$
- Pichon Longueville Comtesse de Lalande Grand Cru / $$$$

CHÂTEAU POUJEAUX

A longtime, not-so-well-kept secret of value-conscious drinkers, Poujeaux provides a consistent, genuine taste of fine Bordeaux. The vineyard's relatively high percentage (up to 40 percent) of Merlot may explain its early-drinking, supple pleasures. The Cuvelier family, who bought the property in 2008, know how to back an underdog—they had previously elevated Clos Fourtet in St-Émilion. Poujeaux's nonclassified-growth status in out-of-the-way Moulis may ensure that its prices stay reasonable.

BOTTLES TO TRY
- La Salle de Château Poujeaux / $$
- Château Poujeaux / $$$

CLOS DUBREUIL

This tiny St-Émilion *garagiste*'s wine commands three-figure prices—if you can find it. In 2002, Clos Dubreuil was purchased by the Trocard family, owners of numerous Bordeaux properties. Benoît Trocard and renowned consultant Michel Rolland have introduced about 10 percent Cabernet Franc to the nearly-all-Merlot blend, but maintained the very ripe, new-oak-imbued, flamboyant opulence that marks many of the *garagiste* super-star wines. In its latest surprise move, the property debuted 100 cases of a Chardonnay (in Bordeaux!) with the 2013 vintage.

BOTTLE TO TRY

● Clos Dubreuil / $$$$

DOMAINE DE CHEVALIER

A Pessac-Léognan aristocrat, Domaine de Chevalier is the rare Bordeaux property to produce both world-class reds and whites. The centuries-old estate, now under the stewardship of the Bernard family (France's leading spirits purveyors), is a secret garden surrounded by the Landes forest. Olivier Bernard has brought onboard luminaries Stéphane Derenoncourt to consult on the reds and Denis Dubourdieu on the whites. The Cabernet-dominated red wines are known for their suave, classical (non-blockbuster-size) weight profile and complex aromatics, while the Sauvignon Blanc–based whites are famously ageworthy.

BOTTLES TO TRY

○ Domaine de Chevalier Grand Cru / $$$$
● Domaine de Chevalier Grand Cru / $$$

VIEUX CHÂTEAU CERTAN

Alexandre Thienpont notes that nearly a century of active obser-vation by his family has brought their 35 Pomerol acres to a state of perfection. Its followers would add that the wine, too, has reached a sublime state: ultra-elegant, often majestic in scale, with effortless power and palate-caressing finesse. Though it doesn't command the off-the-chart prices of its neighbor Pétrus (or of the nearby Thienpont family off-shoot, Le Pin), this is still a much-coveted wine, with a price to match. The second wine, La Gravette de Certan, can be a steal if you can track it down.

BOTTLES TO TRY

● La Gravette de Certan / $$$
● Vieux Château Certan / $$$$

BURGUNDY

CLAIM TO FAME

Burgundy's inconsistent weather means that vintages can vary wildly in quality. Its patchwork of regions (and subregions, and sub-sub-subregions) takes some effort to grasp. And few of its wines are bargain-priced. So why bother? Because no other place on Earth can match Burgundy for the alluring grace of its finest wines. It is the world model for Pinot Noir and Chardonnay, and in great vintages, its ethereal reds and majestic whites offer both polish and seemingly effortless aromatic intensity.

REGIONS TO KNOW

CHABLIS This cool northern subregion is geologically more similar to Champagne than to the rest of Burgundy, resulting in wines (all Chardonnay) that can have a minerally austerity. Unlike other white Burgundies, most Chablis wines are unoaked or lightly oaked, which emphasizes their freshness and fruit, backed by a steely crispness. The best bottles are labeled with *grand* or *premier cru* vineyard names; lesser wines are labeled *Chablis*. Petit Chablis wines are from less prestigious subregions.

CÔTE CHALONNAISE Much red is made here, but this region on the Côte d'Or's southern border has long been known for affordable Chardonnay. Prices have crept up, though, and wines from its four top villages—**Givry, Mercurey, Montagny** and **Rully**— are the costliest. Mercurey and Givry also make notable reds.

CÔTE D'OR The Burgundy heartland is split into two subregions. Specializing in Pinot Noir, the northern **Côte de Nuits** contains most of Burgundy's red *grands crus*, including those in legendary villages like **Chambolle-Musigny** and **Gevrey-Chambertin**. The southern **Côte de Beaune** makes some of the world's most compelling Chardonnays, from villages such as **Meursault** and **Puligny-Montrachet,** and a single *grand cru* red, **Corton.**

MÂCONNAIS This southern Burgundy region turns out affordable, mosty reliable white wine. Much of it is entry level, but ambitious, small-scale vintners are boosting quality. Top Mâconnais offerings come from all-Chardonnay **Pouilly-Fuissé.**

❦ KEY GRAPES: WHITE

CHARDONNAY Most Burgundy white wines are made from Chardonnay, although styles differ greatly among the subregions. Reflecting varying climates and soils as much as different wine-making traditions, Burgundy Chardonnays range from the flinty, high-acid whites of Chablis in the north to the rich, oak-aged offerings of the Côte d'Or.

SAUVIGNON BLANC & ALIGOTÉ Small amounts of these grapes grow in a few spots around Burgundy: Sauvignon Blanc in the northern village of St-Bris, and Aligoté in the Côte Chalonnaise.

❦ KEY GRAPES: RED

PINOT NOIR With its silky texture, endlessly unfolding depth and violet, cherry and earth aromas, fine red Burgundy is typically considered Pinot Noir's pinnacle. Unfortunately, disappointing red Burgundy can be just as pricey, so choosing bottles wisely is key. Pinot Noir vines planted in well-drained limestone soil on sunny slopes tend to yield the most powerful, long-lived wines.

WINE TERMINOLOGY

Burgundy ranks wines by the vineyards from which they originate, not by the producer who made them (as in Bordeaux). Burgundy labels list the region; some also list the subregion, and the most prestigious include a vineyard name. Generally, the more specific the locality on a label, the finer the wine, but vintage is also very important when assessing quality.

BOURGOGNE Burgundy's most basic wines are labeled with just the name of the region, Bourgogne, and occasionally with the grape. Quality ranges from so-so to surprisingly wonderful.

DISTRICT A district appellation (such as Chablis or Mâconnais) is the next step up in quality after AOC Bourgogne. The grapes must be grown exclusively in the named district.

VILLAGE A wine may take the name of a specific village if all of its grapes have been grown within that village's boundaries—for instance, Meursault or Nuits-St-Georges. These are more prestigious than district-wide appellations but not necessarily better. Those from multiple villages within a larger region can append

Villages to that region, as in Côte de Nuits–Villages (used for reds and a bit of white) and Côte de Beaune–Villages (always red). Terrific introductory wines, Côte de Nuits–Villages often offer the best values in this pricey slice of Burgundy.

GRAND CRU Vineyards designated as *grand cru,* the highest classification in Burgundy, are so elite that some, like Montrachet, don't even include the *grand cru* title on their wine labels. To capitalize on their prestige, some villages have added the name of the local *grand cru* vineyard to their own names, but their wines are not themselves *grand cru.* (For example, wines from the town of Chassagne became Chassagne-Montrachet, but while many are superb, they're not true Montrachet.)

PREMIER CRU With the second-highest distinction, *premier cru* vineyards have a long history of producing superior wines. Wines labeled simply *premier cru* may originate from several local *premier cru* vineyards; those with designated vineyard names (e.g., Meursault Premier Cru Genevrières) are more prestigious.

NÉGOCIANTS Merchants who buy wine, grapes or must (freshly pressed juice) from small growers and/or producers and create wines under their own names.

Producers/ Burgundy

BOUCHARD PÈRE & FILS

Founded in 1731, Bouchard got a fresh boost when the Henriot family of Champagne fame bought it in 1995. Today, this prominent Burgundy *négociant* is also the Côte d'Or's largest vineyard owner; its 321 acres of vines yield famed *grands* and *premiers crus,* including the signature Vigne de l'Enfant Jésus red. While Bouchard is known for costly single-vineyard wines, its more affordable village and regional bottlings can also be top-notch.

BOTTLES TO TRY

○ Bourgogne Réserve / $$
● Savigny-lès-Beaune / $$$

CHÂTEAU-FUISSÉ

Antoine Vincent turns out serious Mâconnais whites at this ancient estate, owned by the Vincent family since the 1860s (the domaine itself dates back to the 1600s). Most of its vineyards are in Pouilly-Fuissé, the Mâconnais's top subzone, and its most interesting wines may be the single-vineyard cuvées from its home vineyards, Le Clos, Les Brûlés and Les Combettes: Each one brilliantly highlights *terroir*-driven differences in flavor. Its JJ Vincent *négociant* bottlings from Mâcon and Beaujolais are straightforward, affordable wines meant for everyday drinking.

BOTTLES TO TRY

○ Le Clos Pouilly-Fuissé / $$$
○ Tête de Cru Pouilly-Fuissé / $$$

DOMAINE ARMAND ROUSSEAU

This is one of the legendary producers of Burgundy and a bench-mark name in Gevrey-Chambertin (all the more so since wine-maker Eric Rousseau has been managing most of Château de Gevrey-Chambertin's vineyards since 2012). Prices for a single bottle of the iconic *grands crus*—Chambertin or Chambertin Clos de Bèze, for example—can soar into four figures. Behind the prices are not just decades of consistent excellence—long-lived wines that combine depths of flavor with seamless, silky tex-tures—but the fact that the domaine prunes severely to restrict yields on its already shy-bearing 40- to 45-year-old vines.

BOTTLES TO TRY

● Gevrey-Chambertin / $$$$
● Lavaux St-Jacques Gevrey-Chambertin Premier Cru / $$$$

DOMAINE CHRISTIAN MOREAU PÈRE & FILS

An old Chablis family, the Moreaus sold their J. Moreau & Fils wine merchant business in 1985, but held on to a few top vine-yards, producing a far smaller quantity of high-quality wine under the Domaine Christian Moreau name. Today Christian himself (the *père*) and winemaker Fabien (the *fils*) produce mostly estate-grown wines from vines that can be up to 77 years old. Moreau's basic Chablis is reliably satisfying, especially given its reasonable price.

BOTTLES TO TRY

○ Chablis / $$
○ Vaillon Chablis Premier Cru / $$$

DOMAINE DE LA VOUGERAIE

World-spanning wine entrepreneur Jean-Charles Boisset spearheads a company that is one of the largest wine producers in Burgundy, but Domaine de la Vougeraie is a more personal enterprise. Run by Boisset and his sister Nathalie, it is a relatively new (1999) label that brings together the Boisset family's superlative vineyard holdings—nearly 60 parcels in all, a kind of high-level cross section from across the Côte d'Or. The wines, including *grand cru* gems like Corton-Charlemagne and Clos du Roi, are made using meticulous biodynamic methods.

BOTTLES TO TRY

○ **Les Pierres Blanches Côte de Beaune** / $$$

● **Chambolle-Musigny** / $$$$

DOMAINE DUJAC

Jacques Seysses christened his estate with a play on his first name instead of his family name, which even the French find hard to pronounce (for the record, it's "sayss"). His father bought the first property in the Dujac holdings in 1967, and the wines earned nearly instant acclaim for their elegance. These are fresh, lively wines with immediate appeal to a variety of palates, including connoisseurs'. Though still based in—and identified with—Morey-Saint-Denis, the Dujac holdings are considerably expanded, notably with a major purchase in 2005 that added prestigious vineyards in Vosne-Romanée and Chambertin.

BOTTLES TO TRY

○ **Monts Luisants Morey-Saint-Denis Premier Cru** / $$$$

● **Gevrey-Chambertin Premier Cru** / $$$$

DOMAINE FAIVELEY

Following in the footsteps of six generations might intimidate even the most self-assured 25-year-old, but Erwan Faiveley wasn't afraid to make big changes when he took over his family's domaine in 2007. Among much else, he has embarked upon an ambitious program of expansion, including major purchases in Gevrey-Chambertin and Chablis. Faiveley now controls a sprawling portfolio of some 350 acres. This is good news for wine lovers, as recent vintages have been among the best in years.

BOTTLES TO TRY

○ **Bourgogne** / $$

● **Clos des Myglands Mercurey Premier Cru** / $$$

DOMAINE GEORGES ROUMIER

This is one of Burgundy's most revered labels, synonymous with superlative wines from Chambolle-Musigny, a part of the Côte de Nuits that, thanks to limestone-rich soils, yields some of Burgundy's most profound and delicate wines. In typical Burgundy fashion, the domaine's holdings are splintered, but Christophe Roumier works prized small parcels, including *grands crus* in Musigny and Bonnes Mares that are standard bearers for the appellation and for Burgundy itself, with prices to match.

BOTTLES TO TRY

● Bourgogne / $$$$
● Chambolle-Musigny / $$$$

DOMAINE HENRI GOUGES

Gouges's 37 acres contain no *grand cru*, but this is a reference point producer, not just for Nuits-St-Georges, but for Burgundy. Among the first Burgundy domaines to bottle and market its own wine back in the 1930s, Gouges has been cutting its own path ever since. Now under the guidance of fourth-generation family winemaker Grégory, Gouges has scaled back a shade from the more powerful style of the 1990s and before, but the hallmark of the house remains: These are concentrated wines made from very low-yielding vineyards that have an eye more on ageworthiness than being immediately palate-flattering.

BOTTLES TO TRY

○ Bourgogne Pinot Blanc / $$$
● Nuits-St-Georges / $$$$

DOMAINE JOBLOT

In the snob-appeal world of Burgundy, the Côte Chalonnaise isn't prime real estate, which can be very good news for value-conscious wine drinkers who discover talents like the Joblots of Givry. Vincent, Jean-Marc and the latter's daughter Juliette tend their family's 30-plus acres of rocky limestone with assiduous care, following up bud-clipping and summertime bunch-lopping with a severe picking-time selection that has sorted out a staggering 40 percent of some harvests. These are typically wines of purity and bright fruit that drink well above their price levels.

BOTTLES TO TRY

● Clos de la Servoisine Givry Premier Cru / $$$
● Pied de Chaume / $$$

DOMAINE LAROCHE

Happily for the many fans of this important producer—Domaine Laroche's 222 acres scattered throughout Chablis include one of the appellation's top collections of *grands crus*—its wines are in good hands after a 2010 management change. Winemaker Grégory Viennois, who came on board in 2011, brought a long and impressive résumé from out of the region (including stints at Chapoutier and Smith-Haut-Lafitte). He continues to refine Laroche's house style, producing some of the most texturally opulent wines in Chablis.

BOTTLES TO TRY
- ○ Saint Martin Chablis / $$
- ○ Les Blanchots Chablis Grand Cru / $$$$

DOMAINE LEFLAIVE

The white Burgundies produced by this Puligny-Montrachet domaine (not to be confused with the Olivier Leflaive *négociant* firm) are legendary. The wines are made in tiny quantities with biodynamically grown grapes from some of the world's most famous vineyards, including a range of *grands crus* from the white-wine Holy Grail vineyards of Montrachet. For a taste of Leflaive's refined style at a gentler price, look for its Mâcon bottling, which comes from 23 acres near the village of Verzé.

BOTTLES TO TRY
- ○ Mâcon-Verzé / $$$
- ○ Puligny-Montrachet / $$$$

DOMAINE PERROT-MINOT

Christophe Perrot-Minot's domaine in Morey-Saint-Denis has been in the family (under different names) since the 19th century, but it's fair to say that he put it on the collector's map of Burgundy. This is partly through his intense form of viticulture, which involves severe pruning and grape selection to concentrate the juices that go into his satiny and very ripe but rarely overrich wines. His two Cuvée Ultra–designated wines come from ancient plots that yield only a few barrels each. He's also a skilled *négociant* with great contacts, despite his insistence on harvesting everything with his own crew on his own schedule.

BOTTLES TO TRY
- ● Bourgogne Vieilles Vignes / $$$
- ● La Rue de Vergy Morey-Saint-Denis / $$$$

DOMAINE RAMONET

Ramonet is a name—some would say *the* name—to reckon with in white Burgundy. This small, artisan Chassagne-Montrachet estate is run by brothers Noël and Jean-Claude Ramonet. Their 42-acre domaine makes a little red wine, but it's the exuberantly intense whites that have well-heeled collectors knocking on their doors. Ramonet's grapes are sourced chiefly from vineyards in and around the towns of Chassagne-Montrachet and Puligny-Montrachet, and its holdings include parcels of legendary *grands crus*, such as Le Montrachet, Bienvenues and Bâtard.

BOTTLES TO TRY

○ Chassagne-Montrachet / $$$
○ Les Ruchottes Chassagne-Montrachet Premier Cru / $$$$

DOMAINE ROULOT

Among the most celebrated producers in Meursault, the Roulot family has been a champion of the appellation since 1830. After Jean-Marc Roulot took the helm in 1989, the domaine's trajectory has been nothing but upward. Roulot's wines—nearly all white—can certainly be generous, but they are not typically among the richest Meursaults. Instead, they are prized for their combination of purity, elegance and complexity. Those who balk at the three-figure prices for the great *premiers crus* can sample his touch with the conscientiously produced Bourgogne Blanc.

BOTTLES TO TRY

○ Bourgogne Blanc / $$$
○ Meursault / $$$$

DOMAINE SERVIN

François Servin could have kept making the same respectable wines his family's Chablis estate was known for, but he decided to push the envelope. Aided and abetted by his Australian-born export manager Marc Cameron, he began tweaking the model—pouring money into a high-tech winery, densely replanting vines and bottling later and later. These efforts have made Domaine Servin a candidate for Chablis's "most improved" award, which makes it a label to keep an eye on, indeed: The Servins were already one of Chablis's largest owners of *grands crus*.

BOTTLES TO TRY

○ Chablis / $$
○ Les Clos Chablis Grand Cru / $$$$

BEST OF THE BEST PRODUCERS / BURGUNDY
1. ARMAND ROUSSEAU **2.** DUJAC **3.** GEORGES ROUMIER
4. LEFLAIVE **5.** RAMONET

DOMAINE TAUPENOT-MERME

With 32 vineyard acres spread over 20 appellations, Taupenot-Merme is relatively large by Burgundy standards, though its top wines, from *grands crus* like Clos des Lambrays and Mazoyères-Chambertin, are made in very small quantities. Since taking over the family domaine in 1998, siblings Romain and Virginie Taupenot have brought finesse to the varied portfolio, which includes the family's splendidly sited Côte de Nuits vines.

BOTTLE TO TRY
● Chambolle-Musigny / $$$$

MAISON JOSEPH DROUHIN

Drouhin's cellar is like a taste tour of Burgundy, with wines from nearly 90 appellations. The firm's own 182 acres of vines stretch from Chablis south to the Côte Chalonnaise and include such revered names as Clos des Mouches and Montrachet Marquis de Laguiche. Casual drinkers are more likely to come upon Drouhin's array of village and regional wines, many made from purchased grapes and available at far gentler prices.

BOTTLES TO TRY
○ Domaine de Vaudon Chablis / $$
● Laforêt Bourgogne / $$

MAISON LOUIS JADOT

Few wineries in the world can match this *négociant*'s ability to turn out such a dizzying array of both reliably tasty, value-priced wines and world-class cuvées. American-owned for three decades, Jadot has been ably guided in France by the Gagey family, with Pierre-Henry seamlessly taking the reins from his father and overseeing the transition from longtime vintner-guru Jacques Lardière. The portfolio is a mix of owned properties and purchased grapes and wines, with gems up and down the line.

BOTTLES TO TRY
○ Pouilly-Fuissé / $$
● Pommard / $$$

MAISON ROCHE DE BELLENE

You don't have to follow Nicolas Potel's complicated story—he doesn't make the wines labeled under his own name anymore—to appreciate the beauty and purity of the wines he creates under the Maison Roche de Bellene brand. Founded in 2009, Potel's self-described "haute couture" *négociant* operation focuses on *premier cru* and *grand cru* bottlings from old-vine wines. Though hardly bargain-basement-priced, they tend to represent strong values for high-quality Burgundy.

BOTTLES TO TRY

○ Bourgogne / $$
● Les Suchots Vosne-Romanée Premier Cru / $$$$

PATRICK PIUZE

Bitten by the wine bug, Piuze left his native Quebec in 2000 and moved to Burgundy. After stints with Olivier Leflaive, Maison Verget and Jean-Marc Brocard, he fell in love with the possibilities of Chablis, specifically how small differences in *terroir* could affect the Chardonnay grape. His rise was swift: In 2008, he arrived on the scene with 21 different, tiny-volume bottlings of Chablis, all made with his let-the-grapes-shine, non-interventionist winemaking style. Piuze's star continues to rise as he hones his skills in selecting old-vine grapes, often from hard-to-pick slopes he hand-harvests himself.

BOTTLES TO TRY

○ Terroir de Chablis / $$
○ Blanchots Chablis Grand Cru / $$$$

PIERRE-YVES COLIN-MOREY

Pierre-Yves Colin and his wife, Caroline Morey, founded their label as a "micro-*négociant*" in 2001. After Colin left his family winery in 2005, they launched their enterprise in earnest at Chardonnay ground zero in Chassagne-Montrachet. Now making about two-thirds of the wine from his own vineyards, Colin is a fast-rising star among cognoscenti for his confident, natural winemaking. Among other things, he employs native yeasts and does no filtration, which often means his whites can take as much time to soften into drinkablity as other producers' reds.

BOTTLES TO TRY

○ Bourgogne / $$$
○ Les Baudines Chassagne-Montrachet Premier Cru / $$$$

VINCENT DAUVISSAT

This superstar estate's wines are virtually unmatched in Chablis for prestige and price, yet even its best bottles cost a fraction of what their Côte d'Or counterparts command. Sourced from some of Chablis's top sites and lightly oaked, Vincent Dauvissat wines offer stony purity and fresh, minerally acidity. These qualities can make the wines seem a bit austere when young; even the Petit Chablis usually tastes better with a little bottle age.

BOTTLES TO TRY

○ Petit Chablis / $$$
○ Les Preuses Chablis Grand Cru / $$$$

BURGUNDY

BEAUJOLAIS

CLAIM TO FAME

Although it's considered part of Burgundy, Beaujolais has a profile all its own, with a different climate (warmer) and a different soil (granite, schist and sandstone) from the rest of the region. It also features a different signature grape: Gamay. Producers' efforts, starting a generation ago, to capitalize on tanker-loads of the grapey, simple, Gamay-based red called Beaujolais Nouveau backfired, obscuring the region's often far more worthy non-Nouveau wines in the public mind, and creating some wonderful bargains. In particular, the deeply lush, floral-edged reds of Beaujolais's 10 named *crus* (see below) are some of the most underrated, food-friendly wines in the world.

KEY GRAPES: RED

GAMAY Supple tannins and juicy, exuberant fruit define this easy-to-love variety. Lighter wines from cooler vintages showcase tangy cranberry and strawberry tones; riper, more concentrated grapes yield medium-bodied, graceful red wines loaded with mouth-filling raspberry and cherry flavors.

WINE TERMINOLOGY

BEAUJOLAIS Basic Beaujolais accounts for nearly half of the region's wine output. Quality varies considerably, but in general, wines labeled *Beaujolais* tend to offer more substance than Beaujolais Nouveau, with fruity berry flavors and succulent acidity.

BEAUJOLAIS NOUVEAU Designed to be consumed within weeks of harvest, Beaujolais Nouveau is as light-bodied and simple as red wine gets. By French law, it is released the third Thursday of every November, conveniently coinciding with the start of the US holiday season.

BEAUJOLAIS-VILLAGES Only wines made with grapes sourced from 38 villages occupying the gentle hills at the center of the region can be designated Beaujolais-Villages. Typically produced with more care and precision than basic Beaujolais, these wines exhibit bright, red-berry flavors as well as an added depth of mineral and spice.

CRU BEAUJOLAIS The region's finest wines come from 10 hillside villages in the northern part of Beaujolais, where granite and schist soils and sunny slopes yield riper, more concentrated wines. Deep flavors and ample tannins give the best bottles the ability to age, unlike most other Beaujolais. *Cru* Beaujolais labels often list only the village name: Brouilly, Chénas, Chiroubles, Côte de Brouilly, Fleurie, Juliénas, Morgon, Moulin-à-Vent, Régnié or St-Amour, and fans will endlessly argue the merits of each.

Producers/ Beaujolais

CHÂTEAU DES JACQUES

One of Beaujolais's most respected names, Château des Jacques has been part of the Louis Jadot stable since 1996. The domaine boasts vineyards spanning six subregions, including the flagship offerings from its home appellation of Moulin-à-Vent, where its holdings include five ancient, walled vineyards. Just a few barrels' worth of the single-vineyard Moulin-à-Vent *crus* is imported to the US, but the basic Moulin-à-Vent bottling, which blends grapes from all five sites, is comparatively easy to find and consistently great, as is the richly fruity Morgon.

BOTTLES TO TRY
- Morgon / $$
- Clos de Rochegrès Moulin-à-Vent / $$$

GEORGES DUBOEUF

Georges Duboeuf has largely turned over the reins to his son Franck, and the ship sails on. Even more remarkable than this *négociant*'s huge output (some 2.5 million cases of Beaujolais yearly) is that so much of it is so delicious. Duboeuf helped to create the Beaujolais Nouveau craze in the 1970s, but the lineup also includes many later-released bottlings, including the well-known "Flower Label" Beaujolais-Villages wines, plus *cru* wines offering more serious drinking pleasure. At the top end are the Cuvée Prestige wines from Beaujolais and Pouilly-Fuissé.

BOTTLES TO TRY
- Domaine des Quatre Vents Fleurie / $$
- Moulin-à-Vent / $$

JULIEN SUNIER

This artisan producer describes his approach to farming as "agro-ecology." The Burgundian Sunier moved south to found his winery in 2008, and he now holds about 10 acres in Morgon, Fleurie and Régnié, all organically tended (the vineyard in Fleurie is so steep and rocky, it has to be worked by hand with pickaxes). His approach to winemaking is similarly natural, and these beautifully structured, vibrant wines have given him an avid following that Gamay wines don't often attract.

BOTTLES TO TRY
- Fleurie / $$
- Morgon / $$

LOIRE VALLEY

CLAIM TO FAME

White wines star in this château-dotted river valley, France's longest. The Loire Valley produces more whites than any other French region. They range from the flinty, citrusy Sauvignon Blancs of Sancerre and Pouilly-Fumé to complex Chenin Blancs of Vouvray to brisk, shellfish-friendly bottlings from the coast, where the Loire River meets the cold Atlantic, just past Muscadet. But don't overlook Loire reds—Chinon's Cabernet Francs, the Pinot Noirs of Sancerre or other rarer pleasures. Thanks to the valley's cooler climate, its reds are refreshingly crisp and food-friendly, and often very well priced for their quality.

REGIONS TO KNOW

ANJOU, SAUMUR & SAVENNIÈRES Chenin Blanc is the most important quality-wine grape in these central Loire regions. In Anjou, it is often made into well-respected sweet wines. The incredibly concentrated dry (and sweet) whites of Savennières are among the greatest examples of the Chenin Blanc grape. Red and rosé wines from Anjou and Saumur highlight the fresh side of Loire Cabernet Franc with bright acidity and green-herb notes. **Saumur-Champigny** is exclusively a red wine region offering Cabernet Franc–based blends.

MUSCADET France's largest white wine appellation, Muscadet relies entirely on the Melon de Bourgogne variety, which thrives in the region's relatively cool, coastal climate and sandy soil—conditions that would prove disastrous for most grapes. However, the best Muscadet bottlings—there is an ongoing quality revolution here—come from grapes grown on rocky soil, not sand. In 2011, a new designation based on soil types was introduced, called *cru communal* (see Wine Terminology, opposite).

SANCERRE & POUILLY-FUMÉ Benchmark whites made from Sauvignon Blanc are the calling card of these sister appellations in the upper Loire. Sancerres tend to be lighter and more perfumed, while Pouilly-Fumés are often fuller-bodied, with smoky mineral, herb and citrus tones. For Sauvignon Blanc made in a similar style at a more affordable price, look to the satellite regions of **Menetou-Salon, Quincy** and **Reuilly.** Although it is renowned for white wines, Sancerre produces small amounts of rosé and red wine from Pinot Noir.

TOURAINE This large region centered on the midvalley town of Tours grows a dizzying array of red and white grapes, including Sauvignon Blanc, Gamay, Pinot Noir, Cabernet Sauvignon, Malbec (known locally as Côt) and a local specialty, Pineau d'Aunis. But none of the wines made from them compare to the legendary Chenin Blanc–based white wines of the premier subregion, **Vouvray.** Whether bone-dry or sweet, sparkling or still, they're among the world's most enthralling (and long-lived) whites. Touraine is also responsible for the Loire Valley's best red wines (in the subregions of **Chinon** and **Bourgueil**), which are smoky renditions of Cabernet Franc.

KEY GRAPES: WHITE

CHENIN BLANC Is there a grape more versatile than Chenin Blanc? Its wines range from light and mouth-puckeringly tart to sweet, fruity, full and rich, and come in sparkling, still and dessert bottlings. Their common thread: bright acidity, which gives the best Chenin Blancs amazing longevity.

MELON DE BOURGOGNE Coastal Muscadet's signature grape yields light-bodied, fairly neutral and refreshing whites with light citrus flavors and a hint of salty sea spray. Ambitious producers buck the norm, making top-notch small-lot cuvées from old vines that offer intense, chalky minerality and richer fruit. The best examples even age well, making this category a bargain for budding collectors.

SAUVIGNON BLANC In contrast to more exuberantly tropical and herbaceous Sauvignon Blancs from elsewhere in the world, Loire examples combine the grape's refreshing acidity and trademark citrus tones with smoky mineral and chalk aromas.

KEY GRAPES: RED

CABERNET FRANC The Loire's most distinctive red variety yields wines with red-fruit, herb and pepper notes typical of cool-climate reds, and, often, a smoky tobacco edge. Their high acidity and sometimes astringent tannins mean they're built for food.

WINE TERMINOLOGY

CRU COMMUNAL Specific to Sèvre et Maine, Muscadet's largest and best-known subregion, this new designation identifies that zone's top *terroirs* and sets standards governing yields (lower), ripeness levels (higher) and time spent aging on lees (longer). Three *crus communaux*—Clisson, Gorges and Le Pallet—were approved in 2011; more are in the process of approval.

SEC Meaning "dry," this term indicates a wine with little to no residual sugar—although Chenin Blanc, with its honey and fruit notes, can give the impression of sweetness even when sec.

DEMI-SEC Though this term translates as "half-dry," a demi-sec wine is more accurately described as falling halfway between dry (sec) and sweet.

SUR LIE Appearing on Muscadet's better bottles, this term (pronounced "suhr LEE") indicates that a wine has been aged on its lees, the sediments left over after a wine's fermentation. The dead yeasts give the wine a creamier texture and a slight nutty edge.

VIN DE PAYS DU VAL DE LOIRE Much of the Loire's everyday wine is produced under this region-wide designation, which is also an umbrella term for many smaller *vin de pays* designations within it. These wines list a grape variety as well as a vintage.

Producers/
Loire Valley

BERNARD BAUDRY

Bernard Baudry and his son Matthieu turn out some of the Loire's best Cabernet Francs from this 75-acre estate in the Chinon AOC. The notable red Chinon cuvées are distinguished by the vineyards' diverse terrain. The farming here has been sustainable for many years. The winemaking is also throwback-traditional, using natural yeasts and often no fining or filtering. All of the wines, including the whites and rosés, reflect the Baudrys' preference for supple, classically elegant Chinon.

BOTTLES TO TRY
- Chinon Rosé / $$
- Les Granges Chinon / $$

CATHERINE & PIERRE BRETON

This small estate near Bourgeuil has developed a following partly for the honesty of its natural, biodynamic production practices and largely for the delicious results: Chinons, Bourgeuils and Vouvrays with character, authenticity and energy. The Breton line has three tiers: natural wines for everyday drinking; classic wines that typify specific subregions; and wines of *terroir* (like the top Chinon St. Louans and Bourgeuil Clos Sénéchal) that are meant to mature and gain complexity in the cellar.

BOTTLES TO TRY
- La Dilettante Vouvray / $$
- Beaumont Chinon / $$

CHARLES JOGUET

This familiar label is a welcome sight to value-minded Americans who have come to expect graceful red wines at gentle prices from the Chinon AOC. Those who explore further will be rewarded with some of the Loire's most impressive Cabernet Francs. Now retired, Charles Joguet was a pioneer in estate-bottling Chinon wines, as opposed to selling them in bulk to *négociants*. The domaine that carries on his legacy bottles seven *terroir*-based Chinon cuvées, as well as small portions of AOC Touraine whites from Chenin Blanc and a rosé from Cabernet Franc.

BOTTLES TO TRY
- Cuvée Terroir Chinon / $$
- Les Petites Roches Chinon / $$

DOMAINE CHAMPALOU

Founded in 1983 by husband-and-wife team Didier and Catherine Champalou (now joined by daughter Céline), this house has become one of the best known in the Vouvray appellation. In the US particularly, it is a sommelier favorite, in part because Champalou's lineup provides a kind of sensory textbook to the often underappreciated Chenin Blanc grape: Champalou makes reference-quality Chenin Blancs in all four major style categories, with wines ranging from crisp aperitifs to sensational dessert wines, plus demi-sec (off-dry) and sparkling bottlings.

BOTTLES TO TRY
○ La Cuvée des Fondraux Vouvray / $$
○ Vouvray / $$

DOMAINE DES BAUMARD

Anjou does not routinely produce world-famous wines, but Domaine des Baumard is breaking the mold. The property, which has been in the family since 1634, is currently run by Florent Baumard, whose portfolio is a tour de force of Loire winemaking. The image-makers are the silky, complex, dry, still Chenin Blanc wines from Savennières, as well as the sweet Chenins from the Coteaux du Layon and a range of Crémant de Loire sparkling wines that are gaining increased attention, not least for their strong price-to-quality ratio.

BOTTLES TO TRY
○ Carte d'Or Coteaux du Layon / $$
○ Savennières / $$

DOMAINE DIDIER DAGUENEAU

Didier Dagueneau crafted some of the most riveting and complex Pouilly-Fumés and Sancerres ever made. He died when his ultralight plane crashed in 2008, but his son, Louis-Benjamin, has kept the estate's wines at the same exalted level. Extremely low vineyard yields, biodynamic farming and, atypically, the use of oak-barrel aging result in some of the planet's greatest Sauvignon Blancs. With silken texture, crystalline purity and stony minerality, these whites are ravishing, with prices to match.

BOTTLES TO TRY
- Blanc Fumé de Pouilly / $$$$
- Silex Blanc Fumé de Pouilly / $$$$

DOMAINE HUET

This estate's reputation as one of Vouvray's finest was forged by Gaston Huet, "the pope of Vouvray," who was a World War II hero and town mayor for more than 40 years. His son-in-law Noël Pinguet continued the tradition while converting the vineyards—including legendary sites such as Clos du Bourg, Le Mont and Le Haut Lieu—to biodynamic farming. Cellarmaster Jean-Bernard Berthomé became head winemaker upon Pinguet's retirement in 2012; he also crafts dry and semisweet sparkling and dessert wines that are notable for their purity and balance, and which keep the estate at the forefront of the appellation.

BOTTLES TO TRY
- Le Mont Demi-Sec Vouvray / $$
- Clos du Bourg Sec Vouvray / $$$

DOMAINE PASCAL JOLIVET

As a skilled winemaker and ambitious entrepreneur, Pascal Jolivet came from a winemaking family but opted to found his own wine business from scratch in 1987, purchasing grapes from all over Sancerre and Pouilly-Fumé. Today he's one of the largest exporters of wine from both regions, and Jolivet is able to obtain about half of his grapes from vineyards he owns himself, which allows him to fine-tune the farming. His lively, food-flexible entry-level Sancerre is a familiar and welcome sight on US restaurant lists.

BOTTLES TO TRY
- Sancerre / $$
- Clos du Roy Sancerre / $$$

DOMAINES LANDRON

Jo Landron has been a catalyst in the quality revival of the Muscadet appellation since he began producing wines alongside his father in 1979. He maintained that the underloved—outside of Muscadet—Melon de Bourgogne grape would respond well to lower cropping, meticulous farming and winemaking based on the soil and vintage the grapes came from. Landron's oyster wine, the Amphibolite Nature, is fresh and crisp, a reflection of its stony soils and the fact that it doesn't spend much time on its lees, unlike the richer Le Fief du Breil.

BOTTLES TO TRY
○ Amphibolite Nature Muscadet Sèvre et Maine / $$
○ Le Fief du Breil Muscadet / $$

NICOLAS JOLY

Nicolas Joly's business card reads "Nature Assistant," which is how this Savennières winemaker prefers to describe his role; he's known for being France's most vocal evangelist for biodynamics. His famed Clos de la Coulée de Serrant hails from Savennières-Coulée-de-Serrant, a legendary Chenin Blanc vineyard that is its own appellation. Joly's daughter Virginie has brought more consistency to recent vintages, which offer Savennières's trademark qualities: tart acidity, a silky, rich texture and alluring notes ranging from citrus to minerals to flowers and honey.

BOTTLES TO TRY
○ Clos de la Bergerie Savennières-Roche-aux-Moines / $$$
○ Clos de la Coulée de Serrant Savennières-Coulée-de-Serrant / $$$$

OLGA RAFFAULT

This winery, probably more than any other, is responsible for introducing American wine drinkers to the pleasures of Chinon. Raffault's Cabernet Franc wines are distinct from Bordeaux and California versions, combining earthiness with classic violet and cassis aromatics, and deceptively light colors and moderate alcohol levels with surprising body and flavor intensity. The flagship of this estate, now run by Raffault's granddaughter Sylvie and her husband, Eric de la Vigerie, is the classically structured (not to say firmly tannic) Les Picasses bottling, made from 50-year-old vines on the steep banks of the Vienne River.

BOTTLE TO TRY
● Les Picasses Chinon / $$

RHÔNE VALLEY

CLAIM TO FAME

From the exalted, powerful reds of the northern Rhône, including the famous Hermitage, to the southern Rhône's suppler, berry-rich red blends like Châteauneuf-du-Pape, the Rhône Valley offers wines that rival those of Bordeaux and Burgundy in quality, but with dramatically different flavor profiles. Northern Rhône reds get their spice and brooding dark-fruit flavors from the Syrah grape; in contrast, southern Rhône red wines are multivariety blends typically based on Grenache. The region's often-overshadowed white bottlings are highly sought after by wine cognoscenti.

REGIONS TO KNOW

NORTHERN RHÔNE A narrow stretch of steep and often terraced hills, the northern Rhône occupies a transitional zone between cooler-climate Burgundy to the north and sunnier Mediterranean climes to the south—a position that's reflected in its wines' alluring mix of finesse and robust flavor. Though responsible for less than 5 percent of the Rhône Valley's total production, the northern Rhône is the source of many of its most celebrated wines. The top northern Rhône subregions for reds include **Côte-Rôtie** ("roasted slope," a reference to its sunny exposure), **Cornas** and **Hermitage.** The tiny **Condrieu** appellation turns out coveted, voluptuous white wines from Viognier. The northern Rhône's largest subzone, **Crozes-Hermitage,** produces about half of the region's wine; much of it is ordinary, but most of it is well-priced. The **St-Joseph** appellation is a good source for bargains.

SOUTHERN RHÔNE Some 35 miles south of the northern Rhône's Hermitage hill, the sunnier southern Rhône begins. Many grapes are permitted in its various subregions, most selected for their ability to withstand the hotter Mediterranean climate. The prestigious, and increasingly pricey, wines of **Châteauneuf-du-Pape** are usually based on Grenache but can be blended with up to 13 varieties. The **Gigondas** and **Vacqueyras** appellations produce mostly red wines similar to (but less profound and costly than) those of Châteauneuf. Across the river, the **Lirac**

and **Tavel** districts are best known for outstanding rosés and, increasingly, some solid reds. Farther afield, the satellite regions of **Ventoux, Luberon** and **Costières de Nîmes** make wines similar to basic Côtes du Rhône (see below).

KEY GRAPES: WHITE

GRENACHE BLANC, CLAIRETTE & BOURBOULENC Used only in the southern part of the Rhône Valley, these plump grape varieties typically get blended with Marsanne, Roussanne and Viognier to create the region's medium-bodied, white peach– and citrus-inflected wines.

MARSANNE & ROUSSANNE These fragrant varieties are usually blended to make the northern Rhône's full-bodied, nutty, pear-scented white wines. In the southern Rhône, they are frequently used to complement Viognier. Though not high in acidity, the resulting wines often have the ability to age remarkably well.

VIOGNIER Lush and fragrant, the honeysuckle-scented Viognier is best known as the grape behind the celebrated whites of the northern Rhône's Condrieu appellation.

KEY GRAPES: RED

GRENACHE The southern Rhône's darkly fruity, full-bodied reds are made primarily with Grenache, often bolstered by some combination of Cinsaut, Syrah, Mourvèdre and/or Carignane.

SYRAH The only red grape permitted in northern Rhône wines, Syrah can achieve great power and complexity, expressing a mix of dark fruit accented by black pepper and meat flavors. Most northern Rhône reds may include a small portion of regional white grapes, except in Cornas, where Syrah must stand alone.

WINE TERMINOLOGY

CÔTES DU RHÔNE This is the Rhône's most basic category, representing the vast majority of its wines, both red and white. Most Côtes du Rhône wines come from the south, although the entire valley is permitted to use the designation. Very little basic Côtes du Rhône wine comes from the north; most northern Rhône bottlings meet higher standards and are entitled to label their wines with one of the region's eight *crus*.

CÔTES DU RHÔNE VILLAGES This designation identifies wines made from grapes grown in the dozens of southern Rhône villages that satisfy stricter quality requirements than those for the basic Côtes du Rhône designation. Of these villages, 18 have earned the right to append their name to the wine label— for example, Côtes du Rhône Villages Cairanne. All reds and rosés with the *villages* designation must be at least 50 percent Grenache; whites are based on Grenache Blanc, Clairette, Marsanne, Roussanne, Bourboulenc and Viognier.

Producers/ Rhône Valley

ALAIN GRAILLOT

This estate is a star of the Crozes-Hermitage appellation in the northern Rhône, demonstrating the lively, concentrated, "junior Hermitage" potential of Crozes. Graillot and his son Maxime organically farm 52 acres of old vines in Crozes, and some well-regarded parcels in often underrated St-Joseph. Though not exactly priced for everyday drinking, the top-of-the-line La Guiraude cuvée, assembled from the best barrels in the cellar, is a very strong value for luscious Rhône Syrah.

BOTTLES TO TRY
- La Guiraude Crozes-Hermitage / $$$
- St-Joseph / $$$

CAVE YVES CUILLERON

Success hasn't spoiled Yves Cuilleron; he keeps his hand in all aspects of an operation that produces nearly 32,000 cases from six northern Rhône AOCs and a range of IGP and Vin de France bottlings. He's added to his vineyard holdings (now up to 145 acres), including parcels in Cornas and Crozes-Hermitage, and he broke ground on a new winery in 2014. The estate is arguably more famous for its lush whites from Condrieu and St-Joseph, but its Côte-Rôtie and St-Joseph reds are sought after as well.

BOTTLES TO TRY
- ○ Les Chaillets Condrieu / $$$$
- L'Amarybelle St-Joseph / $$$

CHÂTEAU RAYAS / CHÂTEAU DES TOURS

Rayas soared into the pricing stratosphere by unlikely means: This modest estate is not overly blessed with Châteauneuf's famous rocks (the soil is sandy); it is dominated by the single Grenache variety; and its late presiding genius, Jacques Reynaud, was said to hide when he saw visitors approach. Yet its wines are like nothing else in the world—shifting, complex, by turns earthy and sublimely elegant. Reynaud's nephew Emmanuel continues to turn out these astonishments, and even the second wine, Pignan, is very expensive. For a sense of the genius, try the Vacqueyras from sister estate Château des Tours.

BOTTLES TO TRY

- Château des Tours Vacqueyras / $$$
- Pignan Châteauneuf-du-Pape / $$$$

DELAS FRÈRES

An all-star team of winemaking talent plus a cash infusion from corporate parent Louis Roederer have transformed this *négociant's* once-lackluster portfolio into a treasure trove. From its base near St-Joseph, Delas offers an array of memorable wines from the northern and southern Rhône that have gone from strength to strength. Under managing director Fabrice Rosset and enologists Jacques Grange and Jean-François Farinet, Delas is living up to the potential of its superb vineyards at the top end, and delivering terrific value in everyday bottlings.

BOTTLES TO TRY

- ○ La Galopine Condrieu / $$$
- Saint-Esprit Côtes du Rhône / $

DOMAINE BRUSSET

Now led by third-generation Laurent Brusset, this domaine is best known internationally for the highly regarded Gigondas cuvées it produces from its terraced vineyards in the Dentelles de Montmirail hillsides: Tradition le Grand Montmirail and the costlier Les Hauts de Montmirail. But fans of the Brusset family's efforts also keep an eye out for the well-priced Côtes du Rhône Villages wines from Cairanne as well as others from humbler appellations, which can be a distinct cut above the norm.

BOTTLES TO TRY

- Les Travers Cairanne Côtes du Rhône Villages / $$
- Les Hauts de Montmirail Gigondas / $$$

DOMAINE CHARVIN

Though the history of this Châteauneuf-du-Pape estate stretches back six generations, to 1851, it wasn't until Laurent Charvin took control in 1990 that the family began to bottle most of its production itself. Charvin doubled the size of the Châteauneuf holdings (up to 20 acres) and put his winery on wine lovers' maps via a single red, which he describes as a combination of power and finesse—with about 85 percent Grenache and small additions of Syrah, Mourvèdre and Vaccarèse. The often superb Côtes du Rhône bottlings are also worth seeking out.

BOTTLES TO TRY

- Le Poutet Côtes du Rhône / $$
- Châteauneuf-du-Pape / $$$$

DOMAINE DU PÉGAU

Laurence Féraud makes her sleek, modern wines the easier-said-than-done old-fashioned way: Bring in sound grapes, crush them and let them ferment. She credits extremely low yields and old vines for the fabulous concentration of Domaine du Pégau's top-tier wines, which have become emblematic of seductive, richly layered Châteauneuf-du-Pape. Féraud's *négociant* selections are as polished as her estate-grown cuvées, which now include wines from a Côtes du Rhône property named Château Pégau.

BOTTLES TO TRY

- Sélection Laurence Féraud Côtes du Rhône / $
- Cuvée Reservée Châteauneuf-du-Pape / $$$$

DOMAINE DU VIEUX TÉLÉGRAPHE

The Brunier family inhabits a stony, mistral-swept Châteauneuf-du-Pape plateau apparently perfect for an 18th-century telegraph relay tower and, as it turns out, for producing stylish wine. The magisterial top red, La Crau (there's also a very fine La Crau white), has benefited from having a second wine, called Télégramme, which generally absorbs the younger vine fruit. Other Brunier ventures include a second Châteauneuf property, Domaine La Roquète; a top Gigondas estate, Domaine Les Pallières; and the well-priced Le Pigeoulet des Brunier line.

BOTTLES TO TRY

- ○ La Crau Châteauneuf-du-Pape / $$$$
- La Crau Châteauneuf-du-Pape / $$$$

BEST OF THE BEST PRODUCERS / RHÔNE VALLEY

1. CHÂTEAU DE BEAUCASTEL **2.** CHÂTEAU RAYAS **3.** DOMAINE DU PÉGAU **5.** DOMAINE JEAN-LOUIS CHAVE **4.** HENRI BONNEAU

DOMAINE JEAN-LOUIS CHAVE

Jean-Louis and his father, Gérard, create some of the world's most treasured wines, blended from their plots on the granite hill of Hermitage and sold at astronomical prices. Behind these long-lived, layered taste mosaics—both red and white—are the family's prime vineyard parcels and the magic touch of supremely talented winemakers. The domaine's St-Joseph and Mon Coeur Côtes du Rhône bottlings are more affordable.

BOTTLES TO TRY

- Mon Coeur Côtes du Rhône / $$
- Hermitage / $$$$

DOMAINE LA SOUMADE

Dry reds from the Rasteau appellation have been on the official rise, gaining full AOC status in 2010, and this property, worked by the esteemed André Roméro and his son Frédéric, has been at the forefront. The Grenache-based wines, including a Gigondas, are produced in a dense, powerful style that has gained an international following. The top Rasteau cuvées, Confiance and Fleur de Confiance, are made from 50- to 100-year-old vines.

BOTTLES TO TRY

- Cuvée Prestige Rasteau / $$$
- Gigondas / $$$

DOMAINE LES CAILLOUX

From his Châteauneuf-du-Pape vineyards strewn with *cailloux* ("stones"), André Brunel derives red wines (and a small amount of whites) of rare refinement. There are two reds: the often spectacular "regular" bottling and the prized Cuvée Centenaire, from 100-plus-year-old vines. Look also for the excellent Côtes du Rhône values and the Grenache-based wines from the Féraud-Brunel joint venture with Domaine du Pégau's Laurence Féraud.

BOTTLES TO TRY

- ○ Les Cailloux Châteauneuf-du-Pape / $$$
- Les Cailloux Châteauneuf-du-Pape / $$$

DOMAINE ROSTAING

Réne Rostaing, whose name is usually accompanied by words like *classicist* and *perfectionist,* is focused on making northern Rhône wines of purity and grace that reveal their distinctive *terroirs.* It's a goal often stated, but rarely achieved with such success and consistency: Rostaing's top reds, Côte-Rôties from his parcels in the Côte Blonde and La Landonne and his blend Ampodium, have reached the realm of luxury pricing. A baby brother bottling, Les Lézardes Syrah, is a fraction of the price and comes from old vines just outside the Côte-Rôtie district.

BOTTLES TO TRY

○ La Bonnette Condrieu / $$$$
● Les Lézardes Syrah / $$$

DOMAINE SANTA DUC

Until fourth-generation vintner Yves Gras took over his family's Gigondas estate in 1995, Domaine Santa Duc (the name derives from *canta duc,* the Provençal name of a singing owl) sold its wine in bulk. Gras took a bet on estate-bottled wines that has paid off handily. Top cuvées from the estate's vineyards in the foothills of the rugged Dentelles de Montmirail rank among the region's best. The family holdings include vineyards in several Côtes du Rhône Villages appellations; look for high-quality, affordable bottlings, including Les Quatre Terres.

BOTTLES TO TRY

● Les Quatre Terres Côtes du Rhône / $$
● Gigondas / $$$

E. GUIGAL

Third-generation winemaker Philippe Guigal oversees the northern Rhône's preeminent producer from his high-tech yet highly traditional cellar. He turns out magisterial reds in tiny quantities from estate vineyards in Côte-Rôtie, Condrieu and Hermitage, as well as widely available wines from across the Rhône Valley. At the high end are three stunningly pricey Côte-Rôties from La Turque, La Mouline and La Landonne vineyards; the affordable end offers a tour of every key Rhône appellation, all the way down to great values in red and white Côtes du Rhône.

BOTTLES TO TRY

○ Crozes-Hermitage / $$
● Brune et Blonde de Guigal Côte-Rôtie / $$$$

FAMILLE PERRIN / CHÂTEAU DE BEAUCASTEL

The Perrin family's Château de Beaucastel produces definitive Châteauneuf-du-Pape; the savory, fragrant and deep yet buoyant flagship red typically blends all 13 allowed grapes. Collectors also vie for two rare cuvées: a white made from ancient Roussanne vines and the monumental Mourvèdre-based Hommage à Jacques Perrin. Wallet-savvy Rhône fans stock up on the Coudoulet de Beaucastel blends. The family's *négociant* operation also offers consistent values from the Rhône's less prestigious corners, such as the juicy, easy-drinking wines from Luberon and Ventoux under the Vieille Ferme label.

BOTTLES TO TRY

○ Coudoulet de Beaucastel Côtes du Rhône / $$$

● Château de Beaucastel Châteauneuf-du-Pape / $$$$

HENRI BONNEAU

The 12th generation of his family to make wine here, Henri Bonneau is a living legend, famous for his unkempt cellars; for aging wines in old barrels and wooden tanks before bottling them many years after harvest (and after everyone else); and for turning out some of the greatest Châteauneufs ever tasted. Or, in the case of his small-production, luxury super-cuvée, Réserve des Célestins, from the sunstruck, windblown, rocky La Crau plateau, the greatest very few will ever get to taste.

BOTTLES TO TRY

● Cuvée Marie Beurrier Châteauneuf-du-Pape / $$$$

● Réserve des Célestins Châteauneuf-du-Pape / $$$$

JEAN-LUC COLOMBO

Tireless Jean-Luc Colombo first made his name in a laboratory, not a vineyard, advising winegrowers in the then-obscure Cornas region during the 1980s. But Colombo's gift for transforming Cornas's rustic Syrahs into polished, more accessible reds helped popularize the appellation and won him a prestigious roster of consulting clients. His portfolio, partly overseen by daughter Laure, includes four prestigious, estate-grown Cornas wines from the vertiginous 49 acres near his home, and the reliably tasty, modern-style *négociant* bottlings.

BOTTLES TO TRY

○ La Redonne Côtes du Rhône / $$

● Les Ruchets Cornas / $$$$

M. CHAPOUTIER

One of the most influential Rhône winemakers of the late 20th century and early 21st, Michel Chapoutier turned his family's famous, successful wine business on its ear as he became one of the world's more articulate and vocal supporters of biodynamic winemaking. The results in his case speak for themselves, from the often sensational Hermitage and Châteauneuf-du-Pape wines to reasonably priced wines from vineyards elsewhere in the Rhône and southern France. The prolific Chapoutier also makes wine in Portugal and Australia.

BOTTLES TO TRY

○ Les Granits St-Joseph / $$$$

● Les Meysonniers Crozes-Hermitage / $$

PAUL JABOULET AÎNÉ

The Frey family that owns Bordeaux's Château La Lagune (see p. 30) bought this iconic Rhône wine producer and *négociant* in 2006, and has revitalized it, slashing production and building a sleek new winery. Caroline Frey oversees a still-extensive portfolio, ranging from the hallowed Hermitage La Chapelle to the ubiquitous red and white Parallèle 45 Côtes du Rhônes. In between are a wealth of offerings, many at very tempting prices, including Les Domaines–tier bottlings like the Domaine de Thalabert Crozes-Hermitage, and the even more gently priced Vignerons wines, such as Le Grand Pompée St-Joseph.

BOTTLES TO TRY

○ Parallèle 45 Côtes du Rhône / $

● Domaine de Thalabert Crozes-Hermitage / $$$

VIDAL-FLEURY

Guy Sarton du Jonchay has boosted the quality at this Guigal-owned *négociant*, as demonstrated in his trio of popular Côtes du Rhônes (red, white and pink). From its founding vineyard in Côte-Rotie, Vidal-Fleury has been producing wine continuously for over two centuries, making it the Rhône's oldest estate. Today its umbrella covers nearly every major Rhône appellation, with wines ranging from competitively priced bottlings to the estate-grown and elegantly styled La Chatillonne Côte-Rôtie.

BOTTLES TO TRY

● Tavel / $$

● St-Joseph / $$

SOUTHERN FRANCE

CLAIM TO FAME

France's Mediterranean coast and southwest were long known for the quantity, not the quality, of their wines. But ambitious vintners in search of reasonably priced vineyard lands and global demand for affordable wines spurred a change. Southern France still churns out a lot of bulk wine, but it's also a source of exciting cuvées made from rediscovered ancient vineyards and impressive new ones. A varied geography and relatively gentle climate mean that a sweeping variety of grapes can thrive here.

REGIONS TO KNOW

LANGUEDOC-ROUSSILLON France's Mediterranean coast produces vast amounts of mostly red wine, including many terrific values. Both Roussillon (closer to Spain) and the Languedoc (at the center of the coastal arc) are turning out increasingly complex wines at prices that don't carry the "prestige tax" of their northern neighbors. Unlike most parts of France, the Languedoc grows a wide range of grape varieties—some native to the area, others from different French regions. Look to subregions like **Corbières, Côtes du Roussillon, Faugères** and **Fitou** for great red blends, some based on old-vine Carignane and Grenache.

PROVENCE Known for its herb-edged dry rosés, especially those from **Bandol** (**Côtes de Provence** and **Coteaux d'Aix-en-Provence** rosés can be excellent, too), Provence is also an overlooked source of bold reds. Go-to regions include Bandol, **Les Baux-de-Provence** and Coteaux d'Aix-en-Provence. Whites are citrusy and soft; the best are from the area around **Cassis.**

THE SOUTHWEST This area's wines are little known in the US, but that's changing. **Bergerac** reds are made from the same grapes as Bordeaux—Cabernet, Merlot, Malbec and Cabernet Franc—and can exhibit a similar finesse. **Cahors** vintners craft powerful reds from Malbec, known locally as Auxerrois or Côt. **Madiran**'s full-bodied and tannic wines are based mainly on Tannat. Hearty Basque Country wines are blends of local grapes; **Jurançon**, for example, turns out full-bodied whites made from Petit and Gros Manseng grapes in dry and sweet styles.

❧ KEY GRAPES: WHITE

CHARDONNAY Much of southern France is too warm for fine Chardonnay, though straightforward value versions abound.

GRENACHE BLANC One of the Languedoc's most widely planted white grapes, this fairly neutral variety is usually bottled as part of a blend, contributing softness and mouth-filling body.

MACCABÉO This medium-bodied, floral-tinged grape is known as Viura in Spain's Rioja, but it's also common in Roussillon and the Languedoc.

MARSANNE, ROUSSANNE & VIOGNIER Best known in Rhône wines, these grapes also do well in the warm regions farther south, producing round, lush and sometimes spicy whites.

PICPOUL BLANC This minerally grape (the name means "lip-stinger") is behind some of the Languedoc's incredibly refreshing, zesty whites, especially those grown near the town of Pinet.

ROLLE, BOURBOULENC, CLAIRETTE, SÉMILLON & UGNI BLANC Along with Grenache Blanc, Marsanne and a few others, these local grapes create Provence's white blends. Rolle is also common in Roussillon, where it yields zesty whites comparable to those produced in Italy under its alias, Vermentino.

❧ KEY GRAPES: RED

CABERNET SAUVIGNON & MERLOT This duo is mostly used for inexpensive wines destined for export. While a few regions (such as parts of Provence) and some top producers succeed with more ambitious versions, most of these wines are simple and fruity.

CARIGNANE This widely planted variety dominates southernmost France, especially Roussillon. Much Carignane wine is simple and rustic, but the grape can make great fruity, spicy reds. Some of the best come from old vines in Languedoc's Corbières.

CINSAUT Native to Provence (and eaten locally as a table grape), Cinsaut is the signature variety of the region's fresh, fruity rosés. In the Languedoc, it's often blended with Carignane to add perfume to the reds of Minervois, Corbières and Fitou.

GRENACHE & SYRAH Fruity Grenache and firm, tannic Syrah are blended throughout the south. In both Roussillon and the Languedoc, they are combined with Mourvèdre to create hearty reds, such as those of Minervois and Fitou. In Provence, Grenache and Syrah are responsible for noted rosés and reds.

MALBEC This inky dark variety stars in the southwest's Cahors region, where it's called Auxerrois (not to be confused with the white grape of the same name) or Côt. Unlike Argentina's fruity, supple Malbecs, Cahors versions are spicy, earthy and tannic.

MOURVÈDRE The calling-card grape of Provence's prestigious Bandol region (and the same as Spain's Monastrell), Mourvèdre yields spicy, rich reds and robust rosés on its own. Elsewhere, it is often blended with Grenache and Syrah.

TANNAT Widely planted in the southwest, this tough, tannic grape does best in the Madiran subregion. It's also blended with Cabernet Franc and/or Cabernet Sauvignon for the dark, meaty reds of Irouléguy in the Basque region of France.

Producers/ Southern France

CHÂTEAU DE PIBARNON

The late Count Henri de Saint-Victor began his family's Bandol wine enterprise in the late 1970s with yeoman's labor, bulldozing his newly acquired rugged amphitheater property into terraces and planting them to grapevines. From the winery's first release in 1978, de Saint-Victor, his wife, Catherine, and later their son, Eric, who has directed the estate since 2000, worked to understand what their sunny, dry, limestone- and fossil-filled terrain can mean for Mourvèdre. The answer is a full-bodied top red of great longevity; a lovely second-label red, Les Restanques; and a coveted spicy rosé. There's also a luscious local-varieties white.

BOTTLES TO TRY

- Bandol / $$
- Bandol / $$$

CHÂTEAU LAGRÉZETTE

Luxury marketing mogul Alain Dominique Perrin acquired this ancient estate outside the town of Cahors in 1980, poured cash into rehabilitating its vineyards and 15th-century castle, and hired superstar consultant Michel Rolland to mastermind the wines. The resulting Malbec-based reds have made Lagrézette Cahors's most prominent label. Its powerhouse top cuvée, Le Pigeonnier, spends more than two years in new barrels and is very expensive, but a range of wines made from purchased grapes offer an affordable taste of Lagrézette's intense, fruity style.

BOTTLES TO TRY
- Purple / $
- Château Lagrézette / $$$

DOMAINE DU CLOS DES FÉES

A onetime sommelier bitten by the wine bug, Hervé Bizeul founded his winery in Roussillon's Agly Valley on a shoestring and with a lot of sweat to water his rocky, windswept vineyards—his own Clos des Fées ("walled garden of the fairies"). He produces deep, sometimes prodigiously concentrated cuvées from his old-vine vineyards. His entry-level Les Sorcières is a juicy blend of youngish-vine Syrah with 40- to 80-year-old Grenache and Carignan; La Petite Sibérie, from old, bush-vine Grenache, is his cellar-worthy masterpiece.

BOTTLES TO TRY
- ○ Grenache Blanc / $$
- Les Sorcières / $$

DOMAINE GAUBY

This producer in the Pyrenees Mountains in southwest Roussillon—"Northern Catalonia," as the winery says—helped prove that the overlooked region could produce refined dry reds and whites. In this challenging environment, Gérard Gauby does everything the hard way—with biodynamic viticulture, natural fermentations with no additions and bottling without fining or filtering. Since releasing its first experimental estate wines in the late 1980s, Gauby has migrated to an increasingly elegant, less rustic style that makes it a benchmark for the region.

BOTTLES TO TRY
- ○ Vieilles Vignes Vin de Pays des Côtes Catalanes / $$$
- Vieilles Vignes Côtes du Roussillon Villages / $$$

DOMAINE LAFAGE

Jean-Marc Lafage is a sought-after consultant himself, making him something of a rarity in Roussillon, which tends to import wine advice from elsewhere. In the rugged Agly region, with his winemaker wife, Eliane, Lafage produces a wide array of wines, from traditional *vins doux naturels* to clean, modern-style rosés to fresh, lively whites and a series of reds, including the flagship Cuvée Nicolas. Though wine lovers have caught on, the best of these wines still represent astonishing values.

BOTTLES TO TRY
○ Centenaire Côtes du Roussillon / $
● Nicolas / $

DOMAINE TEMPIER

The Peyraud family, owners of Domaine Tempier, came to many wine drinkers' attention as heroes of importer Kermit Lynch's 1988 book, *Adventures on the Wine Route,* but the estate has been setting standards in Bandol for far longer. Ground zero for spicy, sometimes animal/sometimes elegant/sometimes both, full-throttle Mourvèdre, Tempier has gained a cult following for its pricey, single-vineyard red blends, Cabassaou, La Migoua and La Tourtine, with their highly distinct, *terroir*-driven differences. But the winery also makes one of the world's most memorable rosés and an often sensational Bandol Blanc.

BOTTLES TO TRY
● Bandol / $$$
● Bandol / $$$

GÉRARD BERTRAND

Photogenic former rugby star Gérard Bertrand is not hampered by modesty (he nominates himself as "the Ambassador of the Mediterranean Art of Living"). From his family's original property, Domaine de Villemajou in Corbières, he has built a wine empire spanning several estates and wine lines. His Château l'Hospitalet, with its hotel, restaurant and hospitality center, has become a wine-tourism magnet in Languedoc-Roussillon. It also produces worthy wines using only sustainable viticultural methods, as the Ambassador is a serious steward of the land.

BOTTLES TO TRY
● Gris Blanc / $
● Château l'Hospitalet Art de Vivre Coteaux du Languedoc / $$

Italy

It is nearly impossible to think of Italian wines without thinking of food. Conjure up a great Chianti Classico and you'll almost inevitably get a vision of pasta alla Bolognese alongside it. Such associations are a great reason to learn about Italian wines; another is that Italian wines are far more varied than many people think. There are more than 400 official quality-wine denominations and hundreds of native grape varieties, not to mention a history of winemaking that stretches back some 3,000 years. Only a dedicated scholar would study every aspect, but with Italian wine, even the smallest amount of knowledge can be immensely rewarding.

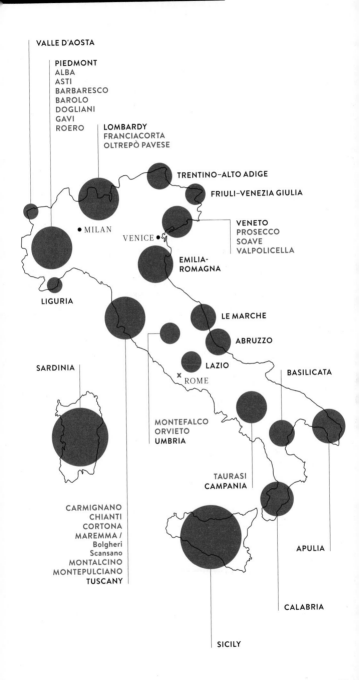

VALLE D'AOSTA

PIEDMONT
ALBA
ASTI
BARBARESCO
BAROLO
DOGLIANI
GAVI
ROERO

LOMBARDY
FRANCIACORTA
OLTREPÒ PAVESE

TRENTINO–ALTO ADIGE

FRIULI–VENEZIA GIULIA

• MILAN

VENICE •

VENETO
PROSECCO
SOAVE
VALPOLICELLA

EMILIA-
ROMAGNA

LIGURIA

LE MARCHE

ABRUZZO

LAZIO

SARDINIA

x ROME

BASILICATA

MONTEFALCO
ORVIETO
UMBRIA

TAURASI
CAMPANIA

CARMIGNANO
CHIANTI
CORTONA
MAREMMA /
Bolgheri
Scansano
MONTALCINO
MONTEPULCIANO
TUSCANY

APULIA

CALABRIA

SICILY

67

WINE TERMINOLOGY

As in France, most Italian wines are labeled by region rather than by grape type, though some list the grape if it defines a region (e.g., Montepulciano d'Abruzzo, made from the Montepulciano grape in Abruzzo). The main quality categories of Italian wines are DOCG, DOC/DOP, IGT/IGP and VdT. These categories dictate standards for growing and making wines, including permitted grape varieties, how much tonnage a vineyard can yield and the finished wine's minimum alcohol content.

DENOMINAZIONE DI ORIGINE CONTROLLATA E GARANTITA (DOCG) This, the strictest classification, includes Italy's most prestigious wines. DOCG wines must pass a blind taste test by experts appointed by Italy's Ministry of Agriculture and carry a numbered government seal around the neck of their bottles.

DENOMINAZIONE DI ORIGINE CONTROLLATA/PROTETTA (DOC/DOP) Equivalent to France's AOC (with local rules differing by area), the DOC category includes most of Italy's better wines. The newer DOP category is meant to replace DOC and DOCG.

INDICAZIONE GEOGRAFICA TIPICA/PROTETTA (IGT/IGP) The IGT and newer IGP categories identify region-specific wines that don't qualify as DOCG or DOC. IGT/IGP wines include ambitious bottlings (such as the famed Super-Tuscans) by vintners determined to buck the restrictions of traditional DOC/G rules.

VINO DA TAVOLA (VDT) Most wines using the Vino da Tavola ("table wine") designation are cheap jug blends, though some quality wines carry the label. VdT wines may come from anywhere in Italy and don't identify their vintage years.

CLASSICO A prestigious subregion, often the original and oldest part of a region whose boundaries were later enlarged.

RISERVA This term indicates a wine that has been aged for a longer period than basic wines of the same designation. Exact requirements differ by region.

SUPERIORE Wines labeled *superiore* are aged longer or have a higher alcohol content and greater concentration than is the norm for their classification.

PIEDMONT

CLAIM TO FAME
Northwestern Italy's Piedmont makes two of the country's most coveted red wines, Barolo and Barbaresco, revered for their ageworthy structure and complex aromatics. But don't overlook Barbera and Dolcetto, the food-friendly reds that locals drink every day. The lesser-known whites are also worth seeking out.

REGIONS TO KNOW
ALBA & DOGLIANI Both zones are sources of top Dolcettos; Alba is also known for good values in Nebbiolo.

BARBARESCO & BAROLO Sourced from a few prized vineyards in the hills around the town of Alba, Nebbiolo-based reds from these two zones have steep price tags reflecting their scarcity. Barolos must be aged three years (18 months in barrel) before release; Barbarescos, two years (nine months in barrel). Many of these bottlings take a decade or more of age to reach their prime.

GATTINARA, GHEMME & LANGHE Go-to zones for Nebbiolo-based reds that offer a taste of this compelling grape at a lower price than Barolo and Barbaresco.

GAVI Gavi's melony whites are lively enough to serve as an aperitif and substantial enough to accompany a wide range of foods.

ROERO This subregion's zesty, minerally, Arneis-based whites are becoming easier to find in the US.

⦂ KEY GRAPES: WHITE

ARNEIS The almond-scented Arneis grape has come back from near extinction; its best wines are from the Roero subregion.

CHARDONNAY Many prominent Piedmont vintners produce worthwhile Chardonnays; they tend to be rich, fruity and fresh.

CORTESE A specialty of southeast Piedmont, Cortese yields tart, citrusy and mostly inexpensive whites. The best come from hillside vines in Gavi, where riper grapes yield fruitier wines.

⦂ KEY GRAPES: RED

BARBERA & DOLCETTO Versatile, high-acid Barbera and fruity, low-acid Dolcetto yield some of Piedmont's most popular wines.

NEBBIOLO The grape behind the majestic wines of Barolo and Barbaresco, Nebbiolo has substantial tannins and firm acidity, which can make these wines difficult to drink when young. With savory, floral aromatics (think tar and roses), it's crafted in a range of styles, from traditional (firm, austere and earthy) to modern (smoother and fruitier). Generally simpler, often more affordable versions are labeled with the Nebbiolo grape name.

Producers/ Piedmont

BRUNO GIACOSA

Now in his eighties, Bruno Giacosa is an icon to collectors around the world, and his wines, under the Bruno Giacosa and Azienda Agricola Falletto di Bruno Giacosa labels, fetch top dollar. The most coveted of his reference-point Barbarescos and Barolos are the rare red-label Riservas from top vintages, although the more common white labels have plenty of takers, too. Giacosa's range of wines includes outstanding—and more accessibly priced—Arneis and Barbera d'Alba bottlings.

BOTTLES TO TRY

● Nebbiolo d'Alba / $$$
● Falletto Barbaresco / $$$$

CANTINA BARTOLO MASCARELLO

If there was concern among Barolo traditionalists that Maria Theresa Mascarello might switch things up when her father, Bartolo, died in 2005, it has been resolved. Mascarello continues to age the winery's flagship Barolo in large neutral barrels, eschewing both the vanilla inflection from small French barrels and the earlier-drinking, fruitier character of new-style Barolos. In fact, many fans believe she has taken the winery's legendarily long-lived flagship blend to new heights. Also wonderful are her lively, full-flavored Dolcetto d'Albas and Barbera d'Albas.

BOTTLES TO TRY
- ● Dolcetto d'Alba / $$
- ● Barolo / $$$$

CAVALLOTTO

Alfio, Giuseppe and Laura are the fifth generation of Cavallottos to produce wine on the family estate, and though they bottle about 11 different wines per vintage, their total output is small: fewer than 10,000 cases a year. The Cavallottos believe in a natural winemaking style that, at its best, captures all of a vintage's nuance. Best known is the lushly complex Barolo Bricco Boschis. Oddly underappreciated, Cavallotto wines rival those of more renowned estates while selling for less.

BOTTLES TO TRY
- ○ Langhe Chardonnay / $$
- ● Bricco Boschis Barolo / $$$$

CERETTO

This relatively large producer keeps a grip on quality by working from four boutique wineries, each tailored to specific cuvées. Brothers Marcello and Bruno Ceretto helped drive the craze for single-site Nebbiolos in the 1970s; today, the next generation crafts wines in the same fruit-focused style. Ceretto's single-site Barolos come from an outpost perched over the legendary Bricco Rocche vineyard, while a tiny cellar in Asili yields two Barbarescos. The vineyard-specific reds are pricey, but Ceretto also crafts more affordable, multi-lot Barolo and Barbaresco bottlings. As for whites, its citrusy Arneis is compulsively drinkable.

BOTTLES TO TRY
- ○ Blangè Langhe Arneis / $$
- ● Barolo / $$$

DAMILANO

The fourth generation of the Damilano family to run this estate has a wealth of Barolo vineyard land to work with: The 150-plus prime acres include parcels in the great *crus* of Brunate, Cannubi, Cerequio and Liste. Fans look for two excellent bottlings, the Barolo Riserva and the Lecinquevigne, blended from five vineyards. High-end collectors seek the single-vineyard Barolos, particularly those from the old-vine Cannubi hillside, whose rare combination of soils imparts both elegance and power.

BOTTLES TO TRY
○ Langhe Arneis / $$
● Lecinquevigne Barolo / $$$

ELVIO COGNO

It's debatable what this tiny producer does best: Elvio Cogno's Barolos, Barbarescos, Dolcetto d'Albas and Barbera d'Albas are all consistently worth tracking down. Cogno himself was the winemaker at the legendary Barolo producer Marcarini until 1990, when he set up his own hilltop, eagle's aerie of an estate in the town of Novello (one of the 11 communes producing Barolo). His daughter Nadia and her husband, Valter Fissore, run the winery today, according to the template established by Cogno. Their powerful, elegant wines balance modern, fruit-focused approachability with earthy, tannic tradition.

BOTTLES TO TRY
● Cascina Nuova Barolo / $$$
● Pre-Phylloxera Barbera d'Alba / $$$

FONTANAFREDDA

Once the hunting grounds of Italy's first king and more recently known as a producer of good, but rarely great, wines, the Fontanafredda estate has been reinvented under Eataly marketplace entrepreneur Oscar Farinetti, who bought the vast property with a partner in 2008. Together with winemaker Danilo Drocco, they've improved quality and spun off two top Barolo *crus* to sister winery Mirafiore. Fontanafredda's own ripe, juicy Briccotondo Barbera has become a perennial overachiever, while the Serralunga d'Alba Barolo showcases muscular, dark fruit.

BOTTLES TO TRY
● Briccotondo Barbera / $
● Serralunga d'Alba Barolo / $$$

BEST OF THE BEST PRODUCERS / PIEDMONT
1. BRUNO GIACOSA 2. CANTINA BARTOLO MASCARELLO
3. GAJA 4. GIACOMO CONTERNO 5. MARCHESI DI GRÉSY

FRANCESCO RINALDI & FIGLI

This bastion of Barolo tradition is run by Paola and Piera Rinaldi, great-granddaughters of the founder. The women have continued the estate's commitment to heritage—still no new oak and extended vatting times, for example—while pushing the wine toward elegance and roundness. There is a strong, full lineup here, but the two single-vineyard Barolos from the noble *crus* Brunate and Cannubi are the pride of the house.

BOTTLES TO TRY
- Roussot Dolcetto d'Alba / $$
- Le Brunate Barolo / $$$$

GAJA

Angelo Gaja became the face of watershed changes in Piedmont a generation ago, famous—or, to traditionalists, notorious—for cutting crop yields to increase intensity, for using new French oak to age Nebbiolo and for planting Cabernet in Piedmont. His lofty reputation rests most squarely on his profound Barbarescos, such as the coveted Sorì Tildìn and Sorì San Lorenzo bottlings. Breathtaking prices are another Gaja trademark.

BOTTLES TO TRY
- ○ Gaia & Rey Langhe / $$$$
- ● Barbaresco / $$$$

G. D. VAJRA

Aldo and Milena Vajra's family-owned winery in Barolo represents fairly priced wines across a range of grapes, including a powerhouse Riesling and the wildly aromatic Kyè bottling from Freisa, an obscure Nebbiolo relative. The Bricco delle Viole Barolo is the top offering. Given a long, natural fermentation and up to four years in large oak barrels, the wine is appreciated for its nuanced delicacy. More accessible is the lovely Albe Barolo.

BOTTLES TO TRY
- ○ Langhe Bianco / $$$
- ● Kyè Langhe Freisa / $$$

GIACOMO BORGOGNO & FIGLI

The Farinetti family (see Fontanafredda, p. 72) bought this Piedmont stalwart in 2008. The Borgogno family had been making Barolos in much the same way since the 1840s. Today, winemaker Andrea Farinetti continues the practice, championing throwback methods—native yeasts, long fermentations, aging in large barrels—while making fresher wines of elegance and roundness. Single-vineyard wines from five top *crus* headline the strong portfolio. No Name, a blend of three vineyards, is so named (or not) as a protest against regulatory authorities.

BOTTLES TO TRY
- No Name / $$$
- Liste Barolo / $$$$

GIACOMO CONTERNO

This is one of the world's most famous wineries. Third-generation winemaker Roberto Conterno is a standard-bearer of the traditionalist school. His powerful, big-boned, seemingly immortal Barolos are macerated for extended periods and aged for up to 10 years in massive old Slavonian oak casks. The summit of Conterno Barolos is the Monfortino bottling, made only in top years from the family's Cascina Francia vineyards in Serralunga. A newer property, a parcel of the famed Cerretta vineyard, yields a Nebbiolo and a Barbera d'Alba worth seeking out.

BOTTLES TO TRY
- Cerretta Barbera d'Alba / $$$
- Cascina Francia Barolo / $$$$

LA SCOLCA

Arguably the best-known producer today of Piedmontese Gavi, La Scolca was among the first to focus on making quality still wines from the white Cortese grape (used to make Gavi), which until the 1970s was associated with mostly forgettable sparkling wines. Owned by the Soldati family, La Scolca benefits from its vineyards' mineral-laden soil, its very old vines and a climate moderated by the Mediterranean Sea. The winery's offerings include the exceptionally tasty entry-level white-label Gavi, and the intense, citrusy, benchmark black-label Gavi.

BOTTLES TO TRY
- "White Label" Gavi / $$
- "Black Label" Gavi / $$$

MARCHESI DI GRÉSY

Grapes have grown on the di Grésy family's Martinenga estate in Langhe since antiquity. But it wasn't until 1973 that Alberto di Grésy built a winery there to take advantage of the family's well-situated vineyards, including the famous Martinenga that's belonged to the Marquis of Grésy since 1797. More top sites were soon added. The three prestigious Barbarescos made from Martinenga grapes each year are still di Grésy's calling card, but winemakers Piero Ballario and Matteo Sasso also have a deft hand with Barbera, Dolcetto and Sauvignon Blanc.

BOTTLES TO TRY

○ Langhe Sauvignon / $$

● Camp Gros Martinenga Barbaresco / $$$$

MICHELE CHIARLO

Michele Chiarlo's silky, palate-flattering single-vineyard Barolos have earned this family-owned, Asti-based estate its place among Piedmont's elite. But Chiarlo is also one of Piedmont's best Barbera d'Asti producers, having helped to create a ripe, oak-inflected style that's worlds away from the thinner versions of decades past. That focus on quality shows across the portfolio, in bottlings such as Tortoniano, a consistently good, multi-vineyard Barolo that's less costly than the rare single-vineyard offerings, and in the estate's fine Gavi and Roero whites.

BOTTLES TO TRY

○ Le Madri Roero Arneis / $$

● La Court Nizza Barbera d'Asti Superiore / $$$

MOCCAGATTA

The roots of this well-regarded Barbaresco producer reach back to the 19th century, but the Minuto brothers and cousins who run it today seem to have taken a page from the modernist playbook of their neighbor Angelo Gaja (see p. 73). Moccagatta's wines, including four Barbarescos and two Chardonnays, all come from the estate's 30 planted acres, which are pruned and given a green harvest to reduce fruit loads and increase intensity. In the winery, the big reds ferment in stainless steel and age in small French oak, resulting in accessible, lushly textured wines.

BOTTLES TO TRY

○ Langhe Chardonnay / $$

● Barbaresco / $$$

PIO CESARE

It takes confidence to make sweeping—and expensive—changes to your father-in-law's winery, but that's exactly what Giuseppe Boffa did when he took over Pio Cesare in the 1940s. Boffa slashed production and began creating ambitious wines, including stunning Barolos and Barbarescos. Boffa's son, Pio, the current proprietor, added new cuvées but preserved the firmly structured style. Pio Cesare's entry-level Barolo is a steal for its price. The wines made with obscure local grapes like Grignolino and Freisa are also worth trying, if you can find them.

BOTTLES TO TRY

○ **Cortese di Gavi** / $$
● **Barolo** / $$$$

PODERE ROCCHE DEI MANZONI

Rocche dei Manzoni's late owner Valentino Migliorini fell squarely in the camp of the Piedmont innovators of the 1970s and '80s, whose style is influential to this day. Perfumed, lively and beautifully crafted, Manzoni wines come from low-yielding, crop-thinned vineyards, with the top Barolos all seeing controlled fermentations and months in French oak *barriques*. The brash exemplar of the winery's modern Piedmont style might be the Barolo called, fittingly enough, Big 'd Big.

BOTTLES TO TRY

● **Bricco Manzoni Langhe** / $$$
● **Big 'd Big Barolo** / $$$$

OTHER NORTHERN ITALY

REGIONS TO KNOW

FRIULI–VENEZIA GIULIA Tucked into the country's northeastern corner, reaching up to the foothills of the Alps, this is one of Italy's premier white-wine-producing regions. The hill country of eastern Friuli is dominated by small, high-quality wineries that make vivid, mineral-laden whites—many from obscure native grapes—plus a few interesting reds, including the violet-hued Refosco. **Collio** and **Friuli Colli Orientali** are the premier appellations. Most of Friuli–Venezia Giulia's Merlot and Cabernet Sauvignon vines grow in the gravelly soils of the plains and valleys; the wines show a crisp, fruit-oriented character.

LOMBARDY Surrounding Milan in north-central Italy, Lombardy derives its reputation for quality wine mainly from the **Franciacorta** region, which makes superb sparklers (see p. 282). The **Oltrepò Pavese** region, a longtime bulk district, is also starting to make fine wine, including reds from the spicy Bonarda grape.

TRENTINO—ALTO ADIGE These adjacent Alpine provinces make distinctly different wines. Trentino is known for fresh, fruity reds made from native grapes; the mostly German-speaking Alto Adige produces terrific whites, including crisp Gewürztraminers and compelling Pinot Grigios and Pinot Biancos.

VENETO The Veneto's wines include **Soave** whites, **Valpolicella** reds and Prosecco sparklers (see p. 283). Soave's Garganega-based whites are often bland, yet those made by better producers in small amounts from low-yielding, well-situated vineyards (especially in the original *classico* subregion) can be subtle and delicious. Valpolicella is made from blends of native red varieties, chiefly Corvina, Molinara and Rondinella. These same varieties go into Amarone, a dry, high-alcohol wine made from ripe, partially dried grapes that give it luscious depth and body. Some vintners infuse their Valpolicellas with pomace (grape seeds, stems and skins) left over from making Amarone—a process known as *ripasso*—to boost alcohol levels and body.

🍇 KEY GRAPES: WHITE

CHARDONNAY Northern Italy's Chardonnays display crisp acidity, thanks to shorter summers and cooler temperatures.

FRIULANO, MALVASIA ISTRIANA, PICOLIT & RIBOLLA GIALLA These aromatic natives are Friuli–Venezia Giulia specialties.

GARGANEGA Soave's wines get their lemon and almond flavors from this indigenous variety.

GEWÜRZTRAMINER, MÜLLER-THURGAU, RIESLING & SYLVANER The prevalence of these German grapes in Trentino–Alto Adige reflects the region's Austrian and Swiss cultural heritage.

GLERA Formerly called Prosecco, this grape is the basis for the Veneto's sparkling Prosecco wines.

PINOT BIANCO, PINOT GRIGIO & SAUVIGNON (BLANC) These international varieties thrive in northern Italy, where they yield whites with intense minerality and a crisp, Alpine freshness.

❧ KEY GRAPES: RED

CORVINA, MOLINARA & RONDINELLA This trio of native grapes provides the basis for three very different Veneto wines: bold, complex Amarone; juicy, medium-bodied traditional Valpolicella; and lighter Bardolino. Using partially raisined grapes for fermentation gives Amarone its sweet-tart flavor and full body.

LAGREIN, SCHIAVA & TEROLDEGO These Trentino–Alto Adige varieties are well adapted to the region's short summers. Schiavas are often light and simple; Lagrein and Teroldego offer more tannins and body, plus crisp acidity.

PINOT NERO (PINOT NOIR) Northern Italian Pinot is typically racy and light. Top regions for the grape include Lombardy's Oltrepò Pavese and Alto Adige.

REFOSCO Friuli–Venezia Giulia's best-known red grape yields plummy, dry wines that range from medium- to full-bodied.

Producers/ Other Northern Italy

ALOIS LAGEDER

Fifth-generation owner Alois Lageder has made this Alto Adige winery one of Italy's most eco-friendly. Lageder and his brother-in-law, winemaker Luis von Dellemann, produce a wide portfolio, divided into three tiers: the Classic wines (varietals like Pinot Grigio, typically from purchased grapes); the Terroirs (such as Haberle and Porer); and the estate wines of the Tenutæ Lageder line. Up and down, the whites are marked by a crisp, mineral-laden freshness and the reds by cool refinement.

BOTTLES TO TRY

○ Porer Pinot Grigio / $$

● Lagrein / $$

FORADORI

Charismatic Elisabetta Foradori has forged her own path since taking over this Trentino estate in the mid-1980s at age 20, after the untimely death of her father. The world's most famous champion of the Teroldego grape (a spicy, high-acid distant cousin of Syrah native to the region), she has progressively upped the ante—replanting to slash yields for greater intensity, going avidly biodynamic in the early millennium and fermenting her sensational top reds, the single-vineyard Teroldegos Sgarzon and Morei, partly in amphorae.

BOTTLES TO TRY
- Teroldego Rotaliano / $$
- Sgarzon Teroldego / $$$

GRAVNER

Friuli's restless Josko Gravner left behind the stainless steel and high technology he himself pioneered in the region for a radically historical take on winemaking that has earned him cult status—among his fans, at least. His wines are fermented old-school style, in *qvevri*, ancient Georgian clay amphorae that are buried in the earth for temperature control. In contrast to typical modern practice, he also ferments the skins and seeds of his whites with the juice, producing deeply colored orange wines, an acquired taste much touted by his deep-pocketed followers.

BOTTLE TO TRY
- ○ Anfora Ribolla / $$$$

JERMANN

Born into a winemaking family in Collio, Silvio Jermann pioneered Friuli's Super-Whites—complex blends of French grapes and native varieties, such as Ribolla Gialla and Picolit. Jermann's rich, creamy flagship cuvée, Vintage Tunina, combines Sauvignon Blanc, Chardonnay and three native varieties in what is perhaps the most famous of the Friuli Super-Whites. His other top wines include the red Blau & Blau, a blend of Blaufränkisch and Blauburgunder (Pinot Nero); the fancifully named, Chardonnay-based Were Dreams; and the rare all-Picolit Vino Dolce della Casa ("sweet house wine").

BOTTLES TO TRY
- ○ Vintage Tunina / $$$$
- Blau & Blau / $$$

LIVIO FELLUGA

In the aftermath of World War II, Livio Felluga faced an uphill battle to reestablish quality winegrowing in the devastated Colli Orientali. His belief in the region resulted in what is today one of northern Italy's most dynamic estates. His Terre Alte Super-White, aged partly in French oak, helped define Friuli's potential for world-class wine; the single-vineyard Abbazia di Rosazzo, debuted in 2009, is the new flagship. Now run by Felluga's four children, the 395-acre estate produces compelling wines made chiefly from traditional grapes.

BOTTLES TO TRY

○ Pinot Grigio / $$

○ Terre Alte / $$$$

MASI

Masi's voluptuous Amarones from the Veneto region are both relatively easy to find and reliably delicious. That consistency is thanks to sixth-generation scion Sandro Boscaini, who has embraced technical rigor while sticking to labor-intensive methods like *appassimento*—the ancient process of air-drying grapes before crushing them. Masi's velvety, seductively styled Amarones are decidedly modern, emphasizing rich, intense fruit. Easier to drink every day are the winery's excellent Valpolicella and humbler IGT wines, all made from traditional local grapes.

BOTTLES TO TRY

● Campofiorin / $$

● Costasera Amarone Classico / $$$

PIEROPAN

A master producer of Soave, Leonildo Pieropan resisted the Veneto's trend toward mass-market wines in the 1980s as well as the push to plant international varieties. Indeed, the Pieropans' fortunes are based on the organic Garganega and Trebbiano grapes that make up their lovely, crisp Soave Classico and more layered La Rocca and Calvarino wines. The newer reds, including a Valpolicella and an Amarone, are already sought-after. The family is restoring the 15th-century Villa Cipolla to serve as a production and hospitality center.

BOTTLES TO TRY

○ Soave Classico / $$

● Ruberpan Valpolicella Superiore / $$

TENUTA J. HOFSTÄTTER

One of the few midsize, family-owned producers left in Alto Adige (where cooperatives dominate), J. Hofstätter farms substantial acreage in a variety of local microclimates and altitudes—up to 2,600 feet. The winery produces two of Alto Adige's most famous and expensive single-vineyard wines: the Barthenau Vigna San Urbano Pinot Nero and the Kolbenhof estate Gewürztraminer. But there are many everyday wines to covet from Hofstätter, too, including the spicy Meczan Pinot Nero, an unusually fruity Lagrein and a range of crisp, lively whites.

BOTTLES TO TRY

○ **Kolbenhof Gewürztraminer** / $$$

● **Meczan Pinot Nero** / $$

VIE DI ROMANS

Gianfranco Gallo's stylish winery typifies the crossroads aspect of Friuli–Venezia Giulia (as the name implies, the winery sits on an old Roman road). Poised between the cool Bora winds from the north and the hot Siroccos from the south, and at the intersection of winemaking traditions from western Europe (Chardonnay, Sauvignon Blanc), Italy (Pinot Grigio), Germany (Riesling) and Friuli itself (Friulano), Vie di Romans has succeeded by producing lushly textured, flavorful wines. The whites benefit from the winery's practice of holding all of the bottles in the cellar for eight months to two years.

BOTTLES TO TRY

○ **Dessimis Pinot Grigio** / $$$

○ **Vieris Sauvignon** / $$$

ZENATO

Overlooking Lake Garda, this Veneto winery began in 1960 as Sergio Zenato's labor of love on behalf of the white Trebbiano di Lugana grape. Under his leadership and now that of his children, Zenato has blossomed into a substantial operation (some 167,000 cases a year, including the Sansonina and S. Cristina labels), famed for its rich reds, such as the Amarone and *ripasso*-style Valpolicella bottlings. For a taste of the original tradition, try the melony white Sergio Zenato Lugana Riserva.

BOTTLES TO TRY

○ **Sergio Zenato Lugana Riserva** / $$

● **Amarone Classico** / $$$$

ZÝMĒ

Celestino Gaspari spent 11 years learning at the side of his father-in-law, iconic winemaker Giuseppe Quintarelli, before releasing his first wines from this winery in 2003. Located in the heart of the Valpolicella zone, Zýmē is a boutique operation with a dozen or so strikingly labeled wines. Though he produces several wines inside the DOC regulations, Gaspari revels in his dark, cellar-demanding (and costly) standard-bearers, Harlequin and Kairos, each made from at least 15 grape varieties.

BOTTLES TO TRY

○ **From Black to White** / $$

● **Kairos** / $$$$

TUSCANY

CLAIM TO FAME

Few wine regions have the global name recognition of Tuscany's Chianti, first legally defined in 1716 (but recognized as a wine region as early as the 14th century). While the boundaries of that original growing district define today's *classico* subzone, the vastly expanded Chianti region now includes seven more subregions. Some of Chianti's most acclaimed wines, however, don't carry its name. Only reds based on the Sangiovese grape can be called Chianti. Rule-breaking Super-Tuscans often include significant portions of international grapes and so carry the humbler IGT Toscana designation. The stellar Brunello di Montalcino wines are grown in warmer vineyards south of the Chianti Classico zone.

REGIONS TO KNOW

CARMIGNANO Vintners in the town of Carmignano have been boosting their Sangiovese-based wines with Cabernet Sauvignon since the 1700s, long before these blends became known as Super-Tuscans. As a result, their reds typically feature lower acidity and firmer tannins than those of Chianti Classico.

CHIANTI Spurred by international competition, Chianti's best vintners have replanted vineyards to better clones and adopted new techniques like aging wines in small French oak barrels. Of Chianti's eight subzones, **Chianti Classico** is the original and most prestigious. Only **Chianti Rufina** and, arguably, **Chianti**

Colli Senesi routinely produce wines to rival Chianti Classico's top bottles. All Chianti wines are based on Sangiovese, which can be blended with native grapes such as Canaiolo and Colorino or locally grown international grapes like Cabernet, Merlot or Syrah. (In Chianti Classico, the latter grapes can make up no more than 20 percent of the blend.) Generic Chianti, with no subzone, is the simplest. *Riserva* Chiantis require at least two years of aging.

CORTONA Established in 1999 and devoted chiefly to international grapes, this DOC has become a source of exciting Syrahs.

MAREMMA Pioneering producers in this coastal region broke with tradition to create the original Super-Tuscan wines in the late 1960s. The Maremma's most famous DOCs are **Bolgheri** and the single-estate DOC, **Bolgheri Sassicaia**. The hilly area around the village of **Scansano** makes reds based on Sangiovese, known locally as Morellino. Basic Morellino di Scansano has improved greatly in recent years and can be a great value.

MONTALCINO Vintners near the town of Montalcino turn out Tuscany's greatest wine, **Brunello di Montalcino**, from a local Sangiovese clone, Brunello. Made from the same grape, **Rosso di Montalcino** reds are younger, lighter versions of Brunellos.

MONTEPULCIANO Though not far from Montalcino, Montepulciano produces lighter wines that can include small amounts of other grapes besides Sangiovese (known locally as Prugnolo Gentile). **Vino Nobile di Montepulciano** wines must be aged two years (three for *riservas*). Like Montalcino, Montepulciano releases younger, baby brother reds under *rosso* designations.

🍇 KEY GRAPES: WHITE

TREBBIANO Tuscany's main white grape variety—and the most commonly grown white grape in Italy—makes mostly light, unremarkable wines, though quality is improving.

VERMENTINO Full of minerality and zesty lime, this white grape thrives in milder coastal subregions like the Maremma.

VERNACCIA A specialty of the hilltop town of San Gimignano, this grape yields crisp, full-bodied and nutty whites.

KEY GRAPES: RED

CABERNET SAUVIGNON, MERLOT & SYRAH These international varieties are popular blending grapes for native Sangiovese.

CANAIOLO, COLORINO & MAMMOLO Vintners typically blend these native red varieties with Sangiovese.

SANGIOVESE Sangiovese is king in Tuscany, where it yields high-acid, cherry- and herb-inflected reds in a range of styles.

Producers/ Tuscany

ANTINORI / SANTA CRISTINA

The scion of a Tuscan wine dynasty stretching back six centuries, Marchese Piero Antinori still makes his home above the family business. That home is Florence's 15th-century Palazzo Antinori, and the business is an iconic brand. Though the Antinori empire stretches across the globe, the wines from its vast Tuscan estates are still its best known. Antinori's groundbreaking Tignanello Super-Tuscan is one of Italy's most prized collectibles; the Santa Cristina Toscana is a consistent red wine bargain.

BOTTLES TO TRY

○ Cervaro della Sala Umbria / $$$
● Santa Cristina Toscana / $

AVIGNONESI

Dating to the mid-1500s, this venerable winery got new wind in its sails when Belgian-born attorney Virginie Saverys gained control of it in 2009. She's converted the estate to sustainable viticulture (all Avignonesi wines come from its own 494 acres), contracted with the University of Bordeaux to micro-map the soils and acquired new vineyards and a cutting-edge winemaking facility. The focus, though, remains on the famed Vino Nobile di Montepulciano and luxury-priced vin santo bottlings.

BOTTLES TO TRY

● Vino Nobile di Montepulciano / $$
● Grifi Toscana / $$$

BADIA A COLTIBUONO

A former abbey, this impressive Chianti Classico estate is now devoted to the secular pursuits of wine and food. Its owners, the Stucchi-Prinetti family, descend from the Florentine banker who bought the property in 1846; the family matriarch today is culinary authority Lorenza de' Medici. But even more impressive than the wines' aristocratic origins is their consistent quality. Badia a Coltibuono's familiar, Sangiovese-based reds stick to a classic style, with firm acidity and bright, fragrant cherry tones.

BOTTLES TO TRY

○ Coltibuono Trappoline Toscana / $

● Chianti Classico / $$

BARONE RICASOLI

The Ricasoli family essentially invented Chianti wine as we know it: In the mid-1800s, the "Iron Baron" Bettino Ricasoli established Sangiovese as the basis of the modern Chianti blend. But it was the 32nd baron, Francesco, who restored the family winery to the upper echelons of Chianti after buying back the brand from an international conglomerate in 1993. He slashed production, replanted vineyards and brought new vitality to Italy's oldest wine estate (some 900 years and counting). He presides today over Chianti Classico's largest winery, whose 3,000 acres produce fine, traditionally structured Chiantis at fair prices.

BOTTLES TO TRY

○ Torricella Toscana / $$

● Brolio Chianti Classico / $$

BIONDI SANTI

The passing of a patriarch like Franco Biondi Santi—Brunello di Montalcino's towering figure died in 2013—might have been catastrophic elsewhere, but Franco was merely the latest in a line of legends in a family credited in some accounts with creating Brunello in the 1800s (Franco's grandfather Ferruccio is said to have isolated the wine's Sangiovese Grosso clone). The *sui generis* company inherited by Franco's son, Jacopo, eschews modern palate-flattering winemaking, creating seemingly immortal Brunellos for appreciative (and deep-pocketed) collectors.

BOTTLES TO TRY

● Brunello di Montalcino / $$$$

● Brunello di Montalcino Riserva / $$$$

CAPEZZANA

Winemaking records at this Carmignano estate date back 12 centuries—the Medicis once owned it—but today's Capezzana is a thoroughly modern winery. Owners Count Ugo and Countess Lisa Contini Bonacossi were pioneers of Cabernet in Carmignano in the 1960s and later led the drive to establish the region as a DOCG. Under the direction of their children, Capezzana today is Carmignano's finest producer, with a lineup ranging from everyday reds—such as the supple, invigorating Barco Reale blend—to a muscular Super-Tuscan, Ghiaie della Furba.

BOTTLES TO TRY
- Barco Reale di Carmignano / $
- Ghiaie della Furba Toscana / $$$

CASTELLARE DI CASTELLINA

Media magnate Paolo Panerai's golden touch has turned even his wine sideline into a thriving business: This Tuscan property is just one of four Panerai estates (see also Rocca di Frassinello, p. 92). Castellare's vineyards are among the highest in altitude and lowest in yield in Chianti Classico. With their bird labels symbolizing Castellare's commitment to environmentally sound practices, the wines range from the well-priced Chianti Classico to the magisterial Super-Tuscan I Sodi di San Niccolò.

BOTTLES TO TRY
- Chianti Classico / $$
- I Sodi di San Niccolò Toscana / $$$$

CASTELL'IN VILLA

This substantial property produces well-regarded, traditionally styled Chianti Classicos—think earthy, spicy, cherry tones—that gain an extra measure of pleasure from being held back in the cellar, typically for two vintages longer than the DOCG requirements. Greek-born, Swiss-raised proprietress Princess Coralia Pignatelli della Leonessa oversees 133 acres of vineyards on a variety of micro-sites, producing three 100 percent Sangiovese Chianti Classicos, including the single-vineyard Poggio delle Rose, and the half Cabernet Sauvignon–half Sangiovese Super-Tuscan Santacroce.

BOTTLES TO TRY
- Chianti Classico / $$
- Santacroce Toscana / $$$$

CASTELLO BANFI

The Long Island–based Mariani family had been importing Italian wine to the US for 60 years under the Banfi name—Riunite, Cella and Bolla are among their brands—when brothers John and Harry Mariani decided to become vintners themselves in 1978. Their holdings now include an entire hamlet surrounding a medieval fortress they named Castello Banfi and thousands of acres across Tuscany. The large Banfi portfolio ranges from everyday bottlings like the basic Chianti Classico to costly Brunellos.

BOTTLES TO TRY
- ○ Centine Toscana / $
- ● Brunello di Montalcino / $$$$

CASTELLO DI MONSANTO

Fabrizio Bianchi began breaking tradition to make great Chianti back in the 1960s. He ripped out white grapes from his Chianti vineyards to concentrate on Sangiovese—a radical idea at the time—and bottled the first single-vineyard Chianti Classico, Il Poggio Riserva, an elegant wine that remains one of Chianti's benchmarks. Today his daughter Laura oversees a lineup that includes the high-end, collector's Nemo Cabernet and classic, Sangiovese-based wines that typically hit the trifecta of reasonable prices, varietal authenticity and consistent quality.

BOTTLES TO TRY
- ● Chianti Classico / $$
- ● Il Poggio Chianti Classico Riserva / $$$

CERBAIONA

Diego Molinari's small estate has been called a "grand cru" of Brunello di Montalcino; fans compare its subtle, multilayered wines to top Burgundies and pay high prices for them. A former Alitalia pilot, Molinari began his wine enterprise in the late 1970s with cuttings and encouragement from Franco Biondi Santi (see p. 85). With grapes from his low-yielding, organic vineyard, Molinari makes wines in the staunch traditionalist style of his mentor—no new French oak here. Somewhat more affordable than the Brunello are the lovely Rosso di Montalcino and the esteemed Toscana red blend.

BOTTLES TO TRY
- ● Toscana / $$$
- ● Brunello di Montalcino / $$$$

CONTI COSTANTI

Costanti counts have deep roots in Montalcino: The family has been on this property since the 16th century; a 19th-century ancestor, Tito, is said to have been one of the first to call a Montalcino red wine by the name Brunello when he presented his 1865 vintage bottling at an 1870 wine exhibition in Siena. Current owner Andrea Costanti has enhanced the estate's reputation for crafting generous-bodied, elegant wines in a largely traditional style, although he does utilize French *barrique* aging for younger wines, like the Rosso and the Vermiglio blend.

BOTTLES TO TRY
- Rosso di Montalcino / $$$
- Brunello di Montalcino / $$$$

FATTORIA SELVAPIANA

A star consultant (Franco Bernabei), a top subregion (Chianti Rufina) and a focused portfolio (four wines, plus vin santo) are just a few reasons why Selvapiana's wines stand out from the pack. Rufina's high elevation and cold nights give Selvapiana's grapes their thick skins and higher acidity, which allow proprietor Francesco Giuntini Antinori and his designated heirs, siblings Federico and Silvia Giuntini Masseti, to create firm, age-worthy reds. The fresh, cherry-driven introductory bottling is a textbook example of Rufina's wines, while the single-vineyard Bucerchiale Riserva offers a serious step up in complexity.

BOTTLES TO TRY
- Chianti Rufina / $$
- Bucerchiale Chianti Rufina Riserva / $$$

FÈLSINA

Though Fèlsina has started planting French grapes (its I Sistri Chardonnay is delicious) and making wines approachable in their youth, it is still best known for deeply flavored Sangioveses of great longevity; top cuvées, such as the Rancia Chianti Classico, will reward decades of aging. And it's not just Fèlsina's wines that are notable for their years: The 100 percent Sangiovese Fontalloro, the Riservas and even the entry-level Chianti Classico are all harvested from sustainably farmed 35-plus-year-old vines.

BOTTLES TO TRY
- I Sistri Toscana / $$
- Berardenga Chianti Classico / $$

FONTODI

Owned by the Manetti family since 1968, Fontodi is one of Tuscany's most highly regarded wineries. The Manettis used to make three Chianti Classicos at their Panzano facility, but in the mid-1990s they dropped the Riserva and now offer just two, one of which is the single-vineyard Vigna del Sorbo. The move raised quality across the board, and freed up juice for Flaccianello, Fontodi's blockbuster IGT Sangiovese. Giovanni Manetti and consulting enologist Franco Bernabei also make Syrah and Pinot Noir from the estate's certified-organic vineyards.

BOTTLES TO TRY
- ● Chianti Classico / $$$
- ● Flaccianello della Pieve Colli della Toscana Centrale / $$$$

GRATTAMACCO

One of three estates (along with Castello di ColleMassari and Poggio di Sotto) run by brother and sister Claudio Tipa and Maria Iris, this Bolgheri hilltop property overlooks steep vineyards that receive full-on summer sun and a nearly constant maritime breeze. The flagship Bolgheri Superiore is a rich, polished, palate-gratifying Cabernet–based blend, liberally aged in new French oak. The little brother Bolgheri Rosso gives a more affordable taste of the style. The winery also takes advantage of its sunshine to make a big-bodied, creamy Vermentino.

BOTTLES TO TRY
- ○ Bolgheri Vermentino / $$$
- ● Bolgheri Superiore / $$$$

ISOLE E OLENA

The adjacent properties that make up this Chianti Classico estate were acquired and combined (hence the name) by the De Marchi family of Piedmont in 1956. Current owner Paolo De Marchi put the place on the map with Cepparello, his single-variety Sangiovese, a wine of finesse but with no shortage of depth and ageability. De Marchi was also a pioneer in bringing French grapes to Chianti Classico, where he now bottles a very fine Cabernet Sauvignon and a barrel-fermented Chardonnay. Value-conscious drinkers should look for the lovely Chianti.

BOTTLES TO TRY
- ○ Chardonnay Toscana / $$$
- ● Chianti Classico / $$

LE MACCHIOLE

Born and raised in Bolgheri, Eugenio Campolmi watched as his sleepy coastal home became Italy's newest world-class wine region, thanks mostly to wealthy outsiders. Campolmi started Le Macchiole in 1980 with 12 acres of vines next door to Super-Tuscan star Ornellaia (see opposite), but the place really took off when Campolmi began working with consulting winemaker Luca d'Attoma in 1991. Their success with single-variety wines like Merlot (Messorio), Cabernet Franc (Paleo) and Syrah (Scrio) helped launch Le Macchiole into the ranks of Tuscany's elite modern estates. D'Attoma and Campolmi's widow, Cinzia Merli, continue to refine its sought-after offerings.

BOTTLES TO TRY
- Bolgheri Rosso / $$$
- Paleo / $$$$

LISINI

Lisini was one of the original founders of the Brunello di Montalcino wine consortium back in the 1960s, and the late matriarch Elina Lisini was an early president. She built the label as a stalwart example of Brunello tradition: All five wines, including the famous, big-shouldered, single-vineyard Ugolaia, are 100 percent Sangiovese Grosso, and the cellar is equipped old-school style, with cement fermenters and large oak-aging casks. Lisini's niece and nephews run this excellent small winery today.

BOTTLES TO TRY
- San Biagio Toscana / $$
- Ugolaia Brunello di Montalcino / $$$$

MARCHESI DE' FRESCOBALDI

The Frescobaldi wine dynasty (now in its 30th generation) is Tuscany's largest vineyard owner—and growing. Yet size hasn't made the dynamic company complacent. Frescobaldi wines, including traditional regional bottlings like the Nipozzano Chianti Rufina Riserva, still win acclaim, as do such impressive upmarket efforts as the opulent Mormoreto, a Bordeaux-style blend from very old vines. The dark-fruited Castiglioni Toscana IGT blend highlights Frescobaldi's modern side.

BOTTLES TO TRY
- Tenuta Frescobaldi di Castiglioni Toscana / $$
- Mormoreto Toscana / $$$$

BEST OF THE BEST PRODUCERS / TUSCANY

1. BIONDI SANTI **2.** FONTODI **3.** LE MACCHIOLE
4. ORNELLAIA **5.** TENUTA SAN GUIDO

ORNELLAIA

This iconic Maremma estate makes two of Italy's most coveted wines: Ornellaia, a Bordeaux-style blend, and Masseto, a single-vineyard Merlot. The Le Serre Nuove red offers a far less costly taste of Ornellaia's style. Though its first vintage was only in 1985, the estate has already belonged to three wine dynasties: Lodovico Antinori founded Ornellaia, then sold it to California's Mondavi family; it's now owned by the Frescobaldis (see opposite).

BOTTLES TO TRY
- Le Serre Nuove dell'Ornellaia Bolgheri / $$$$
- Ornellaia Bolgheri Superiore / $$$$

PODERI BOSCARELLI

When the De Ferrari Corradi family bought this small estate in Montepulciano in the early 1960s, the hilltop town's reputation for great wine had faded into history. The indisputable quality of Boscarelli's Vino Nobile reds helped galvanize a generation of vintners to restore Montepulciano's luster. Bolstered by grapes from the stellar Cervognano vineyard, Boscarelli's reds offer fruity depth and fragrant, polished power.

BOTTLES TO TRY
- Vino Nobile di Montepulciano / $$$
- Vino Nobile di Montepulciano Riserva / $$$

POGGIOTONDO

Globetrotting wine consultant Alberto Antonini took control of his father's 123-acre Chianti property in 2001, and set it on the road to organic viticulture in 2011. His winemaking has also evolved in a natural direction; among other things, he is moving away from stainless steel fermenters to oak and unlined cement ones, which he feels are more "alive." His refined, modern takes on Chianti combine Sangiovese and French-origin grapes.

BOTTLES TO TRY
- ○ Vermentino Toscana / $$
- ● Chianti Riserva / $$$

ROCCA DI FRASSINELLO

The high ambitions of this joint venture between Castellare di Castellina's Paolo Panerai (see p. 86) and Château Lafite's Eric de Rothschild are obvious from its ultra-modern, Renzo Piano–designed Maremma winery. Since the Franco-Italian project's first release about 10 years ago, its six bottlings have been on a steady march toward collector recognition, especially the all-Merlot Baffonero and the flagship Rocca di Frassinello, a blend of Sangiovese, Cabernet and Merlot.

BOTTLES TO TRY
- Le Sughere di Frassinello Maremma Toscana / $$
- Baffonero Maremma Toscana / $$$$

RUFFINO

Ruffino is one of the most consistent of the large Chianti producers, turning out a vast selection of wines sourced from growers across the region and beyond, plus estate bottlings from farms in Chianti Classico, Montalcino and Montepulciano. Launched as a *négociant* in 1877 and hugely successful abroad, Ruffino changed the Chianti industry overnight when it began using modern glass bottles in 1975 instead of the iconic straw-covered fiascos. The fruity, smooth Santedame is made in a modern style; the easy-to-find Riserva Ducale gets its masterful blending of fruit from multiple sites.

BOTTLES TO TRY
- Riserva Ducale Chianti Classico Riserva / $$
- Tenuta Santedame Chianti Classico / $$

TENUTA SAN GUIDO

A lover of thoroughbred horses and Bordeaux wine, Marchese Mario Incisa first planted Cabernet Sauvignon on his Bolgheri estate in the 1940s and went on to create what is now one of Italy's most famous and influential wines, the seductive, velvety-textured and much-imitated Cabernet Sauvignon–Cabernet Franc blend, Sassicaia. Under the decades-long guidance of Incisa's son, Nicolò, San Guido attained international recognition and has added new wines to its portfolio. The second bottling, Guidalberto, is a gorgeous Cabernet-Merlot blend.

BOTTLES TO TRY
- Guidalberto Toscana / $$$
- Sassicaia Bolgheri Sassicaia / $$$$

OTHER CENTRAL ITALY

REGIONS TO KNOW

ABRUZZO This mountainous region has become a terrific source of value-priced reds, led by its signature bottling, Montepulciano d'Abruzzo. (Confusingly, the Montepulciano grape shares a name with the Sangiovese-based wines from Montepulciano in Tuscany.) Often a simple wine with soft, straightforward berry and plum flavors, Montepulciano d'Abruzzo can also be remarkably robust, spicy and tannic. Top vintners are showcasing the grape's polished side at both ends of the style—and price—spectrum. Whites are steadily improving, notably the Trebbiano d'Abruzzo.

EMILIA-ROMAGNA This region's wines are not as famous as its meats and cheeses (e.g., Prosciutto di Parma and Parmigiano-Reggiano), but are worth discovering. Emilia-Romagna's most prominent bottling is Lambrusco, a fizzy, often sweet wine that's usually red but ranges in color from white to deep purple. The best are dry and come from small producers. Quality-focused wineries also turn out fine offerings made from white grapes like Albana, Chardonnay and Malvasia, and reds based on Sangiovese, Barbera, Cabernet Sauvignon and Pinot Nero (Pinot Noir).

LAZIO Located on the outskirts of Rome, Lazio's prolific vineyards have supplied the city's taverns and trattorias with wine for millennia. The region's defining wine, **Frascati**, is a ubiquitous, crisp, citrusy white that's often thin and innocuous, but it can deliver complexity when made with care. Authorities approved two new DOCGs, Frascati Superiore and Cannellino di Frascati, in 2011, which will, in theory, assure higher quality. Reds based on the Cesanese grape have been gaining attention since the **Cesanese del Piglio** zone was elevated to DOCG status in 2008.

LE MARCHE Le Marche juts out from Italy's eastern coast like the shapely calf in the peninsula's boot. The region's top red wines are made from Sangiovese (the signature variety of Tuscany) or Montepulciano. Blends of these two grapes are the specialty of **Rosso Piceno**, a DOC near the port of Ancona; **Rosso Conero** is a bold, smoky red made chiefly from Montepulciano. Le Marche's top white is the zesty, mouth-filling

Verdicchio; the best versions come from the hilltop **Verdicchio dei Castelli di Jesi Classico** subzone. Wines made from little-known native white grapes such as Pecorino and Passerina are turning up more often in the US.

UMBRIA The green hills of landlocked Umbria are home to the light-bodied, usually inexpensive **Orvieto** white, made from a blend of local grapes. Mass-produced bottlings, made chiefly with the Trebbiano grape, are generally forgettable; look instead for versions sourced from old Grechetto vines grown in the soft volcanic rock of Orvieto's *classico* subzone, which can be fantastic. Umbria's best-known reds are bold examples of the Sagrantino grape, grown mainly in the **Montefalco** area.

✿ KEY GRAPES: WHITE

GRECHETTO A white variety presumed to be native to Greece (hence its name), Grechetto is grown chiefly in Umbria and yields refreshing, lime- and peach-flavored bottlings.

PASSERINA & PECORINO Found mainly in Le Marche (and to a lesser extent in Abruzzo), the appley Passerina and minerally Pecorino are increasingly bottled on their own to make some of central Italy's most appealing whites.

TREBBIANO A handful of quality-driven vintners (mostly in Abruzzo) are proving that the Trebbiano grape, widely used for characterless bulk wines (and brandies), can indeed yield whites of distinction.

VERDICCHIO Once bottled chiefly in amphora-shaped bottles, Verdicchio-based wines are typically almond-scented, crisp and citrusy; they're among the world's most seafood-friendly whites.

✿ KEY GRAPES: RED

MONTEPULCIANO Not to be confused with the Sangiovese wines from the Tuscan town of Montepulciano (see p. 83), this plummy, spicy grape is behind some of central Italy's best reds.

SAGRANTINO This native Umbrian grape yields powerful, tannic, long-lived reds. Full of spice, earth and plum notes, Sagrantino does especially well around the Umbrian town of Montefalco.

Producers/ Other Central Italy

ARNALDO CAPRAI

Marco Caprai and his late father, Arnaldo, gained fame for reviving Umbria's native Sagrantino red grape. With such broodingly dark benchmarks as the 25 Anni and Collepiano bottlings, Marco Caprai ranks among the finest producers of Sagrantino wines (Paolo Bea is another; see p. 96). Though the local variety is the star here, Caprai also makes a range of notable reds and whites from grapes originating farther afield.

BOTTLES TO TRY

○ Grecante Colli Martani Grechetto / $$

● Collepiano Montefalco Sagrantino / $$$

FALESCO

The proprietary names, like Tellus (a Syrah) and Montiano (a Merlot), may be obscure, but the names behind them, brothers Riccardo and Renzo Cotarella, are among the most famous in Italian wine. At their Lazio and Umbria estates, the Cotarellas indulge their zeal for experimentation, making a sweeping collection of wines from international grapes and modern versions of local favorites, such as the Trebbiano-based Est! Est!! Est!!!

BOTTLES TO TRY

○ Est! Est!! Est!!! di Montefiascone / $

● Tellus Lazio / $$

FATTORIA LA VALENTINA

As wine quality has risen in Abruzzo in recent decades, La Valentina has been consistently ahead of the curve. Owner Sabatino Di Properzio and consulting winemaker Luca D'Attoma have cultivated the complex side of what's often a simple regional red—Montepulciano d'Abruzzo—by keeping vineyard yields low and using only estate grapes. The most famous site is a 10-acre vineyard that yields a definitive Montepulciano, Binomio.

BOTTLES TO TRY

○ Trebbiano d'Abruzzo / $

● Montepulciano d'Abruzzo / $

FATTORIA LE TERRAZZE

Star consultant Federico Curtaz works with winemaker Ettore Janni at this breakthrough Le Marche winery, owned by one-time physicist and Bob Dylan devotee Antonio Terni (his Visions of J. Rosso Conero and Planet Waves Montepulciano-Merlot blend are rare collectors' wines). Though there are international grapes to be found in its vineyards, Le Terrazze's heart is in the local Montepulciano grape, the sole variety in its Sassi Neri Conero Riserva and the basis of the full-bodied, perfumed Chaos blend, which also includes Syrah and Merlot.

BOTTLES TO TRY
- Rosso Conero / $$
- Chaos Marche / $$$

LUNGAROTTI

The resurgence of Umbrian wine owes much to the late Giorgio Lungarotti, who established his winery in the town of Torgiano in the early 1960s. His innovative Sangiovese-based blend, the violet- and black pepper–inflected Rubesco Rosso di Torgiano, helped put Umbria on the wine world's radar. Now headed by his daughters Teresa and Chiara, Lungarotti is Umbria's largest producer, with a wide range of offerings, including the Torre di Giano whites and the fragrant, cherry-edged Rubesco Vigna Monticchio Riserva, one of the region's most collectible reds.

BOTTLES TO TRY
- Rubesco Rosso di Torgiano / $
- Rubesco Vigna Monticchio Torgiano Rosso Riserva / $$$

PAOLO BEA

Cult Umbrian winemaker Paolo Bea and his sons Giampiero and Giuseppe produce what are arguably the greatest renditions of the stubborn, tannic Sagrantino grape. The Beas' naturalist approach to winemaking includes long aging in large, neutral oak casks, and no fining or filtration. The results can be monumental, as with the dark, spicy, ageworthy Pagliaro Montefalco Sagrantino. The San Valentino Montefalco, a blend of Sangiovese, Montepulciano and Sagrantino, is both more approachable and more affordable.

BOTTLES TO TRY
- San Valentino Montefalco / $$$
- Pagliaro Montefalco Sagrantino / $$$$

SAN PATRIGNANO

One of the world's most unusual high-quality wine endeavors, San Patrignano is a free-of-charge support community for recovering drug addicts near Rimini in Emilia-Romagna. Under the pro bono guiding hand of super-consultant Riccardo Cotarella, the community tends its own vineyards and produces wine from vine to bottle. The flagship wine is the rich, robust Avi, considered one of Romagna's top Sangioveses; the Aulente Rubicone offers major bang for the buck.

BOTTLES TO TRY

- ● Aulente Rubicone / $
- ● Avi Sangiovese di Romagna Superiore Riserva / $$$

VILLA BUCCI

No winery has mastered the Verdicchio grape like Villa Bucci. Located in Le Marche's prestigious Castelli di Jesi subregion, where Verdicchio is the chief white grape, Villa Bucci produces two benchmark Verdicchios as well as two Rosso Piceno wines (blends of Montepulciano and Sangiovese). The rich, creamy Riserva Verdicchio is made only in top vintages, from the estate's oldest vineyards, but even the entry-level Verdicchio provides a palate-pleasing taste of this grape's possibilities.

BOTTLES TO TRY

- ○ Verdicchio dei Castelli di Jesi Classico Superiore / $$
- ● Pongelli Rosso Piceno / $$

SOUTHERN ITALY

CLAIM TO FAME

Once known for bulk wine, southern Italy is now a source of high value-to-quality bottlings, often made from grapes found nowhere else. Mediocre wine is still made here, but the region's top vintners have put the south firmly on wine lovers' maps of Italy.

REGIONS TO KNOW

APULIA This is the home of Primitivo, a plush grape that has gained fame as Zinfandel's Italian cousin (both are clones of the Croatian grape Crljenak Kaštelanski). Less well known are the excellent reds of the **Salice Salentino** and **Copertino** subzones, made chiefly from the dark-skinned Negroamaro grape.

BASILICATA Its spicy, Aglianico-based reds—with their very ancient history—make Basilicata's best case for greatness, especially **Aglianico del Vulture**, from vineyards planted on the slopes and foothills of the extinct Monte Vulture volcano. The newer DOCs of **Terre dell'Alta Val d'Agri** and **Matera** offer red, white and rosé blends based on grapes other than Aglianico.

CALABRIA Cirò, a delicate, floral-scented red based on the Gaglioppo grape, is Calabria's best wine.

CAMPANIA This region is a leader in southern Italy's native grape revival. Campania's *terroir*-driven wines include powerful Aglianico reds (top ageworthy examples come from the **Taurasi** DOCG) and three distinctive whites: expressive Falanghina; lush, nutty **Fiano di Avellino**; and floral, zesty **Greco di Tufo**.

SARDINIA The twin stars of this Mediterranean isle are its fresh Vermentino whites and spicy, supple Cannonau (Grenache) reds, the best of which come from old, low-yielding "bush" vines.

SICILY Sicily's most interesting wines are made from native varieties. Fruity Nero d'Avola is its signature red grape; when blended with Frappato, it yields **Cerasuolo di Vittoria**, the island's only DOCG wine. From Mount Etna's slopes, reds designated **Etna Rosso** offer bold tannins and savory red fruit. White grapes grown in Etna's black soils can yield fresh, minerally wines. Elsewhere, standouts include citrusy whites made from Catarratto, Grillo and Inzolia, and reds based on Frappato.

❖ KEY GRAPES: WHITE

FALANGHINA, FIANO & GRECO BIANCO Wines made from these ancient varieties share crisp floral and mineral notes.

VERMENTINO Grown up and down Italy's coasts, Vermentino produces whites whose racy, lime- and herb-scented flavors make them a terrific match for seafood.

❖ KEY GRAPES: RED

AGLIANICO Responsible for the top reds of Basilicata and Campania, this inky, earthy variety possesses high tannins and acidity that give its wines the ability to age.

CANNONAU, CARIGNANO & MONICA Sardinia's Spanish- and French-influenced history shows in its plantings of these foreign grapes. Cannonau (a.k.a. Grenache) bursts with supple red fruit; the island's top Carignano (Carignane) wines stand among the best examples of this rustic variety. Monica yields simple reds.

FRAPPATO Sicily's Frappato produces alluring, light-bodied reds with fragrant, silky red-fruit tones.

GAGLIOPPO Bottlings of this Calabrian grape are perfumy and supple, with sweet red cherry and floral notes.

NEGROAMARO Depending on how it's used, this Apulian grape can yield simple, light reds or concentrated, muscular wines.

NERELLO CAPPUCCIO & NERELLO MASCALESE Indigenous to the slopes of Sicily's Mount Etna, these varieties offer rich, firm reds.

NERO D'AVOLA Sicilian winemakers prize this native grape for its lush, earthy flavors redolent of sweet blackberries and spice.

PRIMITIVO Plush tannins and rich, brambly red-berry notes are the hallmarks of this Zinfandel relative.

Producers/ Southern Italy

ARGIOLAS

Argiolas set off Sardinia's wine revolution in the early 1990s and is still its top producer. Brothers Franco and Giuseppe Argiolas transformed their family's bulk-wine business; today their children run the large operation. Quality is generally strong across the portfolio, including delicious Vermentinos and ripe, supple reds from Carignano, Monica and Cannonau. The red Turriga blend is a showpiece for Sardinia's winemaking heritage.

BOTTLES TO TRY

○ Costamolino Vermentino di Sardegna / $

● Turriga Isola dei Nuraghi / $$$$

AZIENDA AGRICOLA COS

Few wineries succeed as reliably as COS at crafting benchmark renditions of Sicilian grapes. The biodynamic estate (its name is an acronym of its founders' last names: Giambattista Cilia, enologist Giusto Occhipinti and Cirino Strano) is on the cutting edge of retro-naturalist winemaking. Its Pithos wines, for example, are fermented and aged in clay amphorae. While COS is best known for its peppery, meaty Cerasuolo, it's hard to go wrong with any of its bottlings, including the silky, berry-rich Frappato, which offers pleasing complexity at a slightly lower price.

BOTTLES TO TRY
- Frappato Sicilia / $$
- Cerasuolo di Vittoria Classico / $$$

AZIENDA AGRICOLA PALARI

Artisan producer and architect Salvatore Geraci has reached back into antiquity to create once-typical but now all-but-forgotten blends from obscure Sicilian grapes like Nerello, Nocera, Acitana and Cappuccio. His steep vineyards, terraced more than 1,400 feet above the Straits of Messina, require handwork and some steady nerves to farm. While his proprietary blends are based on ancient tradition, Geraci's soulful modern takes have drawn a new following for wines like the Rosso del Soprano and the complex, elusive Palari Faro collectors' bottling.

BOTTLES TO TRY
- Rosso del Soprano Sicilia / $$$
- Faro / $$$$

CANTINA SANTADI

Widely planted around Mediterranean Europe, and widely ignored by international wine lovers, the Carignano grape can yield exotically spiced, powerful red wines—in the right hands, and Cantina Santadi is one of the world's go-to Carignano producers. Under winemakers Marco Santarelli and Umberto Trombelli, this high-achieving Sardinian cooperative uses old-vine fruit for bottlings like the opulent Terre Brune Carignano del Sulcis. Other specialties from Santadi's 1,235 vineyard acres include fine Vermentino- and Cannonau-based blends.

BOTTLES TO TRY
- ○ Cala Silente Vermentino di Sardegna / $$
- ● Terre Brune Carignano del Sulcis Superiore / $$$

BEST VALUE PRODUCERS / SOUTHERN ITALY
1. ARGIOLAS **2.** MASSERIA LI VELI **3.** SELLA & MOSCA
4. TASCA D'ALMERITA **5.** TENUTA DELLE TERRE NERE

DONNAFUGATA

The Rallo family named their Sicilian estate Donnafugata ("woman in flight") after Maria Carolina, the queen of Naples who took refuge in the area in the early 1800s. Long known for fortified Marsala wine, Donnafugata today is one of Sicily's leading estates thanks to its Nero d'Avola–based offerings. The juicy, dark-fruited Sedàra Nero d'Avola is a terrific introduction to the reds, while the stealth choice is the floral, citrusy Anthìlia white.

BOTTLES TO TRY
○ Anthìlia Sicilia / $
● Sedàra Sicilia / $

FEUDI DI SAN GREGORIO

Since its founding in 1986, this Campania winery has become one of the region's top producers. Although the family owners have invested heavily in everything from clonal research to sleek new cellars and a hospitality center, the winery's soul remains rooted in the volcanic soils of nearby Mount Vesuvius, from which it turns out excellent wines from native grapes like Greco, Falanghina and Aglianico, as well as the costly Pàtrimo Merlot.

BOTTLES TO TRY
○ Falanghina del Sannio / $
● Taurasi / $$$

GULFI

A labor of love by Sicilian-born Milanese businessman Vito Catania, this premier Nero d'Avola producer has assembled more than 170 acres of certified-organic vineyards, including half-century-old, bush-pruned vines. The calling cards are the wonderful, tough-to-pronounce single-vineyard Nero d'Avolas, like Nerobufaleffj and Neromaccarj, but Gulfi is also a leading proponent of lively, subtle whites from the demanding Carricante grape.

BOTTLES TO TRY
○ Carjcanti Sicilia / $$
● Nerobufaleffj Sicilia / $$$

MASSERIA LI VELI

The Falvo family, former proprietors of Avignonesi (see p. 84), bought this 19th-century Apulian property in 1999, and restored its fortress-like buildings. The Falvos have retained the home vineyard's retro plantings of Negroamaro, Primitivo and Aleatico, all certified organic. The family has brought in top consultant Riccardo Cotarella (see Falesco, p. 95) to produce its well-priced wines, like the inky, color-saturated Susumaniello Salento and expressive, floral whites like the Verdeca Valle d'Itria.

BOTTLES TO TRY

○ Verdeca Valle d'Itria / $$

● Susumaniello Salento / $$

MASTROBERARDINO

Ten generations of the Mastroberardino family have guided this preeminent Campania winery, with dapper Piero as the latest scion to do so. Decades ago, his father and grandfather led the region's native-grape revival. Their years of research, as well as the property's vast acreage and high-tech facilities, have resulted in solid bottlings up and down the price scale. Of particular note is Radici, a tannic, complex red that's arguably Campania's greatest Aglianico. Less expensive offerings, like the stony, citrusy Lacryma Christi white from the Coda di Volpe grape, make excellent introductions to Campania's varieties.

BOTTLES TO TRY

○ Lacryma Christi del Vesuvio / $$

● Radici Taurasi / $$$

SELLA & MOSCA

Campari-owned Sella & Mosca boasts one of Italy's largest contiguous vineyards, and it is easily Sardinia's largest wine exporter. Its impressive headquarters near the picturesque port of Alghero is also one of the island's chief wine-tourism destinations. The estate produces some wines from international varieties like Sauvignon Blanc and Cabernet, but the most rewarding bottlings, especially for US wine drinkers, are those made from less familiar indigenous grapes, like the hearty red Cannonau, crisp Vermentino and fresh, elegant Torbato.

BOTTLES TO TRY

○ Terre Bianche Alghero Torbato / $$

● Cannonau di Sardegna Riserva / $

TASCA D'ALMERITA

In the late 1950s, when nearly all Sicilian wine grapes went into jug or bulk wine, Count Giuseppe Tasca aimed higher. He transformed his family's wine estate, founded in 1830, into a quality-driven producer. Now a family of three estates (Regaleali, Capofaro and Whitaker), Tasca d'Almerita sources grapes from roughly 1,500 vineyard acres across the island. Its top wine is the legendary Rosso del Conte. Easier to find and far less costly is Lamùri, a floral, polished red that's also based on Nero d'Avola.

BOTTLES TO TRY
- ○ Regaleali Sicilia / $
- ● Lamùri Sicilia / $$

TENUTA DELLE TERRE NERE

Marco de Grazia, an Italian-American living in Florence, exports an admired portfolio of Italian wine for a living. But he became so enamored of wines from the lava-covered slopes of Sicily's Mount Etna that he started a winery of his own, naming it for the area's black earth (*terre nere*). The minerally whites, made from Carricante, and especially the muscular reds have become stars of Etna's emerging wine industry. Based on the Nerello Mascalese grape, the reds are firm and tight on release; try decanting them if you can't resist opening them right away.

BOTTLES TO TRY
- ○ Etna Bianco / $$
- ● Etna Rosso / $$

TERREDORA DI PAOLO

When a dispute split Campania's Mastroberardino winemaking clan (see opposite) in 1994, Walter Mastroberardino's side gave up the right to make wine under the family name but kept most of the historic vineyards. Today, his beautiful, modern cellars at Terredora look down from the 2,100-foot height of Montefusco over a landscape dotted with nearly 500 scattered acres of estate vines, planted entirely with native grapes. Terredora's definitive bottlings—such as the Fiano di Avellinos, the crisp-but-creamy Falanghinas and the ageworthy Taurasis made from Aglianico—highlight Campania's key grapes.

BOTTLES TO TRY
- ○ Terre di Dora Fiano di Avellino / $$
- ● Fatica Contadina Taurasi / $$$

Spain

Sir Alexander Fleming once wrote, "If penicillin can cure those that are ill, Spanish sherry can bring the dead back to life." Some might say that's an overstatement, even from the man who discovered penicillin, but Spanish wines shouldn't be underestimated. Spain produces remarkable wines at all levels: from the crisp, saline whites of Rías Baixas to the world-class, ageworthy reds from renowned regions like Rioja and Priorat. And those are only three of Spain's more than 65 official wine regions (it's the third-largest wine-producing country, after France and Italy). And, of course, there's sherry. It may not raise the dead, but it wouldn't be a bad idea to buy a bottle or two, just in case.

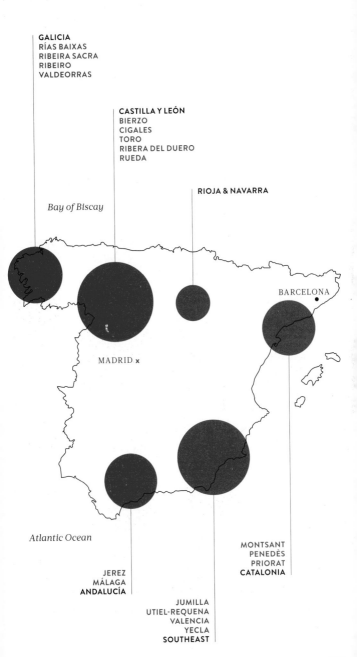

GALICIA
RÍAS BAIXAS
RIBEIRA SACRA
RIBEIRO
VALDEORRAS

CASTILLA Y LEÓN
BIERZO
CIGALES
TORO
RIBERA DEL DUERO
RUEDA

RIOJA & NAVARRA

Bay of Biscay

BARCELONA •

MADRID ×

Atlantic Ocean

MONTSANT
PENEDÈS
PRIORAT
CATALONIA

JEREZ
MÁLAGA
ANDALUCÍA

JUMILLA
UTIEL-REQUENA
VALENCIA
YECLA
SOUTHEAST

WINE TERMINOLOGY

As in France, Spain's appellation-based wine labeling aims to assure the local origin and particular qualities of its wines. But Spain's winemaking traditions also emphasize barrel and bottle aging for its better wines, making the country a great source for old-vine wine and for value-priced wines with extra cellar age.

DENOMINACIÓN DE ORIGEN DE PAGO/VINO DE PAGO The evolving but highly prestigious *vino de pago* classification is given to renowned estate-grown and -bottled wines, originally because some of them did not meet DO regulations. Fifteen *vinos de pago* have been approved since 2003. Confusingly, many wines with *pago* on the label are not in this elite category, and some *vinos de pago* don't say *pago* at all, but simply list the name of the *pago* (estate) after *Denominación de Origen* in place of a regional name, as in *Denominación de Origen Finca Élez*.

DENOMINACIÓN DE ORIGEN CALIFICADA (DOCA) Just two areas, Rioja and Priorat, claim the exalted status of DOCa, the most rigorous regional wine designation.

DENOMINACIÓN DE ORIGEN (DO) Spain's regional DOs set legal standards for permitted grapes, harvest limits and vinification techniques, in addition to geographic sourcing requirements. Most quality export wine belongs to this category.

VINO DE CALIDAD CON INDICACIÓN GEOGRAFICA, VINO DE LA TIERRA, VINO DE MESA In descending order, these are the lowest quality categories of Spanish wine. Vino de Calidad (VCIG) wines are typically from up-and-coming subregions aspiring to DO status.

JOVEN Made to be drunk within a year or two of release, *joven* (young) wines—also called *cosecha*—spend little to no time in oak, which keeps them fresh (and reasonably priced).

CRIANZA Red *crianzas* must be aged at least two years, with six months to one year in oak (requirements vary by region). Whites must be at least 18 months old, with six months in barrel. Top *crianzas* offer great value.

RESERVA This term is applied to a DO or DOCa red with at least 12 months' barrel aging and a total of three years' cellaring. *Reserva* reds typically showcase soft tannins and mellower fruit. White *reservas* must cellar for two years (six months in oak).

GRAN RESERVA Reds in this category are DO or DOCa wines made from top grapes and aged for at least five years, with 18 months in oak (Rioja requires 24 months). Whites must be four years old, with six months in barrel. In the past, these long-aged wines could lack vibrancy and fruit charm, but that's changing.

BODEGA & CELLER Both words mean "winery." The Catalan *celler* is used in Catalonia; the Spanish *bodega*, elsewhere in Spain.

COSECHA & VENDIMIA Spanish for "harvest" and "vintage."

VIÑA & VIÑEDO These Spanish terms for "vineyard" are often part of a winery's name. When not part of the winery name, the words usually refer to a site from which the wine is sourced.

RIOJA & NAVARRA

CLAIM TO FAME

Ruggedly beautiful Rioja, in north central Spain, is still Spanish wines' image-maker, despite newer contenders. The past generation has seen a tug-of-war between traditional producers of earthy, tannic reds that spend long years in oak barrels (usually American) and more internationally minded producers who emphasize fruit and palate richness. Meanwhile, up-and-coming neighbor Navarra has become a go-to source of value reds and *rosados* (rosés).

REGIONS TO KNOW

RIOJA ALAVESA Chalky soils, an Atlantic-influenced climate and a high elevation define this region, home to several of Rioja's top producers. Well-known for their aging ability, Rioja Alavesa wines are not as consistent as Rioja Alta's, but good values abound.

RIOJA ALTA The source of many of Rioja's greatest wines, the Alta ("high") subzone is located in the foothills of the Cantabrian mountains at the region's western end, where Atlantic-driven temperatures and limestone soils yield refined, ageworthy reds.

RIOJA BAJA Winemakers in Rioja Baja, which is adjacent to Navarra, benefit from the warm, dry Mediterranean climate and rely more on Garnacha (Grenache) than on Tempranillo, which is dominant elsewhere. These wines are typically softer, riper and less-structured reds made for early drinking or blending.

KEY GRAPES: WHITE

VIURA Rioja's reputation rests on its reds, but both Rioja and Navarra produce lovely, vibrant whites based mostly on Viura, known elsewhere in Spain as Macabeo. By the 1990s, most white Riojas were made exclusively with Viura. Styles range from barrel-aged and intentionally oxidized to fresh and bright.

KEY GRAPES: RED

GARNACHA (GRENACHE) Supple, sultry and loaded with fragrant red-berry notes, this variety is a key component of many Rioja reds and was, until recently, Navarra's dominant grape. Winemakers use its velvety tannins and plump body to soften Tempranillo's firm, earthy structure in blends.

GRACIANO & MAZUELO Grown in small amounts, these minor grapes are native to northeastern Spain. Graciano is increasingly prized by winemakers for its ability to add acidity and fragrance to a blend, whereas Mazuelo—called Carignane in France and Cariñena elsewhere in Spain—is a tough and tannic grape.

TEMPRANILLO Tempranillo's fragrant cherry flavors, tart acidity and firm tannins have long made it the top grape for Rioja's long-lived blends. Today it's also popular in Navarra, where it recently supplanted Garnacha as the most planted variety.

Producers/
Rioja & Navarra

ARTADI

This cult producer began in the mid-1980s as a co-op in Rioja Alavesa's high-altitude hinterlands. Today, owner Juan Carlos López de Lacalle has wineries in three regions, each producing wines from what he deems the top local varieties. At Artadi, that means Tempranillo for reds and Viura for whites. Viña el Pisón is the triple-digit-priced image-maker, but Artadi turns out balanced, gracefully aromatic wines up and down the line.

BOTTLES TO TRY
- Tempranillo / $$
- Viña el Pisón / $$$$

BODEGAS BENJAMIN DE ROTHSCHILD VEGA SICILIA

The marquee-name partnership between Vega Sicilia (see p. 125) and the Rothschild family's Château Clarke branch spent years assembling nearly 300 acres of old vines in cool Rioja Alta before releasing their two 100 percent Tempranillo wines in 2013. Bordeaux's influence is evident: The wines are all estate-grown, and instead of Rioja's age designations, they're basically ranked as a first wine, Macán, and a second wine, Macán Clasico.

BOTTLES TO TRY
- Macán Clásico / $$$
- Macán / $$$$

BODEGAS FRANCO-ESPAÑOLAS

This large Rioja winery was founded in 1890 when a Bordeaux wine merchant came south looking for phylloxera-free vineyards. Though Spanish-owned for nearly a century, the winery honors its Franco side with the names of its Bordòn (a play on *Bordeaux*) line and upscale Barón D'Anglade red. Franco-Españolas is best known, though, for its straightforward, fruity standard bottlings like the Royal-line reds and the off-dry Diamante white.

BOTTLES TO TRY
- ○ Diamante / $
- Rioja Bordón Crianza / $

BODEGAS MUGA

Although Muga is rightly part of Rioja's old guard (it was founded in 1932), the winery's reputation for traditionalism is only partially valid today. In addition to earthy, long-aged *reservas* and *gran reservas*, Jorge and Manuel Muga's cellars produce prestige wines like Torre Muga and the more recently introduced Aro, whose voluptuousness shows the brothers' skill with a more modern style. Though prices have crept up, the Rioja Reserva is still one of the region's most affordable examples of the layered, age-evolved complexity that draws connoisseurs to Rioja.

BOTTLES TO TRY
- Rioja Reserva / $$
- Torre Muga / $$$$

BODEGAS RODA

Roda has developed a following among well-heeled international wine drinkers for its "neoclassical" Riojas, made from old vines with artisan care and modern techniques, including 100 percent French-oak aging. The two frontline *reservas*, Roda (accessible, lively red fruit) and Roda I (darker, more complex), are silky and palate-flattering. The super-luxury Cirsion cuvée is an all-Tempranillo produced from a vine-by-vine culling in top years. Since the 2008 vintage, there is now a somewhat better-priced second wine, Sela, that showcases Roda's style.

BOTTLES TO TRY
- Roda Reserva / $$$
- Sela / $$$

BODEGAS VALDEMAR

Launched in 1982 by members of the Martinez Bujanda family, who already had nearly a century of winemaking experience in the region, this large brand provides consistent value across the range, with plenty of choices at $20 and under. The entry-level Valdemar wines are fresh and fruity; the flagship Conde Valdemar line includes classically aged *reservas* and *gran reservas*. The Inspiración Valdemar line, which debuted in 2005, offers fruit-forward, modern takes on lesser-exposed regional varieties, like Graciano and Tempranillo Blanco from select Rioja vineyards.

BOTTLES TO TRY
- ○ Inspiración Tempranillo Blanco / $$
- ● Conde Valdemar Crianza / $

BODEGAS Y VIÑEDOS PUJANZA

This new kid on the block in Rioja Alavesa (its doors opened in 2001) has attracted a wine-insider following, thanks to owner Carlos San Pedro's dedication to artisan ideals. It all starts in the vineyard for this Tempranillo specialist, whose vines are low-yielding and old: His Norte bottling comes from high-altitude 25-year-old vines he planted himself as a teenager; the Finca Valdepoleo, from 40-plus-year-old vines; and the top Pujanza Cisma, from nearly 100-year-old vines. Norte's style leans toward Rioja's riper, more robust, modern side, with an extra kick of freshness from a secondary fermentation in steel, not barrel.

BOTTLES TO TRY

- Finca Valdepoleo / $$
- Norte / $$$$

CHIVITE / BODEGAS GRAN FEUDO

One of Navarra's leading wine producers, the Chivite family enterprise dates back to 1647, though the firm is in the midst of a reorganization of its various labels and holdings. The winery's most familiar label—now a stand-alone brand within the Grupo Chivite—is Bodegas Gran Feudo, whose tasty *rosado* introduced Chivite to its many US fans. Gran Feudo wines epitomize some of Navarra's greatest strengths: refreshing, fruity *rosado* and lush, old-vine reds, including Garnacha and Tempranillo.

BOTTLES TO TRY

- Gran Feudo Rosado / $
- Gran Feudo Tinto Reserva / $$$

CVNE

CVNE (the Spanish acronym for Wine Company of Northern Spain) is the umbrella name for a trio of fine wineries. The original anchor-company of the 19th-century group, which is still owned by the founder's descendants, is the Cune winery in Rioja Alta. Among its offerings are the traditionally styled, strong-value Cune line and the *reserva* and *gran reserva* reds of the Imperial label. The Viña Real winery's six bottlings come from Rioja Alavesa, as do the Viñedos del Contino wines, including two prestigious single-vineyard reds crafted by Jesús Madrazo.

BOTTLES TO TRY

- Cune Crianza / $
- Contino Reserva / $$$

LA RIOJA ALTA

Founded in 1890 as a partnership among five of the finest estates of the day, this benchmark producer deftly straddles tradition and modernity. From its very-up-to-date facility emerges a lineup of wines that are still aged in small-cask American—not French—oak, and often for extended periods, meaning that these wines are famously ready to drink when they leave the cellar. The portfolio includes both classically mellowed, old-school bottlings, such as the Gran Reserva 904, and powerful, modern cuvées, like the Viña Ardanza. The silky, well-priced Viña Alberdi Reserva is a perennial overachiever.

BOTTLES TO TRY

- Viña Alberdi Reserva / $$
- Gran Reserva 904 / $$$

MARQUÉS DE MURRIETA

Murrieta's famous wines are sourced solely from its vast, 741-acre Ygay estate at Rioja Alta's southern tip. That's remarkable in Rioja, where most large wineries buy grapes from dozens of growers. The advantage that such control gives Murrieta and its highly regarded winemaker María Vargas is clear in more traditionally styled wines like the graceful, spicy Finca Ygay Reserva, as well as in the winery's modern offering, Dalmau, a smoky, splurge-worthy Tempranillo, Cabernet and Graciano blend.

BOTTLES TO TRY

- Finca Ygay Reserva / $$
- Dalmau Reserva / $$$$

MARQUÉS DE RISCAL

The grand scale of Marqués de Riscal's City of Wine complex—it includes a Frank Gehry–designed hotel and a Michelin-starred restaurant—fits right into this large Rioja producer's high-profile, regional ambassador stature. Founded by a Francophile marquis, Marqués de Riscal produces traditionally styled wines that have helped define Rioja for more than 150 years. The Rioja lineup extends from the light, popular Arienzo Crianza to the collectible Barón de Chirel, a complex and elegant Tempranillo blend, as well as wines from Rueda and Castilla y León.

BOTTLES TO TRY

- Arienzo Crianza / $
- Barón de Chirel Reserva / $$$$

PALACIOS REMONDO

Game-changing visionary Álvaro Palacios wandered far from home to help revolutionize the wine trade of Priorat (see p. 119) and Bierzo. Back at the helm of his family's Rioja Baja winery since 2000, he has decreased production in favor of quality, instituted organic farming and championed the Garnacha grape. Contrary to the trend among most other ambitious Rioja producers, the percentage of Garnacha here *increases* as you go up the line, from 50 percent in the lovely, lively entry-level La Vendimia to 100 percent in the deep, spicily supple Propriedad.

BOTTLES TO TRY
○ Plácet / $$$
● La Vendimia / $$

REMELLURI

The vineyards of this historic estate—it dates back to a 14th-century monastery—are among the highest in Rioja Alavesa, with hardscrabble soils that yield concentrated, ageworthy wines. Remelluri owes its modern-day prominence to Jaime Rodríguez Salis, who bought it in 1967 and began restoring its vineyards. Prodigal son Telmo left the nest to become one of Spain's most acclaimed winemakers, but returned in 2010 to focus on these challenging vines. The three main Remelluri-labeled wines are complex, estate-grown blends; the newer Lindes ("borders") de Remelluri bottlings are sourced from nearby growers.

BOTTLES TO TRY
● Lindes de Remelluri Viñedos de Labastida / $$
● Rioja Reserva / $$$

R. LÓPEZ DE HEREDIA VIÑA TONDONIA

The byword in old-school Rioja, López de Heredia entered this century in high style, with a stunning Zaha Hadid–designed tasting pavilion erected near its iconic 19th-century tower. Back in the cellars, tradition reigns: Extended aging for reds is the norm in Rioja, but López de Heredia is nearly unique in also aging its whites and *rosados* in oak for four or more years, and then in bottles. The use of mostly old, neutral barrels and high-quality fruit results in gorgeously polished and mellow wines.

BOTTLES TO TRY
○ Viña Tondonia Reserva / $$$
● Viña Tondonia Reserva / $$$

VIÑEDOS Y BODEGAS SIERRA CANTABRIA

The vineyards around the Rioja Alta wine town of San Vicente de la Sonsierra have received attention recently, thanks to the high-profile Rothschild–Vega Sicilia partnership (see p. 125). But the six-winery Eguren group, led by vintner Marcos Eguren, has been here for years, turning out consistently high-quality wine with the opposite pricing philosophy. Sierra Cantabria is one of the wine market's reliable bets for strong value. The fresh, ripe, lively reds come almost exclusively from Tempranillo, including the local Tempranillo Peludo ("hairy Tempranillo"). There is also a notable barrel-fermented white blend called Organza.

BOTTLES TO TRY

○ Organza / $$
● Rioja Crianza / $$

GALICIA

CLAIM TO FAME

The green river valleys of Galicia, on northwestern Spain's Atlantic coast, look more like Ireland than Iberia, with drizzly wet weather and Celtic culture to match. But those valleys produce some of Spain's most outstanding white wines, including the vibrant, mineral-laden, Albariño-based offerings of Rías Baixas.

KEY GRAPES: WHITE

ALBARIÑO Most white grapes rot in weather as wet as Galicia's, but this variety thrives in it. Crisp, citrusy, with a hint of sea-salt minerality, Albariño is typically made into unoaked wines meant to be consumed young (preferably with seafood). That said, a handful of ambitious, high-end bottlings (some aged partially in oak) deliver flavors that improve with a few years of bottle age.

GODELLO Rescued from oblivion in the 1970s, Godello is gaining renown among aficionados as a single-variety wine, especially the tangy, quince- and citrus-inflected bottlings made in the interior Valdeorras and Ribeira Sacra subregions.

TREIXADURA The chief grape of the Ribeiro DO (located along the Miño River and its tributaries), Treixadura yields wines with perky acidity and vibrant citrus and apple layers.

❧ KEY GRAPES: RED

MENCÍA It's rare to find a Galician red wine in the US, but if you do, chances are that it is made from this grape (though Mencía-based wines are more likely to be exported from the Bierzo DO of neighboring León). In Galicia's Valdeorras and Ribeira Sacra subregions, Mencía yields light-bodied, high-acid reds with floral and licorice notes.

Producers/ Galicia

BODEGAS VALDESIL

Ancestors of the Prada family were championing the traditional Godello grape in Galicia's inland Valdeorras region back in the 1880s, but succeeding generations sold off nearly all of the old vineyards. Beginning in the 1990s, the family began reassembling a patrimony that includes some of Spain's oldest Godello vines. Bottlings range from the young Montenovo to the Pezas da Portela (fermented in French oak) to the single-vineyard Pedrouzos. The winery also produces elegant reds from Mencía.

BOTTLES TO TRY
- ○ Montenovo Godello / $
- ● Valderroa Mencía / $$

DO FERREIRO

Vintner Gerardo Méndez fashions his Albariños from ancient vines—some more than 200 years old—in the ocean-influenced Salnés Valley, Galicia's coolest and wettest subregion. *Ferreiro* means "ironworker" (the profession of Méndez's grandfather), an appropriate name for an estate whose rocky, granite-based soils give its vibrant wines a steely strength. Méndez uses low-tech, traditional techniques—farming organically, handpicking grapes and fermenting with native yeasts, for example—to create Do Ferreiro's exceptional whites. His old-vines cuvée, Cepas Vellas, offers a complexity few Albariños achieve.

BOTTLES TO TRY
- ○ Albariño / $$
- ○ Cepas Vellas Albariño / $$$

FILLABOA

This winery is owned by the Masaveus, a historic winemaking family that returned to the business by acquiring wineries in Rioja and Navarra, followed by the purchase of Fillaboa in Rías Baixas in 2000. The stylish property features an arched Roman stone bridge and a lovely old-stone mansion. Unusually for Galicia, the family uses only estate-grown fruit, which means that quantities of its two wines—the flagship Albariño and the lees-aged, single-vineyard cuvée, Selección Finca Monte Alto— are inherently limited. Exhibiting rare complexity for the Albariño grape, both are well worth the hunt.

BOTTLES TO TRY

○ Albariño / $$

○ Selección Finca Monte Alto Albariño / $$

PAZO DE SEÑORÁNS

Rías Baixas was invisible on the world's fine-wine radar when Marisol Bueno and her family acquired Pazo de Señoráns in the Salnés Valley in the 1970s. Bueno restored the historic 16th-century property and was instrumental in the campaign to gain DO status (granted in 1988) for the region. The winery's racy, juicy Albariños have long been a Rías Baixas standard-bearer. A rare second wine, Selección de Añada, is made only in great vintages, and is one of the few Albariños that can improve with extended aging in bottle, developing complex, honeyed flavors.

BOTTLES TO TRY

○ Albariño / $$

○ Selección de Añada Albariño / $$$$

RAFAEL PALACIOS

Rafael Palacios (younger brother of icon Álvaro; see p. 119) fell in love with the Godello grapes coming from terraced vineyards of the Valdeorras subregion of Val do Bibei. He came to the Valdeorras in 2004 and began assembling small plots—now 26 different parcels—of mostly old Godello vines, some up to 90 years old. The throwback organic-farming methods on these hard-to-work plots yield wines like the luscious Louro do Bolo and the rich, old-vine flagship, As Sortes.

BOTTLES TO TRY

○ Louro do Bolo Godello / $$

○ As Sortes Valdeorras / $$$

RAÚL PÉREZ

The envelope-pushing Raúl Pérez has developed a cult following for the tiny-lot wines he produces from all over northwestern Spain, notably from Bierzo, where his family's Castro Ventosa winery is the largest grower of the Mencía grape. Pérez's wines tend to have strong personalities, like the exotically spiced Ultreia de Valtuille Mencía and the intense-but-polished Prieto Picudo, from century-old vines in León. The *barrique*-aged Rara Avis Albarín comes from a nearly extinct white grape, and the firm, impressive, often austere Ultreia La Claudina is a different Godello animal entirely from the Valdeorras versions.

BOTTLES TO TRY

○ **Muti Albariño** / $$$
● **Ultreia de Valtuille Mencía** / $$$$

SOUTHEASTERN SPAIN

CLAIM TO FAME

Ambitious winemakers have rediscovered Spain's Mediterranean coast and are turning out terrific offerings from vines both new and very old that thrive in the region's hot, dry conditions. The Monastrells of Jumilla and Yecla and Valencia's Bobal-based wines are the top emerging stars of southeastern Spain, often delivering amazing values.

🍇 KEY GRAPES: RED

BOBAL This distinctive native grape creates dark, brooding reds (plus attractive *rosados*) and accounts for most of the production of the southeast's up-and-coming Utiel-Requena DO.

CABERNET SAUVIGNON, MERLOT & SYRAH Jumilla has spearheaded the adoption of these international varieties in the southeast. They're steadily gaining ground throughout the region.

MONASTRELL (MOURVÈDRE) The signature grape of Jumilla and of the adjacent Yecla DO in Murcia, Monastrell makes spicy, inky, high-alcohol reds.

TEMPRANILLO The southeast's best examples of this cherry-inflected grape come from the Utiel-Requena DO.

Producers/ Southeastern Spain

ÀNIMA NEGRA

This winery on the isle of Majorca off Spain's eastern coast has gained an international clientele for the no-compromise wines it makes with native grapes, such as Callet and Manto Negro, from 30- to 100-year-old, unirrigated, low-yielding, biodynamically farmed vines. Ànima Negra's super-concentrated offerings include the smoky, fruit-spiced Callet flagship wine, Àn; its little brother, Àn/2; and the French *barrique*–aged Son Negre.

BOTTLES TO TRY
- Àn/2 / $$
- Àn / $$$

BODEGAS JUAN GIL

Founded in 1916 and rejuvenated in 2002, the Gil family's Jumilla winery delivers deeply extracted, inky, meaty red wines at remarkably affordable prices. Its specialty is Monastrell, a tough-skinned grape that can cope with drought, intense sunlight and huge temperature extremes. The winery combines old vines and modern winemaking to bottle succulent wines, like the silver-labelled 12 Meses.

BOTTLES TO TRY
- 12 Meses / $
- Honoro Vera Organic Monastrell / $

CASA DE LA ERMITA

Jumilla native Marcial Martínez Cruz made wine all over Spain before returning home in the late '90s to help create this stellar estate. Zeroing in on some of Jumilla's highest-elevation vineyards, he gambled that French grapes could weather the harsh conditions. The base Crianza is a supple, early-drinking blend of Monastrell, Petit Verdot and Cabernet, while the Petit Verdot proves that Jumilla can make luscious, ageworthy reds.

BOTTLES TO TRY
- Crianza / $
- Petit Verdot / $$

CATALONIA

CLAIM TO FAME

Northeastern Spain's Catalonia region is known for sparkling Cava (see p. 283), but it also includes the Priorat DO, a once-obscure area that is now creating some of the country's most prized red wines. Nearby DOs such as Montsant offer similar, if usually less ambitious, blends at a fraction of Priorat prices.

♨ KEY GRAPES: RED

CARIÑENA (CARIGNANE) A good companion to Garnacha, Cariñena delivers structure that boosts Garnacha's soft tannins, giving more power and increased longevity to the blend. It is slowly losing ground in Priorat blends, however, to international varieties like Syrah and Cabernet Sauvignon.

GARNACHA (GRENACHE) Catalonia's star variety grows best on old vines, preferably on hillsides, where lean soils concentrate its plush berry and cherry flavors. Garnacha is usually blended with such grapes as Cabernet, Cariñena, Syrah and Tempranillo.

Producers/ Catalonia

ÁLVARO PALACIOS

In the early 1990s, Rioja native Álvaro Palacios (see p. 113) applied his Bordeaux wine education to Garnacha in the then-forgotten Priorat region. The results were benchmark bottlings—first Finca Dofí, and then L'Ermita, now an icon of modern Spanish wine—that helped establish Priorat as Spain's most exciting wine frontier and Palacios as a superstar. In addition to the luxury-priced L'Ermita, Palacios crafts more affordable wines with a genuine taste of Priorat, such as the plush, black-fruited Camins del Priorat and Les Terrasses, a polished, old-vine blend.

BOTTLES TO TRY

- Camins del Priorat / $$
- Les Terrasses / $$$

ESPELT

Established in 2000, this family operation—three generations of Espelts can be found here—has a "new Spain" sensibility, evident in its cutting-edge winery. With 500 acres of vineyards wedged between the Pyrenees Mountains and the sea, the Espelts espouse organic viticulture and Mediterranean varieties like the 100-year-old vines that produce the elegant Coma Bruna Cariñena and the luscious, unoaked Garnacha-Cariñena Sauló.

BOTTLES TO TRY
- Sauló / $
- Coma Bruna / $$$

TOMÀS CUSINÉ

Tomàs Cusiné, whose family owns the eminent Castell del Remei estate, founded his eponymous winery in 2003, in rugged, high-altitude terrain in the Costers del Segre DO. Here, he implemented progressive winemaking techniques, including slow, low-temperature fermentations and French-barrel aging, and as his 74 acres of vines have matured, so too has his experimentation. Cusiné's reds are typically utilize-the-spice-rack blends: The supple, peppery and floral-perfumed Geol bottling, for example, may combine as many as six grapes. He also bottles two single-variety whites and the multivariety Auzells blend.

BOTTLES TO TRY
- ○ Auzells / $$
- ● Geol / $$

TORRES

In 1962, when Miguel A. Torres joined his family's wine business, its success was built on Sangre de Toro, the red-blend budget wine (known for its kitschy plastic-bull bottle ornament) and the value-priced Coronas label, both from Catalonia. Today, he presides over a wine-and-brandy empire (plus extensive conservation and ecology efforts) spread across Spain, including properties in Ribera del Duero and Rioja, with ventures in Chile and California. Torres wines are emblematic of modern Spain—from the world-class, collector's Cabernet Sauvignon Mas La Plana to terrific everyday reds and whites.

BOTTLES TO TRY
- Sangre de Toro / $
- Mas La Plana / $$$$

CASTILLA Y LEÓN

CLAIM TO FAME

The Castilla y León region, located in north-central Spain, is home to Vega Sicilia (see p. 125), a legendary winery that put the Ribera del Duero DO on the world's fine-wine map nearly a century ago. Vega Sicilia's Único—a Tempranillo–Cabernet Sauvignon blend renowned for its longevity—is among the world's most esteemed (and expensive) red wines. But not until the debut in the 1980s of Alejandro Fernández's Pesquera did interest in Ribera del Duero really take off. Today the nearby Toro region competes with Ribera reds in quality, while the Cigales DO is moving beyond its reputation for *rosados* and turning out an increasing number of bold reds. The long-underrated Rueda DO shines as a source of crisp whites—an anomaly in a region dominated by red wine—and in the Bierzo DO, an influx of winemaking talent is turning out impressive reds from the local Mencía grape.

🍇 KEY GRAPES: WHITE

VERDEJO Once nearly consigned to oblivion, the Rueda region's calling-card grape makes fragrant, citrus-laden white wines that recall Sauvignon Blanc (with which Verdejo is often blended).

🍇 KEY GRAPES: RED

MENCÍA This red grape variety has become increasingly popular with winemakers in recent years. It is best known for giving the fragrant reds of Bierzo their alluring floral aromas, licorice tinge and bright, often rustic cherry notes.

TEMPRANILLO Known locally under a handful of different aliases, including Tinto Fino, Tinta del País and Tinta de Toro, this is the leading grape variety of Castilla y León. Many of Ribera del Duero's savory, spicy, medium- to full-bodied bottlings are pure Tempranillo (although regional regulations permit the addition of small amounts of other varieties). The Tempranillo-based wines of Toro are fuller-bodied and more concentrated than those of Ribera, and they're usually made to be consumed earlier. As in Rioja, Ribera reds often require many years of aging to soften.

Producers/ Castilla y León

AALTO BODEGAS Y VIÑEDOS

Former Vega Sicilia (see p. 125) winemaking legend Mariano García (see Bodegas Mauro, opposite) teamed up with Javier Zaccagnini, a major force in Ribera del Duero in his own right, to found this "Dream Team" winery, which released its first bottles in 1999. Aalto's two sumptuous (and pricey) wines are made entirely from Tinto Fino, the local variant of Tempranillo. García crafts the collectible PS cuvée only in stellar vintages.

BOTTLES TO TRY
- Aalto / $$$
- Aalto PS / $$$$

ABADÍA RETUERTA

Though this sprawling estate lies just outside the Ribera del Duero DO, its wines compete with Ribera's cutting-edge best. Winemaker Ángel Anocíbar is known for Tempranillo-based blends, including the spicy, succulent Selección Especial, the estate's best-known wine. Layering Cabernet Sauvignon and Syrah or Merlot on a Tempranillo base, it's reliably polished and elegant and far easier to find than the luxury-priced Pago reds.

BOTTLE TO TRY
- Selección Especial / $$

BODEGAS EMILIO MORO

This acclaimed, family-owned Ribera del Duero producer is a leader in sustainable winery practices, with three generations of know-how and more than 200 acres of old family vineyards to draw on. Emilio Moro eschews bottle-age designations (e.g., *crianza*) to focus on its own, vineyard-age-oriented scale. The youngest fruit goes to the affordably priced Finca Resalso red, while the oldest vines are dedicated to top-tier cuvées, including the revered Malleolus de Valderramiro bottling.

BOTTLES TO TRY
- Finca Resalso / $
- Malleolus de Valderramiro / $$$$

BODEGAS HERMANOS PÉREZ PASCUAS

This handsome, modern winery, founded by three brothers (*hermanos*) in 1980, produces polished wines from a typically extreme Ribera del Duero environment. The Pérez Pascuas vineyards—alternately frigid and sun-roasted, sometimes on the same day—extend over 333 acres at an elevation of 2,700 feet. The specialty here is old-vine Tinta del País (Tempranillo), with a portion of Cabernet for the top Reserva and Gran Reserva bottlings, in a style that tends toward the traditional: The wines can be austere in youth but blossom with age.

BOTTLES TO TRY
- Viña Pedrosa Crianza / $$$
- Viña Pedrosa Reserva / $$$

BODEGAS MAURO

Mauro's pricey collectors' wines have an avid following, partly due to the estate's wealth of heritage Tempranillo vines, but mostly because of the great winemaker Mariano García (see Aalto, opposite), who founded the winery in 1980. Though labeled for regulatory reasons as humble *vinos de la tierra,* these wines are among the foremost exemplars of powerful, ageworthy Ribera del Duero reds (with a Bierzo white in the mix since 2013). The stylish Tempranillo-Syrah base bottling, Mauro, puts the house style in somewhat more affordable reach.

BOTTLES TO TRY
- Mauro / $$$
- Terreus / $$$$

DESCENDIENTES DE J. PALACIOS

Ricardo Pérez Palacios teamed up with his uncle, Priorat and Rioja winemaking superstar Álvaro Palacios (see p. 113), in 1998 to make red wines in the overlooked Bierzo region. Scouting out grapes from old vines planted on steep hillsides, the pair have helped illuminate the region's tremendous potential, particularly for its signature grape, Mencía. Their single-vineyard reds are Bierzo benchmarks, but are hard to find. Look for the remarkably well-priced entry-level Pétalos, full of wild berry and mineral flavors, or its pricier sibling, Villa de Corullón.

BOTTLES TO TRY
- Pétalos / $$
- Villa de Corullón / $$$

HACIENDA MONASTERIO

Before he grew to cult-star status at his own Dominio Pingus, Peter Sisseck begged some vine cuttings from Vega Sicilia (see opposite) to help Monasterio's owners get this Ribera del Duero estate started back in 1991, and he has been the winemaker ever since. The winery produces three wines from its organic vineyard: a typically silky, intensely aromatic entry-level wine; a Reserva; and in the best years, a Reserva Especial. All are based on the local Tempranillo variant, the big-berried Tinto Fino, with spicings of Cabernet Sauvignon and/or Merlot.

BOTTLES TO TRY
- Hacienda Monasterio / $$$
- Reserva / $$$$

OSSIAN

Ossian could be Exhibit A of the revolution sweeping Spanish wine, where formerly neglected resources—in this case, up-to-200-year-old Verdejo vines—are rediscovered, and reconceived through a combination of local passion and international know-how. Winemaker Ismael Gozalo's ambition is to create Spain's finest white wines from his extraordinary vines, which are organically farmed and planted in sandy soil 3,000 feet up in Rueda. His cellar techniques are Burgundian—including French-oak aging—except when they're German, as with the Verdling bottlings, made with a German Riesling specialist.

BOTTLE TO TRY
- ○ Ossian / $$$

PAGO DE LOS CAPELLANES

This sleek Ribera del Duero winery traces the origins of its 35-parcel vineyard holdings back through centuries of small land donations to the local church. Today's assemblage, bought by the Rodero Villa family when they founded this well-regarded estate in 1996, is planted to Tinto Fino. The winery's enthusiasm for the polish imparted by French-oak barrels can be gauged from the fact that the cellars contain some 22 types, of varying ages and toast levels. Even the base Crianza spends time in French *barriques*.

BOTTLES TO TRY
- Crianza / $$$
- Reserva / $$$

BEST VALUE PRODUCERS / SPAIN
1. BODEGAS JUAN GIL **2.** CASA DE LA ERMITA **3.** CVNE/CUNE
4. TORRES **5.** VIÑEDOS Y BODEGAS SIERRA CANTABRIA

TINTO PESQUERA

Until Alejandro Fernández created his powerhouse Tempranillo, Tinto Pesquera, in 1972, Ribera del Duero wine had only one claim to fame—Vega Sicilia (see below). While Pesquera hasn't quite ascended to those heights, its acclaim helped galvanize the quality-wine revolution in Ribera. Today, Fernández's Grupo Pequera comprises four wineries in emerging areas: Tinto Pesquera and Condado de Haza in Ribera del Duero; Dehesa La Granja in Castilla y León; and El Vínculo in La Mancha. Tinto Pesquera wines remain a benchmark for Tempranillo, with Bordeaux-like nuance and ageability.

BOTTLES TO TRY
- Tinto Pesquera Crianza / $$$
- Tinto Pesquera Reserva / $$$

VEGA SICILIA

This is Spain's most highly esteemed winery. Since 1915, this Ribera del Duero legend has been producing some of the greatest (and most expensive) wines in the world. Vega Sicilia ages its wines in barrel longer than many wines last in bottle, and, once bottled, its best vintages improve for decades more. Its current owners, the Álvarez family, have established sister wineries— Alión in Ribera del Duero (1992) and Pintia in Toro (2001)— and in 2013 launched the Macán project in Rioja, a joint venture with the Rothschild family (see Bodegas Benjamin de Rothschild Vega Sicilia, p. 109). But Vega Sicilia itself produces just three highly coveted wines: Valbuena 5°, Único and a near-mythical multivintage blend, Reserva Especial.

BOTTLES TO TRY
- Único / $$$$
- Valbuena 5° / $$$$

Portugal

For the first time in many, many years, America seems to be waking up to the remarkable quality of Portuguese wines. Once known primarily for inexpensive, innocuous brands like Lancers and Mateus, Portugal has undergone an extraordinary renaissance in quality, and now produces an abundance of spicy, intense reds and vibrant, incredibly refreshing whites. And port, the Douro region's famed sweet wine, continues to be one of the greatest wines in the world, with the best vintage bottlings able to age for decades. The Douro may be a difficult place to get to, but exploring the variety and depth of Portuguese wines is easy–all it takes is reaching for a different bottle or two in your local wine store.

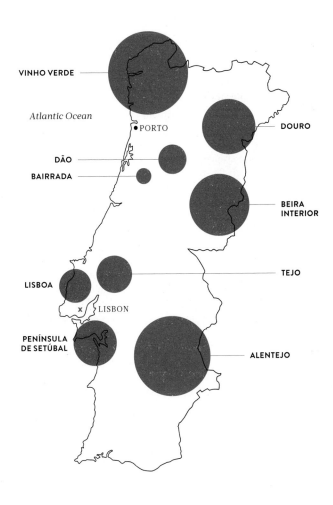

VINHO VERDE

Atlantic Ocean

● PORTO

DOURO

DÃO

BAIRRADA

BEIRA INTERIOR

TEJO

LISBOA

× LISBON

PENÍNSULA DE SETÚBAL

ALENTEJO

REGIONS TO KNOW

ALENTEJO While most of Portugal's winemaking regions are dominated by cool Atlantic Ocean breezes, Alentejo is located in the hot, sunny plains of the country's south. The weather there helps translate grapes into plump, full-bodied red wines with pronounced fruit flavors.

BAIRRADA Best known for inky, full-bodied reds made from the local Baga variety, as well as still and sparkling whites from the fresh, aromatic Maria Gomes grape, Bairrada is now turning out red wines from smoother varieties, such as Touriga Nacional and Cabernet Sauvignon.

DÃO This high north-central plateau is starting to fulfill its great promise. Cool nights and granite soils yield crisp, juicy red blends, ranging from light and simple to complex and ageworthy.

DOURO The oldest officially demarcated wine region in the world, the Douro follows the path of the Douro River from Portugal's border with Spain in the far east toward the Atlantic coast. The region is most famous for long-lived, fortified port wines (see p. 294), but it has a growing international reputation for rich, dry reds, often blended from the same mix of indigenous grapes used to make port.

LISBOA & TEJO Located not far from the capital city of Lisbon, these two regions are dominated by large cooperatives making mostly dull wines. But increasingly, smaller, independent producers in these areas are releasing quality reds at excellent values. (Until recently, the Lisboa wine region was known as Estremadura, and Tejo was known as Ribatejo.)

PENÍNSULA DE SETÚBAL Moscatel de Setúbal, a fortified dessert wine, is this sandy southwest region's signature wine, though dry reds from the peninsula's Palmela zone are gaining notice.

VINHO VERDE This is Portugal's largest winegrowing district. Stretching from the Minho River to south of the Douro River in the country's northwest, the cool, rainy Vinho Verde region is best known for light, dry, slightly spritzy whites with crisp citrus notes. A relatively low alcohol content makes Vinho Verde wines especially refreshing and a great choice for summer drinking.

KEY GRAPES: WHITE

ALVARINHO This aromatic grape (called Albariño in Spain) helps give Vinho Verde wines their bright, citrus-driven flavors. Usually made into light-bodied, crisp whites with mineral-laden notes of white peach and orange rind, uplifted by a slight effervescence, Alvarinho can also yield fuller-bodied, more complex wines.

LOUREIRO & TRAJADURA While both of these grapes are used as supporting players to Alvarinho in Vinho Verde, occasional single-variety bottles of Loureiro are making their way to the US. Similar to Alvarinho, Loureiro offers mouthwatering acidity and floral aromatics.

KEY GRAPES: RED

BAGA The Bairrada region's hallmark grape, thick-skinned Baga produces tannic, often rustic red wines with high acidity.

TINTA RORIZ (TEMPRANILLO) In Spain, this grape yields medium-bodied red wines marked with distinctive cherry flavor. In Portugal, vintners commonly combine it with native grapes like Touriga Nacional and Touriga Franca to craft hardy reds.

TOURIGA FRANCA The most widely planted grape in the Douro, Touriga Franca is rarely bottled on its own; instead it's valued for the fragrant aromas and firm, fine-grained tannins it contributes to red blends.

TOURIGA NACIONAL The country's star grape has a very thick skin that gives wines made from it their firm tannins. This quality, along with the grape's high acidity, also helps give these wines their ability to age—which is why Touriga Nacional forms the backbone of so many ports and dry red blends. It offers spicy depth and juicy black currant, floral and licorice notes, and is increasingly gaining favor as a single-variety wine.

WINE TERMINOLOGY

DENOMINAÇÃO DE ORIGEM CONTROLADA/PROTEGIDA (DOC/ DOP) These classifications apply to wines made in designated regions and vinified according to strict rules covering factors such as maximum yields, winemaking methods and aging periods.

IGP The less stringent IGP ("protected geographical indication") category is increasingly being used by innovative vintners to create fine wines outside the bounds of DOC/DOP rules. Some wineries still prefer the old *vinho regional* (VR) designation.

RESERVA Wines labeled *reserva* must have an alcohol content at least half a percent higher than the minimum for DOC/DOP or IGP wines (minimums vary by region). Some *reserva* regulations specify aging periods and even higher alcohol levels.

QUINTA Portuguese for "farm," "vineyard" or "wine estate."

Producers/ Portugal

ÁLVARO CASTRO

The wines Álvaro Castro and his daughter Maria produce from their estates, notably the Quintas de Saes and da Pellada, provide an instant reference point for the Dão region's emerging potential. The affordable Quinta de Saes and Dão-tier bottlings make a great introduction; old-vine Pellada-vineyard cuvées are a worthy splurge. Deep fruit and finesse define the reds; whites are silky, crisp and minerally. Álvaro also collaborates with Dirk Niepoort (see p. 132) on a delicious cross-regional blend, Doda.

BOTTLES TO TRY

- Dão / $
- Quinta da Pellada / $$$

ANSELMO MENDES

Anselmo Mendes has made a name for himself across Portugal as a wine consultant, but his own game-changing whites are his calling card. These are not your typical light-and-simple Vinho Verdes, but world-class wines of substance. An Alvarinho specialist (he also utilizes the local Loureiro and Avesso grapes), Mendes farms 25 parcels throughout the region. The Muros Antigos line features fine, crisp wines of excellent value. The fuller-bodied Muros de Melgaço Alvarinho and Parcela Única (single-parcel) bottlings are aged in French oak, gaining an extra dose of elegance.

BOTTLES TO TRY

○ Contacto Alvarinho / $$

○ Muros Antigos Alvarinho / $$

AVELEDA

The innovative Guedes family has helped set the standard for wines from the northwest coast since the 1880s. Today, the fourth and fifth generations oversee one of Portugal's largest and most widely exported wine brands. Aveleda is best known for crisp, light and dry Vinho Verdes with reasonable prices and an easy-drinking charm. The sprawling line, produced from estates throughout northern Portugal, has benefited from the consulting help of Bordeaux's Denis Dubourdieu.

BOTTLES TO TRY

○ Casal Garcia Vinho Verde / $

● Follies Touriga Nacional Cabernet Sauvignon / $

HERDADE DO ESPORÃO

A leading producer in the dynamic, emerging Alentejo area, the Roquette family's well-funded Esporão operation owes much of its success to the vision of Australian-born winemaker David Baverstock. The winery's output includes the well-priced Reserva and esteemed Private Selection wines and the blockbuster luxury Torre red blend. In 2008, Esporão took a giant step into the future by acquiring Quinta dos Murças, with vineyards extending along nearly two miles of Douro River cliffs, in the heart of a top port-wine district.

BOTTLES TO TRY

● Reserva / $$

● Private Selection / $$$$

LUIS PATO

The Bairrada region got little notice as a quality wine source until Luis Pato started making headlines at his family estate in the 1980s. Pato adopted modern methods (e.g., destemming grapes and using French barrels) to refine wines made from Baga and other local grapes. A godfather to a generation of quality-minded Bairrada producers, Pato is paving the road to the luxury market with his triple-digit-priced, all-Baga Quinta do Ribeirinho Pé Franco, while also turning out enticing wines with gentler prices, such as the Maria Gomes white and Vinhas Velhas bottlings.

BOTTLES TO TRY
- Vinhas Velhas / $$
- Quinta do Ribeirinho Pé Franco / $$$$

NIEPOORT

Although he's the scion of a centuries-old Dutch port-producing family, Dirk Niepoort has all the dynamism of a Silicon Valley startup guru. Niepoort is a leader of the collective that makes the Lavradores de Feitoria table wines, and he masterminds two of Portugal's greatest modern reds (Batuta and Charme) and a stable of go-to Douro bottlings, including the charming, affordable kitchen-sink blend Twisted. Beyond the Douro, Niepoort makes a fresh, fragrant Vinho Verde and juggles joint ventures with an all-star cast of winemakers from Spain to South Africa.

BOTTLES TO TRY
- Twisted / $$
- Batuta / $$$$

PRATS & SYMINGTON

Bruno Prats seems to like life in the fast lane. While running his family's famous Bordeaux château, Cos d'Estournel, he raced sports cars on the side. After Prats sold Cos d'Estournel in 1998, he teamed up with famous vintners all over the world, including the Symingtons of Graham's and Warre's ports. Prats & Symington created Chryseia, an ambitious Douro red based on native grapes that's notable for its length and elegance, plus a baby brother bottling, Post Scriptum. In 2009, P&S acquired Quinta de Roriz, adding the Prazo de Roriz red and a port to its lineup.

BOTTLES TO TRY
- Post Scriptum / $$
- Chryseia / $$$$

QUINTA DE SOALHEIRO

Along with Anselmo Mendes (see p. 131), Quinta de Soalheiro is a reference-point producer of fine, modern Vinho Verde. Located in an unusually warm, dry corner of the appellation (*soalheiro* means "sunny"), this family-owned winery makes lush, complex, non-fizzy dry whites exclusively from low-yielding Alvarinho. Siblings Luis and Maria João Cerdeira farm their vines organically and use estate-grown fruit. The pricier Reserva tier sees some new French oak, but some drinkers may prefer the "regular" Alvarinho's crisp purity.

BOTTLES TO TRY

○ Alvarinho / $$
○ Alvarinho Reserva / $$$

QUINTA DO CRASTO

Perched on a steep mountain overlooking the Douro River, this well-known port winery owned by the Roquette family had produced only two vintages of non-fortified table wines in 1997 when one of its reds bested thousands of entrants at an international wine competition. That recognition catapulted the winery—and Portugal's dry reds—into the spotlight. Today Crasto is a sought-after name, known for plummy, polished reds made from blends of indigenous grape varieties. The stealth choice, though, is its luscious, minerally white.

BOTTLES TO TRY

○ Crasto / $
● Crasto Superior / $$

SOGRAPE

This mega-producer has spent the past few decades reinventing itself. It built a fortune selling huge volumes of Mateus rosé and, more recently, Sandeman and Ferreira ports. These days, Sogrape owns wineries across Portugal that make terrific non-pink, non-fortified wines, ranging from the low-priced Callabriga bottlings to prime Douro reds from Casa Ferreirinha. The iconic 1751 Ferreirinha estate has reached new heights of international esteem, thanks to the revered, luxury-priced Barca Velha bottling, produced sparingly and only in top vintage years.

BOTTLES TO TRY

○ Gazela Vinho Verde / $
● Casa Ferreirinha Vinha Grande / $$

Germany

In the US, German wine has only one real problem: the German language itself. One word like *Trockenbeerenauslese* (a type of sweet dessert wine) or *Erzeugerabfüllung* (estate bottled) can scare off a hundred potential German wine fans. But there are myriad good things about German wine, with the Riesling grape at the top of the list. Riesling is one of the world's greatest white varieties, and when grown in Germany's ancient, crumbling slate hillsides, it achieves an unmatched mix of stony purity and perfumed elegance. Not that many other German wines come to US stores, but fans of crisp, aromatic reds should definitely look out for German Spätburgunder–or, as it's better known, Pinot Noir.

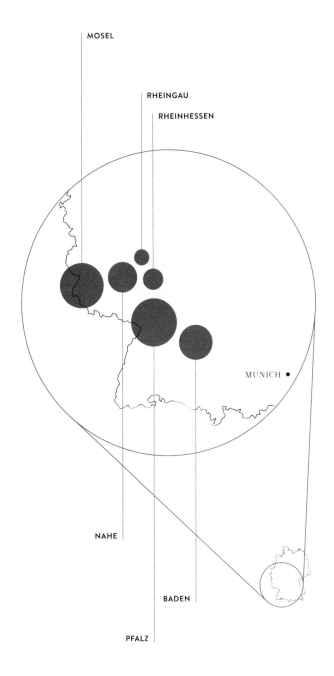

MOSEL

RHEINGAU

RHEINHESSEN

MUNICH

NAHE

BADEN

PFALZ

REGIONS TO KNOW

BADEN, NAHE & PFALZ These relatively warm regions have been the source of some exciting new wines recently, thanks to a generation-long influx of ambitious winemakers. Look for lusher Rieslings and interesting wines from lesser-known grapes, including Grauburgunder (Pinot Gris) and Gewürztraminer. Some of Germany's best Weissburgunder—a.k.a. Pinot Blanc—comes from Baden and the Pfalz. Baden also produces most of the country's Spätburgunder (Pinot Noir).

MOSEL Featuring some of the world's most vertiginous and difficult-to-cultivate vineyards, the south-facing slopes along the Mosel River and its tributaries, the Saar and the Ruwer, make the most of Germany's available sunshine. Vines rooted in rocky slate terraces produce delicate but often intense, minerally Rieslings with racy acidity.

RHEINGAU Home to storied estates with vineyards dating back to Roman times, the Rheingau traces the course of the Rhine River and has an outsize reputation among wine lovers, considering that it bottles less than 3 percent of Germany's wine. Its Rieslings, which are generally fuller-bodied than those of Mosel, its chief rival, display a mineral purity rarely equaled; the best examples are graceful but well-structured whites that improve with age for many years.

RHEINHESSEN The hilly terrain of the Rheinhessen region produces many low-quality sweet wines, but there are excellent bargains to be found among the bulk offerings. The region turns out some of the best examples of Scheurebe and Silvaner—two underrated German white varieties.

⚜ KEY GRAPES: WHITE

GEWÜRZTRAMINER & MUSKATELLER (MUSCAT) These varieties thrive in Germany's cool climate and yield wines marked by floral, intensely fragrant aromas.

GRAUBURGUNDER/RULÄNDER (PINOT GRIS) & WEISSBURGUNDER (PINOT BLANC) Both sweet and dry whites are produced from these varieties, with Weissburgunder being generally dry. Pinot Gris is called Grauburgunder when crafted in a crisp style; sweeter versions are often named Ruländer.

MÜLLER-THURGAU (RIVANER) & SILVANER Wines made with these grapes are rare in the US, mainly because there's not much worth importing. Typically used for simple, refreshing table wines, these popular varieties can sometimes yield sleek, exciting whites when grown for quality rather than quantity.

RIESLING Germany's most widely planted and prestigious grape is made into a vast range of wine styles, from bracingly dry to unctuously sweet, from searingly mineral to fruity and floral. Many connoisseurs consider fine German Riesling to be the epitome of stylish subtlety in the world of white wine.

SCHEUREBE Often used for dessert wines, this unusual white variety displays black currant aromas and citrusy flavors.

⚜ KEY GRAPES: RED

DORNFELDER First cultivated in 1979, this new grape yields juicy, deeply colored reds that are catching on in Germany.

SPÄTBURGUNDER (PINOT NOIR) The German version of Pinot Noir is still far from a household presence in the US, but if you can find them, wines made with Spätburgunder often offer delicate, fresh cherry notes and a pleasing vibrancy.

WINE TERMINOLOGY

There may be such a thing as providing too much information, and Exhibit A could be the German wine label. Clear as ABC to those who can crack the code, it can seem overwhelming (especially when written in Gothic print) to casual drinkers. Labels identify the producer, the place of origin and, sometimes, a ripeness level. If grapes come from a single village, that town is identified and given the suffix *er;* the vineyard name follows if it's also a single-vineyard wine. Sometimes a proprietary cuvée name is included. For wines at the QmP quality level (see below), there is also a ripeness designation at the end of the wine name. So, a wine labeled *Dr. Loosen Wehlener Sonnenuhr Riesling Spätlese,* for example, is produced by the Dr. Loosen estate near the town of Wehlen in the Sonnenuhr ("sundial") vineyard from Riesling grapes that were picked at a Spätlese level of ripeness.

QUALITÄTSWEIN OR QUALITÄTSWEIN BESTIMMTER ANBAUGEBIETE (QBA) This basic category includes the majority of German wines; it's used on everything from bulk wines to solidly made value bottlings.

QUALITÄTSWEIN MIT PRÄDIKAT (QMP) A big step up from QbAs, wines labeled *QmP* are held to higher quality standards; they are further ranked by the grapes' sugar levels, or ripeness, at the time of harvest (see below).

RIPENESS & SWEETNESS LEVELS Grapes with higher sugar levels have the potential to make more flavorful, fuller-bodied wines. Perceived sweetness depends more on the balance between acidity and residual sugar, the amount of natural grape sugar allowed to remain after fermentation. Wines in less-ripe categories are usually drier than those made from riper grapes, though not always. The least-ripe category is Kabinett, which can be vinified as dry or slightly sweet. Spätlese wines, the next designation up, range from dry to sweet with more concentrated flavors than Kabinett. Richer and typically sweeter than Spätleses, Auslese wines come from handpicked grapes that ripen on the vine long after most fruit has been picked. The sweetest designations are Beerenauslese (BA) and Trockenbeerenauslese (TBA). Made with superripe grapes, these opulent, luxury-priced dessert wines can age beautifully for decades.

TROCKEN & HALBTROCKEN Trocken wines taste dry, while halbtrocken ("half-dry") bottlings have a very subtle sweetness. Spätlese trocken means that the wine is dry in style, yet made from grapes picked at Spätlese levels of ripeness.

CLASSIC & SELECTION These terms for Germany's increasingly popular, high-quality dry wines are meant to clear up confusion over designations like Spätlese trocken (see opposite). Classic wines are made from regionally typical grapes and bear the name of the producer but not the vineyard. By regulation, they must be "harmoniously dry," deftly balancing acidity and residual sugar. Selection wines are higher in quality; they must be made from top, low-yielding vineyards and hand-harvested grapes, among other rigorous qualifications. Selection wines list the producer and vineyard.

ERSTE LAGE, GROSSE LAGE & GROSSES GEWÄCHS These newer, elite designations are reserved for top-quality wines sourced from specific vineyards recognized as superior. Erste Lage wines are comparable to the Burgundian *premier cru* (see p. 35). Grosse Lage, a term approved in 2012, is the highest tier—comparable to Burgundy's *grand cru* designation. Grosses Gewächs, abbreviated "GG" on bottles, denotes a relatively dry wine from a Grosse Lage vineyard.

Producers/ Germany

A. J. ADAM

Part of the new generation of true believers in German wine-making, even in challenging terrain, Andreas Adam rejuvenated his family's estate on the Mosel's obscure Dhron River tributary, and is successfully hand-farming steep, windswept terraces above the Dhron, as well as vertiginous old-vine parcels in Piesport's renowned Goldtröpfchen vineyard. Adam's work in the vineyards and his natural-winemaking style yield intense, striking wines with a signature energy that have gained him a devoted following of critics and sommeliers—and clued-in consumers. Look especially for the Dhroner Riesling or the balanced feinherb (off-dry) Rieslings.

BOTTLES TO TRY

○ Dhroner Riesling / $$$
○ Hofberg Riesling Grosses Gewächs / $$$$

DÖNNHOFF

Helmut Dönnhoff's masterfully balanced wines command cult-like devotion from fans, and are priced accordingly. Arguably the finest producer in the small, less-heralded Nahe region, Dönnhoff ranks among the best in all of Germany. Its coveted Eisweins, sweet Rieslings and range of Grosses Gewächs bottlings demonstrate a stunning intensity, with a lift from the winery's signature shimmering acidity. Even Dönnhoff's duo of delicate entry-level Rieslings—one dry (trocken), the other lightly sweet—offer rare precision and purity.

BOTTLES TO TRY

○ Riesling / $$
○ Riesling Trocken / $$

DR. LOOSEN

Every wine region needs a spokesperson like Ernst Loosen, an ebullient, charismatic risk taker who helped revolutionize German winemaking. When he took over his family's Mosel estate in 1988, he focused his efforts on old, ungrafted vines and low yields. In collaboration with winemaker Bernard Schug, Loosen crafts expressive single-vineyard Rieslings that put the estate in the ranks of Mosel's elite. The Dr. L label offers delicious, reliable wines for everyday drinking. In the US, Loosen joined with Washington state's Chateau Ste. Michelle (see p. 214) to produce the top-notch Eroica Rieslings.

BOTTLES TO TRY

○ Dr. L Riesling / $
○ Wehlener Sonnenuhr Riesling Auslese / $$$

EGON MÜLLER

One of Germany's most prominent winemakers, Egon Müller works a Mosel estate that's been in his family since 1797. The house produces only Riesling wines from its own vineyards, including the Scharzhofberg Grosse Lage. Müller's elegant, vibrant approach is on full display in the Scharzhofberger bottlings; the Scharzhof Riesling offers a less costly introduction. Müller's well-priced Château Belá Riesling from Slovakia is made in a broader style that recalls Alsace and Austrian versions.

BOTTLES TO TRY

○ Scharzhof Riesling / $$$
○ Scharzhofberger Riesling Kabinett / $$$$

FRITZ HAAG

This winery in the heart of the Mosel was much lauded under the longtime guidance of Wilhelm Haag, so the transition to his son Oliver in 2005 was closely watched. Any concerns have since dissipated, as the younger Haag has taken this bellwether estate to fresh heights. And speaking of heights: Haag's prime vineyards are on the near-vertical slopes of Brauneberg, a site famed in Roman times that includes the Brauneberger Juffer Sonnenuhr Grosse Lage. An accessible sweet spot in the lineup is the palate-enlivening Brauneberger Riesling Kabinett.

BOTTLES TO TRY

○ Brauneberger Riesling Kabinett / $$
○ Brauneberger Juffer Sonnenuhr Riesling Spätlese / $$$

GEHEIMER RAT DR. VON BASSERMANN-JORDAN

An esteemed Pfalz producer for some 300 years (the winery claims the poet Goethe as a former customer), Bassermann-Jordan entered the 21st century under the ownership of entrepreneur Achim Niederberger. Since his death in 2013, the winery has been led by his widow, Jana, and continues to produce scintillating wines. It is lionized for its Grosses Gewächs and high-end dessert bottlings, but winemaker Ulrich Mell also turns out a broad range of wines from the house's 20 vineyards.

BOTTLES TO TRY

○ Riesling Feinherb / $
○ Riesling Trocken / $$

MAXIMIN GRÜNHAUS

This benchmark Ruwer Valley producer was created when the von Strumm family acquired land from the ancient Abbey of St. Maximin in the 1880s. Farmed naturally under the winemaking eye of Stefan Kraml since 2004, the estate produces filigreed Rieslings that epitomize the Ruwer Valley's delicate, flinty style. Grapes come from a trio of exalted vineyards: Abtsberg, Bruderberg and Herrenberg. Single-site cuvées can be hard to track down; alternatively, look for the estate's two intro-level, multivineyard Rieslings, all with the same wonderfully elaborate old-fashioned labels.

BOTTLES TO TRY

○ Herrenberg Riesling Kabinett / $$
○ Riesling / $$

REICHSGRAF VON KESSELSTATT

This 600-year-old estate has been owned since 1978 by the Reh family and is now under the direction of second-generation Annegret Reh-Gartner. With 90 acres of vines along the Mosel, Saar and Ruwer Rivers at his disposal, winemaker Wolfgang Mertes can be choosy about which vineyards to showcase in the winery's famous site-specific cuvées. Von Kesselstatt's single-vineyard wines from top sites like Bernkasteler Doktor and Scharzhofberger reflect the range of its *terroirs*. Estate vineyards also provide prime material for affordable multivineyard blends.

BOTTLES TO TRY

○ RK Riesling / $

○ Scharzhofberger Riesling Auslese / $$$$

SCHLOSS JOHANNISBERG

Dating back to around 1100, this cornerstone Rheingau estate is virtually synonymous with Riesling. Emperor Franz I of Austria awarded the former Benedictine monastery to the great diplomat Prince Klemens Wenzel von Metternich in 1816. Although the last member of the Metternich clan, Princess Tatiana von Metternich, died at the estate in 2006, it had been acquired in 1974 by the Oetker dynasty of packaged-food magnates. The wines here are aged in casks made from estate forest oaks and receive an extended aging on their lees, which adds a subtle succulence to their fresh, intense Rheingau fruit.

BOTTLES TO TRY

○ Rotlack Riesling Kabinett / $

○ Silberlack Riesling Grosses Gewächs / $$$$

WEINGUT JOH. JOS. PRÜM

Eldest daughter Dr. Katharina Prüm now works alongside her famous winemaker father, Manfred, at this estate in the Mosel village of Wehlen. Established in 1911 by Manfred's grandfather Johann Josef Prüm, the winery is famous for, among other things, a resolute refusal to bow to fashion: The estate's four great vineyard sites produce virtually all sweet wines, and nearly all are built for the long haul. Even the entry-level Riesling Kabinett continues to gain complexity for a decade after release.

BOTTLES TO TRY

○ Riesling Kabinett / $$

○ Wehlener Sonnenuhr Riesling Spätlese / $$$

WEINGUT ROBERT WEIL

Robert Weil's dessert wines are so famous that they can over-shadow the phenomenal dry Rieslings. Although this 140-year-old Rheingau estate was already well regarded, the founder's great-grandson, Wilhelm Weil, has raised its profile even higher. His meticulous methods (e.g., picking a vineyard up to 17 times in order to harvest perfectly ripe grapes) result in Rieslings of rare elegance and intensity. Weil's finest wines come from three superb vineyard sites near the town of Kiedrich; grapes from other locations go into the two basic blends.

BOTTLES TO TRY

- ○ **Riesling Trocken** / $$
- ○ **Kiedrich Gräfenberg Riesling Spätlese** / $$$$

WEINGUT SELBACH-OSTER

Selbach family forebears established this renowned Mosel estate in the 1660s. Today Johannes Selbach and his son Sebastian work with nearly 50 acres of superlative, steeply terraced estate vineyards to make Selbach-Oster's masterful Rieslings. The winemaking here is very natural, resulting in wines of great verve and lift that combine flavor intensity with moderate alcohol. The remarkable Rotlay, Schmitt and Anrecht bottlings come from tiny old-vine parcels.

BOTTLES TO TRY

- ○ **Riesling Kabinett** / $$
- ○ **Schmitt Zeltinger Schlossberg Riesling** / $$$

WEINGUT ST. URBANS-HOF

Named for the patron saint of wine producers, St. Urban of Langres, this family-owned Mosel estate produces two terrific, value-driven Rieslings—the stony, crisp estate bottling and a light, barely sweet Urban cuvée. Even St. Urbans-Hof's more expensive single-site wines, the best of which come from the Piesporter Goldtröpfchen and Leiwener Laurentiuslay vineyards (in the Mosel) and the Ockfener Bockstein vineyard (in the Saar), deliver terrific quality at relatively reasonable prices. The new "from old vines" estate Riesling is a fresh, slightly off-dry bottling from vines averaging 50 years of age.

BOTTLES TO TRY

- ○ **Estate Bottled from Old Vines Riesling** / $
- ○ **Ockfener Bockstein Riesling Spätlese** / $$$

Austria

The skiing may be great in the Alps of western Austria, but for extraordinary wine, head to the eastern edge of this Central European country. The grapes for Austria's most famous wines–peppery Grüner Veltliners and regal, stony Rieslings–grow here, along the banks of the beautiful Danube River. These invigoratingly fresh whites are fantastic complements to food, which may be why US sommeliers have been so obsessed with convincing their customers of the virtues of Austrian wine. Austria's less-well-known reds–particularly its juicy Zweigelts and spicy Blaufränkisches–are also well worth exploring, though they constitute only about 30 percent of the country's production.

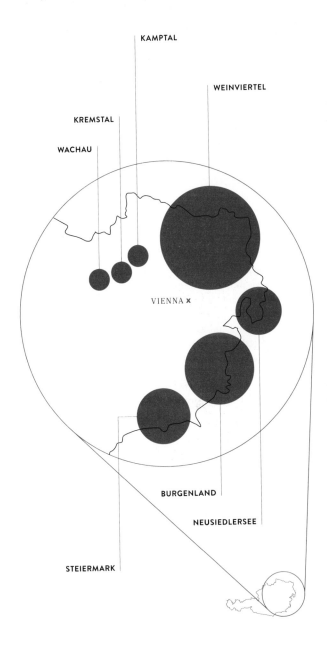

KAMPTAL

WEINVIERTEL

KREMSTAL

WACHAU

VIENNA ✕

BURGENLAND

NEUSIEDLERSEE

STEIERMARK

REGIONS TO KNOW

BURGENLAND South of Vienna and bordering Hungary, this warm zone produces most of the country's reds, along with stunning dessert wines.

NIEDERÖSTERREICH (LOWER AUSTRIA) Austria's great white wines come mainly from this sprawling northeastern province, where vineyards line the Danube River. The dramatically terraced **Wachau** subregion (a UNESCO World Heritage site) turns out many of Austria's richest Grüner Veltliners and Rieslings; neighboring **Kremstal** and **Kamptal** also make stellar examples. The region's largest subzone, **Weinviertel**, is a good source of affordable Grüner Veltliner and reds from grapes like Zweigelt.

STEIERMARK (STYRIA) Austria's southernmost wine region produces vivid, aromatic whites from such varieties as Sauvignon Blanc, Gelber Muskateller, Chardonnay, Weissburgunder and Welschriesling.

WIEN (VIENNA) Wine from the hills just outside Vienna is made from blends of different varieties harvested and crushed together (called *gemischter satz*).

🍇 KEY GRAPES: WHITE

GELBER MUSKATELLER US sommeliers champion this rare grape, which yields delicate, floral-scented whites.

GRÜNER VELTLINER Austria's signature grape—and another sommelier favorite for its food-friendly properties—is a crisp, peppery white bursting with mineral and apple flavors. Top Grüners improve over time, gaining notes of honey and smoke.

MORILLON (CHARDONNAY) & SAUVIGNON BLANC These international white varieties are gaining ground in Austria; Sauvignon Blanc from Steiermark is generally the finest.

MÜLLER-THURGAU (RIVANER) & WELSCHRIESLING These high-yielding varieties are responsible for much of Austria's everyday whites, though a few excellent sweet Welschrieslings are made.

RIESLING Austria's versions of this minerally white tend to be drier than Germany's Rieslings and fruitier than Alsace's.

WEISSBURGUNDER (PINOT BLANC) The most famous Austrian examples of this variety come from Burgenland, where it is the basis of superb dessert wines and many dry whites. Southeast Steiermark is also a good source of dry Weissburgunders.

KEY GRAPES: RED

BLAUFRÄNKISCH (LEMBERGER) This spicy red variety yields medium-bodied wines that are exceptionally food-friendly.

ST. LAURENT Though rarely exported, the red wines made from this local variety may be Austria's most seductive, with lush, smoky flavors and exuberant aromas reminiscent of Pinot Noir.

ZWEIGELT Fresh cherry and licorice tinges and juicy acidity define Zweigelt, Austria's most popular red.

WINE TERMINOLOGY

Austrian wine labels list grape and region, and, except for simple table wines, use rankings similar to Germany's Qualitätswein designations, which define the ripeness of grapes for quality wines and hence the finished wine's potential alcohol level. In 2002, Austria introduced the Districtus Austriae Controllatus (DAC) regional wine-classification system. The Wachau established its own three-category classification system for white wines in 1983.

DISTRICTUS AUSTRIAE CONTROLLATUS (DAC) Similar to the French AOC and Italian DOC classification systems, DAC categories have rules that cover yields, permitted grapes, winemaking requirements and geographic limits for sourcing. The wines must also adhere to local stylistic profiles. DAC designations are meant to ensure that Austrian wines are quality examples of the country's most important regional styles; today there are nine designated appellations.

GEMISCHTER SATZ A wine made from a traditional "field blend" of different grape varieties. For these bottlings, winemakers grow and ferment the grape varieties together, rather than blending them after fermentation. Wiener Gemischter Satz achieved DAC status in 2013.

STEINFEDER A term used in the Wachau to define light, low-alcohol wines that are made for drinking young (and perfect for picnics and parties).

FEDERSPIEL A Wachau name for wines made from riper grapes that are then fermented into medium-bodied dry wines similar to those made in a Kabinett style (see p. 138).

SMARAGD This Wachau term applies to wines made from grapes picked later than those for Federspiel wines (see above). The extra hang time on the vine gives Smaragd wines exceptional richness and body, and occasionally a touch of sweetness.

Producers/ Austria

DOMÄNE WACHAU

The rare large wine cooperative renowned for quality, Domäne Wachau farms one-third of the Wachau's vineyards, yet its wines deliver the consistency more typical of a far smaller operation, with an emphasis on finesse rather than opulence. Prime grapes from prestigious sites like Loibenberg and Kollmitz go into the higher-end, single-vineyard tiers, but even these bottlings are gently priced, and the best of them can rival Wachau's finest.

BOTTLES TO TRY
- Terrassen Grüner Veltliner Smaragd / $$
- Terrassen Riesling Federspiel / $$

F.X. PICHLER

With their legendary depth, concentration and penetrating minerality, F.X. Pichler's Rieslings and Grüner Veltliners inspire cultlike devotion (and are priced accordingly). Franz Xaver and his winemaker son Lucas fashion their richly styled whites from some of the Wachau's most famous vineyards. Lucas has worked in recent vintages to dial back alcohol levels by harvesting earlier, but the wines are still luscious, with pinpoint balance. Collectors snap up top bottlings like the F.X. Unendlich Riesling; look for the enticing Federspiel cuvées, which are easier to find.

BOTTLES TO TRY

○ Loibner Burgstall Riesling Federspiel / $$$
○ Loibner Berg Grüner Veltliner Smaragd / $$$$

HEIDI SCHRÖCK

The Burgenland town of Rust is famous for its sumptuous sweet wines, and vintner Heidi Schröck has been a key figure in the revival of the area's traditional, Tokaji-like Ruster Ausbruch. But it's her dry cuvées made with grapes like Weissburgunder (Pinot Blanc) and Grauburgunder (Pinot Gris) that have made her a star: They expertly balance silkiness and spice, delicacy and lushness. Schröck has also been acclaimed for influential wines from less-well-known grapes, such as Gelber Muskateller and Hungary's Furmint, which are reaching broader audiences thanks to the enthusiasm of wine insiders.

BOTTLES TO TRY

○ Weissburgunder / $$
○ Furmint / $$$

MORIC

Moric's Roland Velich spent years studying the storied domaines of Burgundy and Barolo in order to bring that level of greatness to Austrian reds. He's achieving just that with Blaufränkisch grapes from Burgenland's rolling hills. Instead of treating the local variety as a heat-loving grape like Cabernet (i.e., aging it in new oak and extracting maximum concentration), Velich uses a delicate touch suited to cool-climate grapes like Pinot Noir. The result: spicy, silky reds with captivating finesse.

BOTTLES TO TRY

● Blaufränkisch / $$
● Blaufränkisch Reserve / $$$

SCHLOSS GOBELSBURG

Until 1996, Michael Moosbrugger was just an obsessive young wine collector. Then Willi Bründlmayer (see below) gave him the opportunity of a lifetime: to lease the vineyards at Schloss Gobelsburg, a 12th-century monastery with vines in some of Kamptal's finest *terroir*. Since then, the quality of Gobelsburg's wines has soared, and Moosbrugger has made the leap from novice to star. Committed to letting the vineyard shine through, he farms organically and carts his wines gently about the cellar in wheeled barrels rather than pumping them with machines.

BOTTLES TO TRY

○ Gobelsburger Riesling / $$
○ Tradition Grüner Veltliner / $$$

WEINGUT ALZINGER

In only 25 years, the Alzinger family's winery has climbed into Wachau's upper ranks, thanks to wines of compelling elegance and precision. Leo Alzinger's parents founded the vineyard in 1925 and sold grapes to the local cooperative for six decades; today Leo and his son (also Leo) fashion estate-grown whites, many from old vines, that are as celebrated as they are scarce. The winery's top stars are its plantings of Riesling (higher up the slopes) and Grüner Veltliner (lower down) in the Loibenberg and Steinertal vineyards.

BOTTLES TO TRY

○ Frauenweingarten Grüner Veltliner Federspiel / $$
○ Steinertal Riesling Smaragd / $$$$

WEINGUT BRÜNDLMAYER

Bründlmayer is a name to remember in Austrian wine—partly because Willi Bründlmayer makes wines that are consistently ranked among Austria's finest. It's also because, in a country where most family estates are tiny, Bründlmayer owns nearly 200 vineyard acres in the heart of Kamptal, making his wines easier to find. Heiligenstein-vineyard Rieslings are the estate's standouts, but the quality is terrific across the portfolio, including Grüner Veltliners, acacia-barrel-aged reds and fine sparklers that, by themselves, would put the place on the map.

BOTTLES TO TRY

○ Zöbinger Heiligenstein Alte Reben Riesling Reserve / $$$$
● Zweigelt / $

WEINGUT EMMERICH KNOLL

A leading figure in Austria's wine renaissance of the 1980s, Emmerich Knoll II (now with son Emmerich III) farms 37 acres of steep vineyards along the warmer, eastern stretch of the Wachau Valley (the two also run the family's 400-year-old wine-country restaurant, Loibnerhof Familie Knoll). Knoll's wines, with their striking gold Baroque labels depicting Saint Urban, combine freshness, power and stony minerality, resulting in some of Wachau's most ageworthy whites: Top cuvées from sites like the Loibenberg vineyard and Pfaffenberg (just across the Wachau border in Kremstal) can improve for many years.

BOTTLES TO TRY
- Loibner Grüner Veltliner Federspiel / $$
- Ried Loibenberg Riesling Smaragd / $$$

WEINGUT FRANZ HIRTZBERGER

There is a changing of the guard at this renowned Wachau estate, as Franz, Jr., takes the reins from his father. One thing that won't change is the intensive work the family puts into its vineyards—they make up to five passes to pick only the ripest grapes. It's a difficult, thigh-burning task: The fruit grows on some of the region's steepest terraces, towering over the Danube. This obsessiveness means that even the Federspiel (lighter) wines are among the most impressive of their kind, while the seductive Smaragds offer silky richness and seamless balance.

BOTTLES TO TRY
- Rotes Tor Grüner Veltliner Federspiel / $$$
- Hochrain Riesling Smaragd / $$$$

WEINGUT HIRSCH

While still in his twenties, Johannes Hirsch convinced his family to let him rip out every red variety growing in their Kamptal vineyards—never mind that their reds were among the region's best. Continuing on his progressive streak, Hirsh converted the estate to biodynamic farming and became Austria's first vintner to use screw caps for all of his wines. His stellar Grüners and Rieslings include the juicy, compulsively drinkable Veltliner #1 and minerally whites from the famed Heiligenstein vineyard.

BOTTLES TO TRY
- Veltliner #1 / $$
- Heiligenstein Riesling Reserve / $$$

WEINGUT JAMEK

While many of his fellow vintners were churning out sweetened wines for the export market in the 1950s, the Wachau's Josef Jamek was creating then-unheard-of single-vineyard Rieslings and naturally dry cuvées that helped galvanize Austria's quality-wine revolution. Since 1996, his daughter Jutta and her husband, Hans Altmann, have run this iconic estate (Jamek passed away in 2011). The winery boasts a who's who collection of noble Wachau vineyard sites, including parcels of Achleiten, Klaus and Pichl, planted chiefly to Riesling and Grüner Veltliner.

BOTTLES TO TRY
○ Ried Achleiten Grüner Veltliner Smaragd / $$$
○ Ried Klaus Riesling / $$$

WEINGUT LOIMER

Fred Loimer, Jr.'s Kamptal winery, a minimalist black glass box, sits on top of vaulted-brick tunnels that once belonged to the local castle, and some of the surrounding vineyards are plowed by horse, not tractor. These contrasts embody Loimer's edgy-yet-traditionalist approach, which has put him at the forefront of both Kamptal's new guard and Austria's biodynamic movement. Benefiting from some of Kamptal's finest Erste Lage (first growth) vineyards, Loimer's wines aim for balance over sheer power, with succulent freshness prized as much as richness.

BOTTLES TO TRY
○ Lois Grüner Veltliner / $
○ Langenlois Steinmassl Riesling Erste Lage Reserve / $$$$

WEINGUT NIGL

First-generation star winemaker Martin Nigl makes Rieslings and Grüner Veltliners on his family's Kremstal estate that are impressive enough to compete with those of the region's more prestigious—and more expensive—neighbor, the Wachau. Nigl's grapes are all sustainably and organically farmed; those from the estate's oldest vineyards are reserved for the more expensive Privat line. Though they are layered with complex flavors, even Nigl's top wines retain a sense of delicacy; he often uses steel tanks rather than barrels to mature them.

BOTTLES TO TRY
○ Freiheit Grüner Veltliner / $$
○ Privat Riesling / $$$$

WEINGUT PRAGER

Franz Prager helped found the game-changing Vinea Wachau association, though his daughter Ilse and her husband, Vienna-born biologist turned winemaker Toni Bodenstein, have arguably been even more influential in turning Prager into one of the Wachau's most sought-after names and emulated producers. The estate's top bottlings come from the Achleiten vineyard, a revered ancient site planted with Riesling and Grüner Veltliner. But its newest vineyards, painstakingly scouted and analyzed by Bodenstein, are in cooler high-elevation sites—conditions that help preserve a wine's bright flavors and acidity in the face of Austria's increasingly warm summers.

BOTTLES TO TRY

○ Steinriegl Riesling Federspiel / $$$
○ Achleiten Grüner Veltliner Smaragd / $$$$

WEINGUT RUDI PICHLER

Since taking over his family's winery in 1997, Rudi Pichler has steadily transformed it into one of the Wachau's very best, partly through the intensive concentration he lavishes on his stony, old-vine vineyards (he calls himself a wine-caretaker, not a winemaker). In his handsome, modern cellar, he also employs a signature technique: Freshly pressed grape juice gets an extended pre-fermentation maceration on the skins after crushing. This gives Pichler's savory, minerally, very dry Rieslings and Grüner Veltliners an extra layer of complex aromatics.

BOTTLES TO TRY

○ Grüner Veltliner Federspiel / $$$
○ Weissenkirchner Achleithen Riesling Smaragd / $$$$

Greece

Greece has a longer winemaking history than any other European nation, going back more than 4,000 years. Maybe that's why, despite the world's fascination with Cabernet and Chardonnay, Greek winemakers have concentrated on evocative local grapes, using them to express the historic character of their country. Greece's Santorini whites fully capture that island's clear, sparkling sunlight and seaside freshness (and they're fantastic with fish, whether grilled, baked or fried). In Macedonia, fragrant Xinomavro reds suggest the rugged mountain slopes; in the Peloponnese, ripe, rich Agiorgitikos reflect the Mediterranean sun and soft hillsides. If you haven't tried Greek wines recently, you're missing out on some of the great wines of the world.

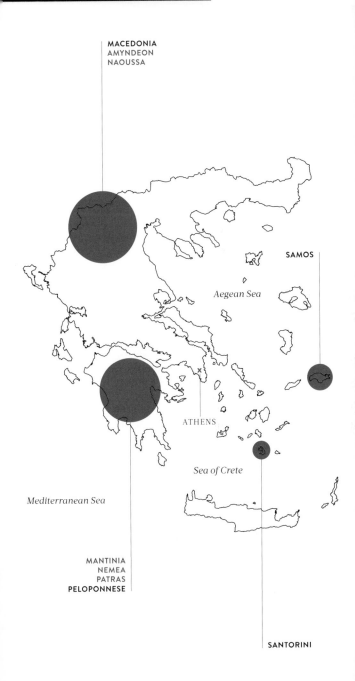

MACEDONIA
AMYNDEON
NAOUSSA

SAMOS

Aegean Sea

✕
ATHENS

Sea of Crete

Mediterranean Sea

MANTINIA
NEMEA
PATRAS
PELOPONNESE

SANTORINI

REGIONS TO KNOW

MACEDONIA This mountainous northern zone produces young, fruity reds as well as tannic, ageworthy ones from native Xinomavro grapes. The best come from **Naoussa** and **Amyndeon.**

PELOPONNESE This large peninsula in southwestern Greece is a go-to zone for aromatic reds based on the Agiorgitiko grape and floral Moschofilero-based whites. Top subzones include **Nemea,** for reds, and **Mantinia,** for whites.

SANTORINI Arguably Greece's finest whites come from this small island, where rainless summers, volcanic soils and native grapes (especially Assyrtiko) give its wines a minerally intensity.

KEY GRAPES: WHITE

ASSYRTIKO A Santorini specialty, Assyrtiko yields bone-dry, minerally wines that, at their best, can improve for decades.

ATHIRI This ancient white grape, often blended with Assyrtiko, is the source of succulent, citrusy whites.

MALAGOUSIA Revived in the late 1970s, this native grape yields satiny-textured wines with lush, full-bodied, stone-fruit flavors.

MOSCHOFILERO This pink-skinned Peloponnesian native stands out for crisp, low-alcohol white and rosé wines with floral, lightly spicy qualities reminiscent of Gewürztraminer.

ROBOLA The same grape as Friuli's Ribolla Gialla, Robola grows mostly in the mountainous island of Cephalonia, where it is responsible for minerally, citrus-inflected whites.

RODITIS A bulk-wine staple, Roditis also produces charming, floral whites in the Peloponnese's Patras appellation.

SAVATIANO This common variety is the usual basis for retsina, the simple, ubiquitous white wine flavored with pine resin.

KEY GRAPES: RED

AGIORGITIKO Also known as St. George, this grape is the source of some of Greece's top reds. A lush texture and juicy cherry notes are its hallmarks, whether it's made into fresh rosés or rich reds.

XINOMAVRO Macedonia's signature grape yields bold, ageworthy reds marked by savory black olive and herb notes.

WINE TERMINOLOGY

Greek wine labels typically list regions rather than grape varieties, as a wine's region tends to determine its main grapes. Greek wine regulations recognize two broad categories: the more strictly controlled Protected Designation of Origin (PDO) wines and basic table wines. The latter category includes wines entitled to a Protected Geographical Indication (PGI) designation, as well as the Traditional Appellation specialty wines: retsina and the multivarietal white verdea.

Producers/ Greece

ALPHA ESTATE

In Amyndeon, near the Albanian border in the northwest, vintner Angelos Iatridis and vine guru Makis Mavridis craft powerful, fruity, modern-style wines. Amyndeon's cool climate means that these wines retain vibrant acidity, despite their ripeness. Alpha's top bottling is Xinomavro; the Reserve, crafted from nearly 90-year-old vines, is a refined, supple wine that may spend up to 24 months in French oak and another 24 in bottle before release.

BOTTLES TO TRY

- Axia Syrah-Xinomavro / $$
- Xinomavro Reserve / $$

BOUTARI

Family-owned since 1879, Boutari has six wineries in Greece that occupy strategic spots in the top wine zones, making it one of the country's largest producers. It's also one of the best, thanks to Constantine and Yannis Boutari, who transformed their family's successful *négociant* into a premium winegrower after taking over in the 1980s; they've since influenced a generation of winemakers to focus on indigenous grapes. Boutari makes what may be Greece's most famous example of the Xinomavro grape—its firm, savory Grande Reserve Naoussa bottling—as well as terrific Moschofilero whites and innovative blends.

BOTTLES TO TRY

○ Moschofilero / $
● Grande Reserve Naoussa / $$

DOMAINE SIGALAS

Paris Sigalas is a Sorbonne-educated mathematician who spent much of his childhood on the island of Santorini and became fascinated with its wines, especially those made from ancient varieties. Inspired in part by the stellar wines he drank while studying in France, Sigalas started winemaking as a hobby, applying French techniques to Santorini grapes. In 1991, he went commercial, and today he's one of the country's most respected winemakers, thanks to chiseled Assyrtiko-based whites and elegant reds made from local grapes.

BOTTLES TO TRY

○ Assyrtiko Santorini / $$
○ Barrel Santorini / $$$

DOMAINE SKOURAS

Trained in France, George Skouras was among the first in Greece to blend the plush Agiorgitiko grape with Cabernet Sauvignon. The resulting elegant, tightly wound red has lived up to its name, Megas Oenos ("great wine"), becoming one of the definitive bottlings of the current Greek wine renaissance. The Nemea-based winery works with both French and native grapes to turn out top-quality wines that can be a steal for the price, like the minerally, medium-weight Moschofilero white.

BOTTLES TO TRY

○ Moscofilero / $
● Megas Oenos / $$

DOMAINE TSELEPOS

Native Cypriot Yiannis Tselepos started his Peloponnesian winery with his wife, Amalia, in 1989, after studying enology in Dijon and working for several Burgundy wineries. One of the central figures of the Greek fine-wine resurgence, Tselepos is known for championing the taut, fragrant Moschofilero grapes he grows in rocky clay soil, in a chilly vineyard at 2,100 feet. He also makes a world-class Gewürztraminer and notable reds, including his well-priced all-Agiorgitiko Driopi Classic and Reserve wines, plus Merlot and Cabernet Sauvignon bottlings.

BOTTLES TO TRY

○ Moschofilero Mantinia / $
● Driopi Classic Nemea / $$

ESTATE ARGYROS

Yiannis Argyros inherited his family's modest winery in the Santorini hills in 1974 and turned it into one of Greece's most prominent, in part by producing extravagant aged vin santos from sun-dried indigenous grapes harvested from 150-year-old vineyards. You can experience Argyros's quality in a drier style and for far less than the luxury prices the top vin santos command with the entry-level Atlantis-series wines: an Assyrtiko-based white and rosé and a silky red from the Mandelaria grape.

BOTTLES TO TRY

○ Atlantis / $$
● Mavrotragano / $$$

GAIA WINES

A research trip to the island of Santorini opened the eyes of then-Boutari enologist Yiannis Paraskevopoulos. The Bordeaux-trained PhD recognized potential for great wine when he saw it and tasted it, and he joined forces with vineyard expert Leon Karatsalos to found Gaia in 1994. Thalassitis, their pure, razor-sharp Santorini Assyrtiko bottling, made the winery an instant success. The partners have since branched out, producing the polished, velvety Gaia Estate Agiorgitikos from a hillside vineyard they acquired in Nemea in 1996, and the affordable Peloponnese white and red they bottle under the Notios label.

BOTTLES TO TRY

○ Thalassitis / $$
● Notios / $

NEW
WOR

162
UNITED
STATES

222
AUSTRALIA

256
CHILE

266
SOUTH
AFRICA

LD

United States
Australia
New Zealand
Argentina
Chile
South Africa

238
NEW
ZEALAND

248
ARGENTINA

United States

Forty years ago, California was producing spectacular wines–the only hitch was that the world didn't know that. Today, though, its top wines are some of the world's most sought-after, and names like Napa and Sonoma are almost universally known. What happened over the last four decades was a US wine revolution. There are now more than 600 wineries in Oregon, over 850 in Washington and more than 4,000 in California (and additional wineries in every other state in the nation), producing everything from pricey collector bottlings to some of the greatest wine values on the planet. It is truly a sensational time to be drinking American wine.

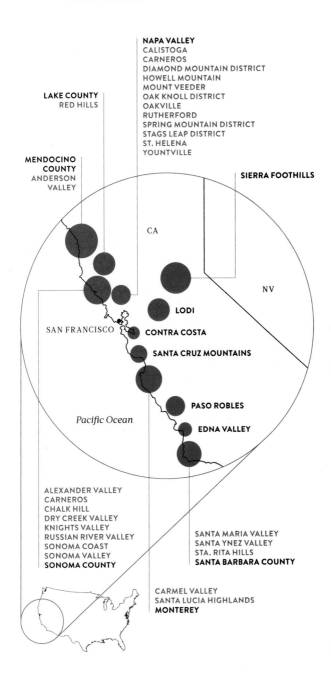

NAPA VALLEY
CALISTOGA
CARNEROS
DIAMOND MOUNTAIN DISTRICT
HOWELL MOUNTAIN
MOUNT VEEDER
OAK KNOLL DISTRICT
OAKVILLE
RUTHERFORD
SPRING MOUNTAIN DISTRICT
STAGS LEAP DISTRICT
ST. HELENA
YOUNTVILLE

LAKE COUNTY
RED HILLS

**MENDOCINO
COUNTY**
ANDERSON
VALLEY

SIERRA FOOTHILLS

CA

NV

LODI

SAN FRANCISCO

CONTRA COSTA

SANTA CRUZ MOUNTAINS

PASO ROBLES

EDNA VALLEY

Pacific Ocean

ALEXANDER VALLEY
CARNEROS
CHALK HILL
DRY CREEK VALLEY
KNIGHTS VALLEY
RUSSIAN RIVER VALLEY
SONOMA COAST
SONOMA VALLEY
SONOMA COUNTY

SANTA MARIA VALLEY
SANTA YNEZ VALLEY
STA. RITA HILLS
SANTA BARBARA COUNTY

CARMEL VALLEY
SANTA LUCIA HIGHLANDS
MONTEREY

WINE TERMINOLOGY

AMERICAN VITICULTURAL AREA (AVA) Most US labels carry an AVA, showing the legally defined region from which the wine comes. Unlike many European designations, AVAs don't stipulate how a wine must be produced, which grapes may be used or the maximum yields allowed per vineyard. Rather, US law dictates that at least 85 percent of the grapes in a wine labeled with an AVA must come from that region. If an AVA wine lists a vintage date, 95 percent of the fruit is required to be from that year's harvest. Wines with the name of one grape, often called varietal wines, must contain 75 percent of that grape variety. Some states go beyond these requirements. Oregon, for example, mandates a higher minimum percentage for most varietal wines and for geographic designations.

MERITAGE Pronounced like "heritage," this category recognizes multivariety blends made from traditional Bordeaux grapes—chiefly Cabernet Sauvignon and Merlot in reds and Sauvignon Blanc and Sémillon in whites. Many producers use proprietary names for these wines, e.g., Robert Mondavi's Opus One.

OLD VINES The US government does not regulate the phrase *old vines* on labels, meaning that vintners can define it however they like. Many vintners agree that vines older than 35 years qualify as old, though some believe only those a half century or older make the cut.

RESERVE Another term that has no legal definition, *reserve* can be applied to any wine regardless of its age or how it was made; how much the designation is actually worth depends entirely on the brand.

VITIS LABRUSCA Native to North America, this hardy grape species has largely been supplanted in the US by European *Vitis vinifera* grapes. The *Vitis labrusca* species includes such varieties as Concord and Catawba.

VITIS VINIFERA All of Europe's so-called "noble" grape varieties, such as Chardonnay, Cabernet Sauvignon, Sauvignon Blanc and Pinot Noir, belong to this grape species.

CALIFORNIA

CLAIM TO FAME
California's wine history can be divided into three main eras: the promising years before Prohibition; the decades after repeal, when the business was dominated by large-scale, low-priced producers; and the years since the landmark opening of the Robert Mondavi Winery in 1966, when ambitious artisan and high-end producers showed the wine world what the state's vineyards could produce at their best. Today, California's 3,800 wineries are America's powerhouse, bottling 90 percent of US wines. Many of the best regions hug the coast, with vines depending on ocean-driven wind and fog to chill the grapes nightly and to help create complexly flavored fruit. But vineyards grow across much of the state. And while plantings are dominated by international varieties such as Cabernet Sauvignon and Chardonnay, California's experimental winemakers work with a vast array of other grapes, producing wines of every type and style.

REGIONS TO KNOW
CARNEROS Straddling the southern ends of Napa and Sonoma Counties, Carneros has a blustery climate that's perfect for Chardonnay and Pinot Noir; sparkling versions are a specialty.

CENTRAL COAST Not to be confused with the scorching-hot Central Valley (largely bulk-wine country), this stretch of the Pacific Coast is a premium growing region extending between San Francisco and Santa Barbara. Of its 39 subregions, a few stand out. Occupying a peninsula south of San Francisco, **Monterey** specializes in Chardonnay and Pinot Noir (aromatic whites like Sauvignon Blanc and Riesling grow well here, too).

South of Monterey, inland **Paso Robles** offers bold, fruity reds, especially Zinfandel, Rhône varieties (Syrah, Grenache, Mourvèdre) and Cabernet. Southern California's **Santa Barbara County** owes its success with cool-climate grapes (notably Chardonnay, Syrah and Pinot Noir) to a geological oddity: coastal valleys that run east–west and serve as superhighways for chilly ocean air. Subregions include the **Santa Maria** and **Santa Ynez Valleys** and the latter's **Sta. Rita Hills** zone.

LAKE COUNTY This district has long been a fine source of delicious Sauvignon Blanc; now its **Red Hills** subzone is gaining fame for Napa-like Cabernets at refreshingly gentle prices.

LODI & THE SIERRA FOOTHILLS Lodi, located inland and east of San Francisco Bay, in the Central Valley, and the Sierra Foothills region are particularly famous for old-vine Zinfandels.

MENDOCINO COUNTY This rugged North Coast region grows an unlikely mix of grapes ranging from Charbono to Carignane. Easier to find are its fantastic old-vine Zinfandels and cherry-driven Pinot Noirs. The cool, rainy subregion of **Anderson Valley** has emerged as an excellent source of silky Pinot Noirs, crisp Chardonnays and refined sparkling wines.

NAPA VALLEY California's most prestigious wine region produces benchmark Cabernet Sauvignons that are among the world's finest reds. (It produces great Merlot and Cabernet Franc, too.) Northeast of San Francisco, Napa, which includes 16 subregions, is blocked from the Pacific by the Mayacamas Mountains, making it warmer than its western neighbor Sonoma County. The most tannic, powerful Cabernets come from hillside vineyards on famous slopes such as **Howell, Spring** and **Diamond Mountains;** more plush, generous versions, like those from **Oak Knoll District, Stags Leap District** and **St. Helena,** are typically made from grapes grown on the valley floor or on benchlands.

NORTH COAST This large umbrella region encompasses all of Northern California's best-known AVAs, including those in Napa, Sonoma, Mendocino and Lake Counties. The designation is typically used for larger-production blends sourced from multiple vineyard areas.

SANTA CRUZ MOUNTAINS Though it's home to Ridge Vineyards, one of the finest US producers, this forested district south of San Francisco remains under the radar. But that's slowly changing as boutique vintners discover its superb terrain, particularly for plantings of Chardonnay and Pinot Noir.

SONOMA COUNTY Thanks to its varied soils and microclimates, Sonoma's million-plus acres grow heat-seeking Cabernet and Merlot as well as more heat-shy grapes like Pinot Noir and Sauvignon Blanc. Located an hour north of San Francisco, the county is hemmed in between the Pacific and the Mayacamas Mountains, which funnel ocean-driven fog. The prestigious **Russian River Valley** turns out world-class Pinot Noir and Chardonnay, as does the sprawling **Sonoma Coast** AVA. Warmer regions, such as parts of the **Alexander Valley** and **Knights Valley,** produce polished Cabernet and Merlot and some lush Chardonnays. One of Sonoma's warmer subregions, **Dry Creek Valley** is ideal for Zinfandel, as well as Cabernet and Syrah. **Sonoma Valley** yields perhaps the most diverse wines, with firm reds coming from hillside vines and cool-climate grapes thriving in the valley's southern end.

🍇 KEY GRAPES: WHITE

CHARDONNAY The state's most planted wine grape makes wines that range from rich and heavily oaked to minerally and crisp.

MARSANNE, ROUSSANNE & VIOGNIER Often blended to create lush, fruity white wines, these Rhône Valley varieties are most associated with the Paso Robles and Santa Barbara regions.

PINOT GRIGIO/PINOT GRIS Most California Pinot Grigio used to be pretty bad, but today winemakers are crafting some delicious, citrusy wines with the grape, particularly from cooler regions. The designation Pinot Gris typically indicates a wine made in a somewhat fuller-bodied, creamier French style.

RIESLING The popularity of this crisp, aromatic white has been rising, along with its producers' skill. Though a few wineries have been making ambitious, small-lot Rieslings for decades, they're joined now by many larger wineries that are producing fresh, fruity, often lightly sweet bottlings, many from Monterey.

SAUVIGNON BLANC California bottlings of this zippy white variety typically display succulent tropical fruit and citrus flavors, which distinguish them from grassier New Zealand versions and minerally white Bordeaux.

KEY GRAPES: RED

CABERNET SAUVIGNON This is the grape that put California on the international map in the 1970s, and Cabernet remains the state's iconic wine. Though world-class Cabernets are made in many top West Coast regions, Napa Valley's complex, ageworthy examples still set the standard, at least for prestige and price.

MERLOT Although its reputation took a hit as a result of over-production in the 1990s, Merlot has bounced back in quality and, somewhat less quickly, in prestige—which means shrewd shoppers can now find great Merlots that are much less expensive than Cabernets.

PETITE SIRAH A traditional grape often misidentified in field blends, most California Petite Sirah is actually Durif, a French-originated cross of Syrah with the humble Peloursin. The spicy grape is used primarily to add color and tannin to blends. On its own, Petite Sirah has a small but passionate following.

PINOT NOIR A cool climate is essential for good Pinot, and the state's best bottles come from coastal regions, including western Sonoma, the Anderson Valley and Santa Barbara County.

SYRAH Syrah is the most important Rhône red in California. Often blended with Grenache and/or Mourvèdre, it thrives in the California sun, particularly in the so-called Rhône Zone around Paso Robles. Syrahs made in warm regions like Paso Robles are lush and fruity; taut, elegant bottlings are made in cooler areas such as Santa Barbara.

ZINFANDEL Although Zinfandel is not actually a native variety (it's an obscure Croatian grape related to Italy's Primitivo), California winemakers have given it a distinctively rich, spicy American identity. Paso Robles, Sonoma County's Dry Creek Valley, Mendocino County and Contra Costa County are top spots for the grape.

Producers/ California

ALBAN VINEYARDS

In Edna Valley, far from the Napa-Sonoma limelight, paradigm-shifting winemaker John Alban was on the cutting edge of planting Rhône varieties—including Viognier, Roussanne, Grenache and Mourvèdre—when Rhône wasn't cool. Though relatively few drinkers will get to taste his intense single-vineyard Syrahs, the influence they and Alban's other top wines have had on his peers has been profound.

BOTTLES TO TRY
- ○ Central Coast Viognier / $$
- ● Patrina Syrah / $$$

ANTICA NAPA VALLEY

It's taken a while—an earlier Sangiovese-focused venture did not meet expectations—but the long-held ambition of Tuscany's Antinori wine dynasty (see p. 84) to produce Antinori wine in Napa Valley has been realized with their Antica (*Anti*nori *Ca*lifornia) project. Over the past decade, Antica has been producing sensational Cabernets and estimable Chardonnays that pair Napa power with Tuscan food-complementing finesse.

BOTTLES TO TRY
- ○ Chardonnay / $$$
- ● Cabernet Sauvignon / $$$

AU BON CLIMAT

Jim Clendenen's wines are sleek and coolly elegant, with a structure that bears the stamp of his formative stint in Burgundy in 1981, the year before he founded Au Bon Climat in Santa Barbara County. Today his trailblazing work yields some of California's most flavorful but refined Chardonnays and Pinot Noirs. The Santa Barbara County entry-level bottlings are striking bargains for their quality.

BOTTLES TO TRY
- ○ Santa Barbara County Chardonnay / $$
- ● La Bauge Au-dessus Pinot Noir / $$$

BEAULIEU VINEYARD

Founded in 1900, this landmark Napa Valley winery helped define world-class California Cabernet Sauvignon for decades with its Bordeaux-inspired Georges de Latour Private Reserve bottling. The winery passed from family hands in 1969, ultimately becoming the property of beverage giant Diageo. BV currently fields a sprawling range of wines sourced from vineyards in Napa Valley and other areas of the state. The Napa-sourced wines in particular constitute a very solid line, including the intro-level BV Napa Valley Cabernet Sauvignon and the pricier Tapestry blend.

BOTTLES TO TRY

○ Chardonnay / $$
● Napa Valley Cabernet Sauvignon / $$

BEDROCK WINE CO.

Bedrock's Morgan Twain-Peterson crushed his first wine at the tender age of five, with some help from his famous winemaker dad, Ravenswood founder Joel Peterson. Now 35 years old, Sonoma-based Twain-Peterson has an expert hand with grapes that include Zinfandel, Syrah, Cabernet Sauvignon and Pinot Noir. He has a particular passion for heirloom grapevines (e.g., old-vine Zinfandel), as well as Graves-style whites (Sauvignon Blanc and Sémillon) and fine rosé.

BOTTLES TO TRY

○ Judge Family Vineyard Sauvignon Blanc / $$
● Old Vine Zinfandel / $$

BENZIGER FAMILY WINERY

Mike Benziger and his late father, Bruno, founded their name-sake Sonoma Mountain winery in 1980 and went on to farm the 85-acre estate according to rigorous biodynamic principles. Best known for its Cabernet Sauvignons—from the bargain-priced Sonoma County bottling to the top-end Tribute blend—the winery scored an early success with the super-affordable (and long-since-sold) Glen Ellen brand. The Wine Group bought Benziger Family Winery last year, but fans should expect little change, if any, in the high quality of its offerings.

BOTTLES TO TRY

○ North Coast Sauvignon Blanc / $
● Sonoma County Cabernet Sauvignon / $$

BERINGER VINEYARDS

Napa Valley's oldest continuously operating winery was founded by brothers Jacob and Frederick Beringer in 1876. Today, as part of Australia-based Treasury Wine Estates, Beringer's portfolio ranges from mass-market White Zinfandel to Cabernets and Chardonnays (like the Private Reserve bottlings) that compete with Napa's best. Beringer's sweet spot lies in its midprice wines, especially the Napa Valley line and those sourced from the winery's vineyards in Knights Valley, just over the Sonoma line. But few large wineries anywhere rival Beringer's ability to put dependable value into the bottle at every price level.

BOTTLES TO TRY

○ Founders' Estate Chardonnay / $
● Knights Valley Cabernet Sauvignon / $$

BERNARDUS WINERY

In the late 1980s, Dutchman Ben (Bernardus) Pon set out to rival Bordeaux with his pioneering Carmel Valley winery. The lineup's top end consists of estate-grown Bordeaux-style wines, including the signature Marinus, and Burgundy-style wines from cooler Santa Lucia Highlands sources, including highly regarded bottlings from such prestigious sites as Pisoni and Rosella's Vineyards. The Monterey County Pinot Noir, Chardonnay and Sauvignon Blanc bottlings are typically strong values.

BOTTLES TO TRY

○ Monterey County Chardonnay / $$
● Marinus / $$$

BONTERRA ORGANIC VINEYARDS

This Mendocino County winery was organic before organic was cool (starting in 1990), and it has not only stayed the course, but upped the ante, with several hundred acres of its McNab Ranch, Butler Ranch and Blue Heron vineyards, plus the winery itself, now certified biodynamic. The wines, especially the notable Zinfandel and Viognier, tend to overdeliver for the price. Except for the very fine premium-priced flagships—the Rhône-style The Butler; The McNab, a Bordeaux blend; and The Roost, a Chardonnay—Bonterra wines generally sell for under $20.

BOTTLES TO TRY

○ Viognier / $
● The Butler / $$$

BREWER-CLIFTON

Greg Brewer and Steve Clifton are two very talented winemakers whose skills are also on display at the Italian varietal project Palmina (Clifton) and the Burgundy-Rhône-centric Melville (Brewer). They convene at Brewer-Clifton to celebrate the Cal-Burgundian possibilities of Pinot Noir and Chardonnay in the cool-climate Sta. Rita Hills of Santa Barbara County; all of the fruit they use comes from 10 vineyards in the appellation. Their track record in producing sophisticated, intense, full-bodied wines has placed them in the forefront of this intriguing region.

BOTTLES TO TRY

○ Sta. Rita Hills Chardonnay / $$$
● Sta. Rita Hills Pinot Noir / $$$

BUEHLER VINEYARDS

The Buehler family purchased this remote property with its pre-Prohibition ghost winery on a Napa Valley hillside near the foot of Howell Mountain way back in 1971. The estate's low-yielding, dry-farmed Cabernet Sauvignon and Zinfandel vineyards are more than 30 years old now, and produce outstanding wines at very reasonable prices. Proprietor John Buehler, Jr., and winemaker David Cronin reach out to the cool Russian River Valley and Carneros regions for the Chardonnays, but stick closer to home for the signature reds.

BOTTLES TO TRY

○ Russian River Valley Chardonnay / $$
● Zinfandel / $$

BUENA VISTA WINERY

Founded in 1857 by California pioneer Agoston Haraszthy, the state's oldest winery has had its ups and downs. A new era began in 2011 with its acquisition by the Boisset family (see DeLoach Vineyards, p. 177), which funded such improvements as the renovation of the winery's historic cellars. Jean-Charles Boisset, a Burgundian at heart, has recommitted the winery to Chardonnays and Pinot Noirs from the cool Carneros region, while restoring the luster of the Private Reserve tier of Chardonnay, Pinot Noir, Cabernet Sauvignon and Zinfandel.

BOTTLES TO TRY

○ Chardonnay / $$
● Pinot Noir / $$

CALERA WINE COMPANY

Josh Jensen spent two years in the early 1970s scouring the West Coast for an outcropping of the limestone rock he associated with the great vineyards of Burgundy. He found what he was looking for in this remote spot in the Gavilan Mountains southeast of Santa Cruz. Jensen's boldly flavored Mt. Harlan wines are Calera's specialties, but it's the single-vineyard estate Pinot Noirs, like the Jensen and Selleck bottlings, that have made him one of California's most respected vintners. The Central Coast line, produced from purchased fruit, offers great value.

BOTTLES TO TRY

○ Mt. Harlan Chardonnay / $$$

● Central Coast Pinot Noir / $$

CAMERON HUGHES WINE

A man with a plan since he began selling wine out of his station wagon in 2002, Cameron Hughes is a *négociant* who buys wine from others and sells it, typically at a fraction of the wine's price under its original name. Consumers have responded to his eye for a bargain, evident in his five globe-spanning labels, from the anonymous Lot Series (each wine is assigned a unique lot number) to the grapes-to-glass Hughes Wellman line. The San Francisco–based venture is a family affair, with Hughes's co-founder and wife, Jessica Kogan, overseeing marketing and sales.

BOTTLES TO TRY

○ Lot Series Arroyo Seco Chardonnay / $

● Zin Your Face Zinfandel / $

CARLISLE WINERY & VINEYARDS

At his Sonoma County winery, former software developer Mike Officer is committed to husbanding old-vine vineyards, preserving their distinctions in his wine and selling it at realistic prices. His approach has worked: Production rose from five gallons of Zinfandel made in Officer's kitchen to Carlisle's current 9,000-plus cases. Officer quit his day job in 2004 and, with college pal Jay Maddox as co-winemaker, got on with making some of California's most compelling Zinfandels and Rhône-style reds, including benchmark Syrahs, all in a bold, full-flavored style.

BOTTLES TO TRY

○ The Derivative / $$$

● Zinfandel / $$$

CAYMUS VINEYARDS

Caymus's Special Selection Cabernet Sauvignon helped create the California cult wine phenomenon in the 1970s. The company is now in its third generation under the Wagner family, whose holdings include 350 Napa Valley vineyard acres and an array of brands, including Mer Soleil, Conundrum and Belle Glos. But the Caymus name itself remains indelibly associated with full-bodied, polished reds: The Special Selection Cab is the luxury-priced flagship, but the basic Cabernet and small-lot Zinfandel offer a more affordable taste of Caymus's bold style.

BOTTLES TO TRY
- Zinfandel / $$$
- Cabernet Sauvignon / $$$$

CHALK HILL

This 1,340-acre Sonoma County estate added another chapter to its four-decade history in 2010 when it was acquired by William Foley for his Foley Family Wines. Talented Steve Nelson came on board as winemaker in the spring of 2015, joining longtime viticulturist Mark Lingenfelder, who has provided the continuity that's enabled the new regime to get off to a strong start. Chardonnay—including the exclusive $100-plus old-vine Founder's Block bottling—is the star, but the Bordeaux-style reds have a justifiable following as well.

BOTTLES TO TRY
- ○ Sonoma Coast Chardonnay / $$
- Estate Red / $$$$

CHAPPELLET WINERY

When Donn and Molly Chappellet founded their winery in 1967, they had the vision to terrace a steep hillside in the Vaca Mountains. But they couldn't have guessed what Pritchard Hill would become today, with neighbors like Colgin, Bryant Family Vineyard and Ovid. Following in the footsteps of stellar winemakers like Philip Togni, Tony Soter and Cathy Corison, longtime incumbent Phillip Corallo-Titus keeps the Pritchard Hill bottlings at the forefront of Napa Cabs. Whites—Chardonnays and a luscious Chenin Blanc—can be very good here, too.

BOTTLES TO TRY
- ○ Chenin Blanc / $$$
- Mountain Cuvée / $$

BEST OF THE BEST PRODUCERS / CHARDONNAY
1. FAR NIENTE **2.** HANZELL VINEYARDS **3.** KONGSGAARD
4. MOUNT EDEN VINEYARDS **5.** VARNER WINE

CHATEAU MONTELENA WINERY

Chateau Montelena vaulted to stardom when its Chardonnay bested an array of prestigious Burgundies in the famous 1976 Judgment of Paris tasting. That wine was only the second vintage for the revived 1882 Calistoga estate, which had been bought and rehabilitated by Jim Barrett. Today, under the longtime direction of his son Bo, Montelena continues to bottle lovely, somewhat restrained Chardonnays and a bouquet of fine reds.

BOTTLES TO TRY
○ Chardonnay / $$$
● Cabernet Sauvignon / $$$

COBB WINES

Pinot Noir guru Ross Cobb began bottling hands-on, small-production wines from his family's Coastlands Vineyard in 2001. Coming from the "true" (i.e., foggy, cold and ultra-challenging to farm) Sonoma Coast, Cobb's already small production gets even tinier in difficult vintages, so lovers of nuanced, dramatically aromatic, anti-jammy Pinot Noir should be quick to put their names on this list.

BOTTLES TO TRY
● Coastlands Vineyard Pinot Noir / $$$$
● Diane Cobb: Coastlands Vineyard Pinot Noir / $$$$

CONTINUUM ESTATE

Following the sale of their family's Robert Mondavi Winery (see p. 196), Tim Mondavi and sister Marcia (brother Michael has separate ventures) set up shop in tony Pritchard Hill to make a single, limited-production wine. Their luxury-priced Cabernet Sauvignon–based Continuum has gone from strength to strength. The volcanic hillsides provide tiny yields of intense grapes that give the wine its core, while Cabernet Franc and Petit Verdot contribute to its gracefully layered elegance.

BOTTLE TO TRY
● Continuum / $$$$

COPAIN WINES

Francophile Wells Guthrie turns out exceptionally graceful and subtle Pinot Noirs, Chardonnays and Syrahs. Though his winery is located in Sonoma County's Russian River Valley, Guthrie sources most of the grapes for his flavorful, moderate-alcohol wines up north in cool, coastal-influenced Mendocino County. The top bottlings are the single-vineyard Pinots from the flagship Kiser vineyard. The multivineyard Tous Ensemble Chardonnay, Syrah and food-friendly Pinot Noir are notable bargains.

BOTTLES TO TRY

○ Brosseau Chardonnay / $$$
● Tous Ensemble Pinot Noir / $$

CORISON WINERY

Highly regarded winemaker Cathy Corison lent her talents to such producers as Chappellet (see p. 174) and Staglin Family (see p. 200) before devoting herself to her boutique Napa Valley label. She produces small bottlings of five wines, including the Corazón Gewürztraminer and Helios Cabernet Franc, but her signature offerings are the Cabernet Sauvignons: the single-vineyard Kronos and Napa Valley bottlings. In both, Corison takes a hands-off approach that lets the vineyard shine; the results are expertly balanced, assured wines that target finesse and harmony over sheer strength.

BOTTLES TO TRY

○ Corazón Gewürztraminer / $$
● Napa Valley Cabernet Sauvignon / $$$$

DALLA VALLE VINEYARDS

This ambitious winery above the Silverado Trail burst on the scene in the 1980s with intense, concentrated wines based on Cabernets Sauvignon and Franc, made by a succession of wine-making all-stars. Current winemaker Andy Erickson, a Screaming Eagle alumnus, is assisted by famed French consultant Michel Rolland. This is a world-class operation with prices to match. The hillside vineyards yield three Bordeaux-style reds: the cult wine Maya, the Dalla Valle Cabernet Sauvignon and the younger-vines Collina Dalla Valle.

BOTTLES TO TRY

● Cabernet Sauvignon / $$$$
● Collina Dalla Valle / $$$$

DASHE CELLARS

From their base in downtown Oakland, husband-and-wife team Michael and Anne Dashe—Michael honed his craft working with the great Paul Draper at Ridge Vineyards (see p. 196)— seek out old vines, rocky hillsides and special locales for their *terroir*-based, small-production wines. The winery is best known for its single-vineyard Zinfandels, in styles ranging from the chewy, deeply concentrated Todd Brothers Ranch bottling to a sweet, late-harvest version. Les Enfants Terribles is a line of limited-production wines from cool-climate vineyards.

BOTTLES TO TRY

○ **Dry Riesling** / $$
● **Dry Creek Valley Zinfandel** / $$

DELOACH VINEYARDS

The 2003 purchase of Sonoma County's DeLoach by French wine entrepreneur Jean-Charles Boisset gradually shifted the venerable brand's focus from Zinfandel and Chardonnay to Pinot Noir, although it retains strong footholds in both of those varietals. Boisset's passion for biodynamic viticulture and Burgundian winemaking (low intervention, limited new oak) have brought a fresh attention to detail to the top bottlings, which include the Vineyard Designate, Estate Wines and O.F.S. (Our Finest Selection) lines.

BOTTLES TO TRY

○ **California Chardonnay** / $
● **Russian River Valley Pinot Noir** / $$

DIAMOND CREEK VINEYARDS

In 1968, the late Al Brounstein created a Napa Valley winery that was the exception to every rule. He produced Cabernet-based wines (in a Chardonnay era) that were profoundly *terroir*-driven, when that was barely a concept yet in California, and he crafted them in a style that could be austere and sometimes take years to open up. Brounstein's stubbornness and bedrock belief in his vineyards—Volcanic Hill, Gravelly Meadow, Red Rock Terrace and the elusive Lake—paid off in giving Diamond Creek a lasting, passionate, deep-pocketed following.

BOTTLES TO TRY

● **Gravelly Meadow Cabernet Sauvignon** / $$$$
● **Volcanic Hill Cabernet Sauvignon** / $$$$

DOMINUS ESTATE

Dominus owner and art patron Christian Moueix is one of Bordeaux's leading winemakers (Château Pétrus) and tastemakers. His Napa Valley estate's 124 dry-farmed acres are centered on the famous Napanook Vineyard, first planted by Yountville's original settler, George Yount, in the early 19th century. Today it yields the Cabernet Sauvignon, Cabernet Franc and Petit Verdot grapes that go into the winery's two world-class Bordeaux blends: the complex, structured Dominus and a more accessible, though typically superb, second bottling, Napanook.

BOTTLES TO TRY
- Napanook / $$$
- Dominus / $$$$

DRY CREEK VINEYARD

David Stare set up shop in Sonoma County's Dry Creek Valley in 1972, determined to make Loire-inspired wines. Two Loire varieties, Chenin Blanc and Sauvignon Blanc, are used to make some of the most popular wines in Dry Creek Vineyard's lineup. Very fine single-vineyard and old-vine Zinfandels are another Dry Creek specialty—its Heritage Vines bottling is one of the best Zin deals around. Fans also seek out the winery's high-quality, reasonably priced Cabernet-based blends, made in the fruit-forward, juicy Sonoma style.

BOTTLES TO TRY
- ○ Dry Chenin Blanc / $
- ● Heritage Vines Zinfandel / $$

DUCKHORN VINEYARDS

Dan and Margaret Duckhorn founded their St. Helena winery in 1976 and struck gold with Merlot, especially their iconic Three Palms Vineyard bottling. The winery also makes palate-flattering Cabernets and some of Napa's finest Sauvignon Blancs. Duckhorn's spin-off brands include Goldeneye, a game-altering Pinot-centric producer in Anderson Valley; Paraduxx, offering unique blends; and the more affordable Decoy line. Today, under the stewardship of GI Partners, a private equity firm, Duckhorn continues to produce at a consistently high level.

BOTTLES TO TRY
- ○ Napa Valley Sauvignon Blanc / $$
- ● Napa Valley Merlot / $$$

DUNN VINEYARDS

Having honed his craft at Caymus (see p. 174) in its early years, Randy Dunn, with his wife, Lori, bought their own vineyard on Howell Mountain in the late 1970s and went on to create a mountain style of Cabernet: broodingly dark, big-scaled wines with massive but supple tannins. Though the family's holdings have expanded from that original five-acre vineyard, Dunn still produces a limited amount (4,500 cases) of much-sought-after wine, typically in just two bottlings: the highly structured, long-distance runner Howell Mountain and the softer Napa Valley.

BOTTLES TO TRY

● Howell Mountain Cabernet Sauvignon / $$$$
● Napa Valley Cabernet Sauvignon / $$$$

DUTTON-GOLDFIELD WINERY

Steve Dutton is the son of the legendary winegrower Warren Dutton, who assembled the 1,300 acres of Dutton Ranch in the Russian River Valley. Under Steve's management, the estate still supplies fruit to many of the region's most esteemed wineries, but he and winemaker-partner Dan Goldfield cherry-pick some of the top Chardonnay and Pinot lots—plus vineyard designates from elsewhere in the Northern California coast—for this joint venture. Among their specialties are old-vine, dry-farmed Chardonnays first planted by Warren in the cool Green Valley.

BOTTLES TO TRY

○ Dutton Ranch Chardonnay / $$$
● Freestone Hill Vineyard Pinot Noir / $$$

ETUDE WINES

Tony Soter runs his namesake winery in Oregon (see p. 289), but over 30 years ago, he founded Etude in Napa, with the aim of making great Pinot Noir. He planted numerous clones and low-yielding heirloom varieties at his Carneros estate, and they remain the basis for some of Etude's top bottlings. Long since acquired by Beringer Blass Wine Estates (now part of Treasury Wine Estates), Etude has expanded its offerings. Winemaker Jon Priest fields a consistently fine lineup that includes excellent Cabernets and one of California's top Pinot Gris.

BOTTLES TO TRY

○ Pinot Gris / $$
● Carneros Pinot Noir / $$$

FAILLA WINES

Rhône-trained Ehren Jordan left his longtime job at Turley Wine Cellars to focus on multi-appellation winemaking at Failla, which is named for his wife and partner, Anne-Marie Failla. Though the winery is in Napa, nearly all of its often superb Pinot Noirs (plus some Chardonnay, Viognier and Syrah) are sourced from the cool, foggy Pacific Coast, mostly in the rugged coast range of Sonoma County. The flagship Pinots are grown in marginal climates and made with low-tech, traditional methods.

BOTTLES TO TRY

○ **Estate Vineyard Chardonnay / $$$**
● **Sonoma Coast Pinot Noir / $$$**

FAR NIENTE

The late Gil Nickel acquired this landmark 1885 Napa estate—abandoned since Prohibition—in 1979 and lavishly restored it. The gardens and vintage cars offer pleasant distractions, but the wines are the real draw. Far Niente offshoots include Dolce (dessert wine), Nickel & Nickel (single-vineyard wines) and EnRoute (Sonoma Coast Pinot Noir and Chardonnay), but the parent winery itself produces just two wines: Cabernet and Chardonnay. Prices were set high early on, and so were the ambitions—the silky, layered Cabernet and juicy Chardonnay, vibrant with melon and exotic fruit, are some of California's finest.

BOTTLES TO TRY

○ **Chardonnay / $$$**
● **Cabernet Sauvignon / $$$$**

FLOWERS VINEYARDS & WINERY

Among the earliest believers in the grape-growing potential of the extreme Sonoma Coast, Walt and Joan Flowers planted the first vineyards on their rugged, ocean-cooled property in 1991, then upped the challenge by farming the land biodynamically. Now owned in part by Quintessa's Huneeus family, Flowers is a go-to source for vibrant, leaner, more European-style wines. The estate vineyards, Camp Meeting Ridge and Sea View Ridge, are among California's most promising; the Sonoma Coast wines, while not inexpensive, are a more wallet-friendly entry point.

BOTTLES TO TRY

○ **Sonoma Coast Chardonnay / $$$**
● **Sea View Ridge Pinot Noir / $$$$**

FOXEN VINEYARD & WINERY

Bill Wathen and Dick Doré founded Foxen Winery in 1985 in Santa Maria Valley on land once owned by Doré's great-great-grandfather William Benjamin Foxen. They were major quality pioneers here, favored early on by insiders for their silky, full-flavored yet restrained Chardonnays, Pinot Noirs and Syrahs. Today, their vineyard-focused small lots of character-filled, cool-climate wines are still superb. Wathen and Doré showcase their Bordeaux and Cal-Ital wines at their historic Foxen 7200 tasting shack, while the core Burgundy-Rhône wines can be sampled at their solar-powered winery down the road.

BOTTLES TO TRY

○ Block UU Chardonnay / $$$
● Santa Maria Valley Pinot Noir / $$$

FRANCISCAN ESTATE

Since its opening in 1973, Napa Valley's Franciscan Estate—now a 300,000-plus-case operation belonging to Constellation Brands—has kept the focus on value. The six entry-level Napa Valley wines are perennial good deals. Franciscan's top-end bottlings deserve at least a footnote in valley history: The easy-to-appreciate Magnificat Bordeaux blend was among the earliest of the Meritage wines (see Wine Terminology, p. 164); the winery's all-out Burgundy-method Cuvée Sauvage Chardonnay is said to be Napa's first wine to be fermented with native yeasts.

BOTTLES TO TRY

○ Cuvée Sauvage Chardonnay / $$$
● Merlot / $$

FRANCIS FORD COPPOLA WINERY

The director's non-film business empire now includes the magnificent Inglenook winery in Napa. Coppola also bought Sonoma's Chateau Souverain facility (not the brand) and turned it into a "wine wonderland," as he puts it. The winery, in Geyserville, features swimming facilities and a movie museum. And, oh yes: wine. The place bottles at least 10 showily labeled lines, including Sofia (named after Coppola's daughter), food-friendly Su Yuen and the limited-production Director's Cut.

BOTTLES TO TRY

○ Director's Cut Chardonnay / $$
● Sofia Rosé / $

FROG'S LEAP

Former Stag's Leap Wine Cellars vintner John Williams started his Napa Valley venture on a site that was once a frog farm, hence the playful name. Since the 1980s, Frog's Leap has set a high bar for eco-friendly farming, forgoing chemicals, pesticides and even—unusual for Napa Valley—irrigation: Frog's Leap dry-farms more than 200 vineyard acres. The sophisticated wines hold to a restrained, food-friendly style. Though much of the winery's production is Sauvignon Blanc, Williams also has a deft hand with reds, notably Zinfandel and Cabernet.

BOTTLES TO TRY

○ Sauvignon Blanc / $$
● Zinfandel / $$

GALLO SIGNATURE SERIES / GALLO ESTATE WINES

Winemaker Gina Gallo and her brother Matt team up on these two distinct, higher-priced tiers that provide the local-*terroir* face of the global megabrand E. & J. Gallo Winery. The Signature Series utilizes Gallo's extensive vineyard holdings around the state to produce AVA-specific wines, among them a Napa Valley Cabernet, a Pinot Noir from Santa Lucia Highlands and a Russian River Valley Chardonnay. The limited-production Gallo Estate wines are a Cabernet and a Chardonnay sourced from the best of the company's Sonoma vineyard holdings.

BOTTLES TO TRY

○ Estate Chardonnay / $$$
● Signature Series Cabernet Sauvignon / $$$

GRGICH HILLS ESTATE

After clobbering the French with his 1973 Chateau Montelena Chardonnay at the famous 1976 Paris tasting, Mike Grgich founded his own winery with coffee heir Austin Hills. Grgich's creamy, full-flavored Chardonnays helped set the California standard in the 1980s. They remain the winery's headliners but may not actually be Grgich's best offerings. Try the lively Fumé Blanc or the graceful Cab or Zinfandel to understand the winery's approach to making wines of finesse. True to his convictions, Grgich uses only his own, naturally farmed grapes.

BOTTLES TO TRY

○ Fumé Blanc / $$
● Napa Valley Cabernet Sauvignon / $$$$

HANZELL VINEYARDS

Hanzell's Burgundy-loving founder, James Zellerbach, planted some of California's first post-Prohibition Chardonnay and Pinot Noir in Sonoma County in 1953. Today, thanks in large part to the four-decade tenure of its late winemaker, Bob Sessions, the winery carries on its founder's vision. Under current winemaker Michael McNeill, Hanzell wines are still closer to the European ideal than to the California mainstream (i.e., they're not loaded with sweet fruit and oak). Tightly wound when released, these long-lived wines typically benefit from extended cellaring.

BOTTLES TO TRY

○ **Chardonnay / $$$$**
● **Pinot Noir / $$$$**

HIRSCH VINEYARDS

David Hirsch was the pioneering visionary of far-western Sonoma County. His wind-scoured mountaintop vineyards lie less than a mile from the San Andreas Fault, subject to every peril, from frost to flood to earthquake. His very low-yielding vines produce enough fruit for six extraordinary Pinot Noirs and a tiny amount of Chardonnay (plus the small-lot Hirsch Vineyard designates sold to other top producers); their flavors all reflect the marginal climate and jumble of soils along the fault zone. Hirsch has had a string of talented winemakers; Ross Cobb (see Cobb Wines, p. 175) is the eminent incumbent.

BOTTLES TO TRY

○ **Chardonnay / $$$$**
● **San Andreas Fault Pinot Noir / $$$$**

HONIG VINEYARD & WINERY

The struggling garage operation Michael Honig took over in 1984 has become a multigenerational family success story. A rare American winery that made its reputation on Sauvignon Blanc, Honig produces three versions: the lively Napa Valley bottling, aged mostly in stainless steel to retain freshness; the Rutherford reserve bottling, which gets some barrel aging; and a dessert wine. With (sustainably farmed) acreage in the heart of Rutherford's Cabernet country, Honig also bottles very fine reds.

BOTTLES TO TRY

○ **Sauvignon Blanc Reserve / $$**
● **Cabernet Sauvignon / $$$**

HOURGLASS

Wine collectors held their breath when Hourglass owner Jeff Smith parted company with his star winemaker, Bob Foley, in 2012. Fortunately, Smith was able to enlist another top talent, Tony Biagi, to continue the winery's way with ripe, richly flavored, massively built Bordeaux-style wines that somehow come across as seamlessly balanced. The flagship vineyard is a special piece of land at the narrowest pinch of Napa Valley's hourglass shape. The winery's second vineyard, Blueline, is also proving to be a stunning site for Bordeaux varieties.

BOTTLES TO TRY
- Blueline Estate Merlot / $$$$
- Cabernet Sauvignon / $$$$

HUNDRED ACRE

Jayson Woodbridge's brimming self-confidence not only made him a successful investment banker, but it enabled him to plunge into the luxury wine business in 2000 with zero experience. His tiny-production Hundred Acre wines (he also owns the value-oriented Layer Cake; see p. 188) are rarefied, hard-to-obtain cult reds with triple-digit price tags. The stars are the single-vineyard, 100 percent Cabernet Sauvignon bottlings from Napa Valley, but the collector's buzz really builds around such specialty projects as Deep Time, a Cabernet that may spend up to 40 months in barrel.

BOTTLES TO TRY
- Arc Vineyard Cabernet Sauvignon / $$$$
- Kayli Morgan Vineyard Cabernet Sauvignon / $$$$

J. LOHR VINEYARDS & WINES

Jerry Lohr, a sometime real estate developer and the son of South Dakota farmers, has an obvious passion for land. His sprawling wine venture includes 1,327 estate acres in Monterey County devoted to cooler-climate grapes; 2,302 acres in Paso Robles planted to Cabernet Sauvignon and other reds; and 35 acres in Napa Valley. The output is similarly diverse: the J. Lohr tiers, headlined by the Cuvée Series; value-priced wines under the Cypress Vineyards label; and the Ariel nonalcoholic wines.

BOTTLES TO TRY
- ○ Arroyo Vista Chardonnay / $$
- Los Osos Merlot / $

JOSEPH PHELPS VINEYARDS

Few new faces on the luxury Napa wine scene are likely to establish the glittering track record of Insignia, the world-class Cabernet-based wine launched by the late Joe Phelps in 1974. His son Bill heads the winery today, with Damian Parker, Ashley Hepworth and Justin Ennis as winemakers. After a major renovation completed in 2015, the original St. Helena winery remains focused on Bordeaux varieties and Syrah from biodynamically farmed estate vineyards. The 2007 Sonoma Coast facility is dedicated to Burgundy-style Pinot Noir and Chardonnay.

BOTTLES TO TRY

○ Sauvignon Blanc / $$$

● Cabernet Sauvignon / $$$$

JUSTIN VINEYARDS & WINERY

An upscale hub of Central Coast wine tourism, Paso Robles's Justin was started by former investment banker Justin Baldwin in 1981 (and sold to the owners of Fiji Water in 2010). Though it produces a range of bottlings, Justin is mainly a Cabernet Sauvignon specialist, with the Bordeaux-style Isosceles as its image-maker. The Cabernet Franc–Merlot blend Justification is also worth seeking out, as is the varietal Cabernet bottling.

BOTTLES TO TRY

○ Chardonnay / $$

● Cabernet Sauvignon / $$

KENDALL-JACKSON

This Sonoma-based megabrand (the foundation of Jackson Family Wines) has a straightforward formula for maintaining quality despite its huge size: Source grapes from estate-owned vineyards; judiciously use high-end techniques (like barrel aging), even on inexpensive wines; and rely on winemaster Randy Ullom to mastermind the cellar. Kendall-Jackson is best known for the ubiquitous Vintner's Reserve Chardonnay, but its deep portfolio also features single-vineyard offerings. The top wine is the limited-production Bordeaux-style blend Stature, whose stellar Napa and Sonoma vineyard sources demonstrate Kendall-Jackson's impressive reach.

BOTTLES TO TRY

○ Grand Reserve Chardonnay / $$

● Vintner's Reserve Zinfandel / $

KONGSGAARD

John Kongsgaard is a guru whose road to enlightenment is much admired but little emulated, at least in its entirety. He takes his gorgeously layered Chardonnays, for example, to the extreme edge, leaving them for months-long fermentations, in a process he calls "death and resurrection" that would cause other winemakers to lose sleep—if not their jobs. Through the years, though, he's mentored a remarkable roster of winemakers, and avid fans snap up his Napa winery's tiny lots of Chardonnay, Cabernet-Merlot blends, Syrah and Viognier-Roussanne.

BOTTLES TO TRY

○ **Chardonnay / $$$$**
● **Syrah / $$$$**

KOSTA BROWNE WINERY

Founded in the late 1990s by Dan Kosta and Michael Browne (later joined by Chris Costello), this onetime shoestring operation moved into a sleek new winery complex in Sebastopol in 2012. With a series of capital infusions (the winery passed from one private equity group to another with its sale to J.W. Childs Associates in 2014), Kosta Browne has expanded production of its full-flavored, polished Pinots and Chardonnays, but still struggles to keep up with demand. Be ready to wait up to six years for the option to buy some of these coveted wines.

BOTTLES TO TRY

○ **One Sixteen Chardonnay / $$$$**
● **Russian River Valley Pinot Noir / $$$$**

KUTCH

A former NASDAQ trader at Merrill Lynch, Jamie Kutch was used to risky work. But in the mid-2000s, he took up an arguably more nerve-racking challenge by throwing his hat into the luxury Pinot Noir ring. It's a crowded field, but Kutch has made a big impression with his young, artisan-scale operation. This is partly because he has a talent for producing luscious, transparently pure Pinot Noir, and partly because he has the good sense to source it from tiny-crop vineyards that yield sensational grapes, like the McDougall Ranch on the far Sonoma Coast.

BOTTLES TO TRY

● **McDougall Ranch Pinot Noir / $$$**
● **Sonoma Coast Pinot Noir / $$$**

BEST OF THE BEST PRODUCERS / CABERNET

1. CONTINUUM ESTATE **2.** DALLA VALLE VINEYARDS **3.** DIAMOND CREEK VINEYARDS **4.** DOMINUS ESTATE **5.** RIDGE VINEYARDS

LARKMEAD VINEYARDS

One of the few Napa Valley heritage properties to operate continuously since the 19th century, Larkmead today is a top-notch, if somewhat under-the-radar, producer of Bordeaux-style reds. The family-owned property's all-estate-grown portfolio includes the distinctive, luxury-priced LMV Salon, Solari and The Lark reds. The more wallet-friendly Firebelle Merlot-based blend can be superb, but it's also heading skyward in price.

BOTTLES TO TRY
- Firebelle / $$$$
- The Lark / $$$$

LAUREL GLEN VINEYARD

From the first vintage in 1981, Laurel Glen's elegant, firmly structured Sonoma Mountain wines helped prove that Napa's neighbor could produce top-tier Cabernet. The winery focuses on two estate-grown, all-Cab bottlings: the pricey flagship and the more affordable Counterpoint. Its two even-more-limited-production offerings are an old-vine field-blend rosé and The Laureate, made from the cellar's richest Cabernet lots.

BOTTLES TO TRY
- Counterpoint Cabernet Sauvignon / $$$
- Cabernet Sauvignon / $$$$

L'AVENTURE WINERY

Armed with a French wine degree (and experience owning Bordeaux châteaus), Stephan Asseo founded this Paso Robles estate in 1998. His silky, full-throttle reds, such as the coveted flagship Estate Cuvée and Côte à Côte bottlings, are now among the appellation's most renowned, their concentration due to very low-yielding vines. The Syrah–Cabernet–Petit Verdot Optimus blend is a more accessible entry point.

BOTTLES TO TRY
- Rosé / $$
- Optimus / $$$

LAYER CAKE WINES

Layer Cake's goal of offering "luxury everyone can afford" is amply met in its supple, palate-flattering, remarkable-value wines, sourced from five countries on four continents. Owner-winemaker Jayson Woodbridge (he's also the proprietor of Napa Valley's luxury-priced Hundred Acre; see p. 184) shows considerable ingenuity in putting layers in the Layer Cake: The California Cabernet, for example, is blended from one vineyard in Sonoma's Alexander Valley and another in Paso Robles.

BOTTLES TO TRY

○ Virgin Chardonnay / $
● Cabernet Sauvignon / $

LIOCO

Former Spago Beverly Hills sommelier Kevin O'Connor and his buddy Matt Licklider, a onetime wine importer, share a passion for Chardonnay and Pinot Noir with lithe, vibrant flavors—the kind grown in Burgundy and in California's coolest wine regions. In 2005 they teamed up to create their own versions with Sonoma-based LIOCO, a label focusing on Pinot Noir and Chardonnay—and a few less-appreciated varieties, such as old-vine Carignane—sourced from a handful of top vineyards. The often outstanding wines are all native-yeast-fermented, low- to non-oak-impacted and bottled with minimal intervention.

BOTTLES TO TRY

○ Sonoma County Chardonnay / $$
● Hirsch Pinot Noir / $$$$

LITTORAI WINES

Ted Lemon well deserves his reputation as one of America's most talented winemakers. In the cold, often foggy reaches of coastal Sonoma and Mendocino Counties, Littorai's owner-winemaker found the perfect place to make genuinely Burgundian Pinot Noirs and Chardonnays: wines that maintain a tension between ripe and unripe with a racy vibrancy. Lemon's approach—he seeks out superb small-vineyard sources and practices sustainable farming and winemaking, with minimal handling—makes this one of the great small wineries of the New World.

BOTTLES TO TRY

○ Mays Canyon Chardonnay / $$$$
● The Haven Vineyard Pinot Noir / $$$$

LOKOYA

From its start in 1995, this Jackson Family Wines project aimed to push the envelope, both in quality and in price. Longtime winemaker Christopher Carpenter's four stratospherically priced Cabernets come from mountain vineyards in four appellations: Diamond Mountain, Howell Mountain, Mount Veeder and Spring Mountain. With their massive payloads of flavor and aroma, these wines are meant to knock drinkers' socks off.

BOTTLES TO TRY

- Howell Mountain Cabernet Sauvignon / $$$$
- Spring Mountain District Cabernet Sauvignon / $$$$

LOUIS M. MARTINI WINERY

A focus on big, bold Cabernet Sauvignons has reinvented this Napa Valley producer, which started out making jug wines in 1933. Under the auspices of Gallo, which bought Martini in 2002, third-generation Mike Martini, grandson of Louis M. and the winemaker for nearly 40 years, crafts five exemplary Cabernets, including the famous flagship Monte Rosso, from an estate vineyard 1,000 feet up in the Mayacamas range, and the amazingly value-priced Sonoma County bottling. Martini has a well-deserved reputation for Zinfandel, too; the Gnarly Vine, also sourced from the Monte Rosso Vineyard, is superb.

BOTTLES TO TRY

- Sonoma County Cabernet Sauvignon / $
- Gnarly Vine Zinfandel / $$$

MARSTON FAMILY VINEYARD

Michael and Alexandra Marston began acquiring this property on the southern slopes of Napa Valley's Spring Mountain in 1969, with some of the original turn-of-the-century vineyards still in production. They became full owners in 1976 and brought on star winemaker Philippe Melka in 1998 to craft the exceptional estate-bottled Cabernet Sauvignons for which they're best known today. The estate vineyard is situated above the fog line at elevations of up to 1,100 feet, which give it a cooler, extended growing season. With the 2010 vintage, Melka handed over the reins to Sierra Leone–born winemaker Marbue Marke.

BOTTLES TO TRY

- ○ Albion / $$$
- Cabernet Sauvignon / $$$$

MARTINELLI WINERY & VINEYARDS

Martinelli's longtime collaboration with celebrated consultants Helen Turley and John Wetlaufer resulted in massively scaled, exuberantly full-flavored wines that shot into the collector's stratosphere. Turley and Wetlaufer have moved on, but their protégés Bryan Kvamme and Erin Green oversee the lineup of estate-produced, small-production Zins, Chardonnays, Pinot Noirs and Syrahs. The Martinelli family has been growing grapes in the Russian River Valley since the 1880s, and they still sell about 90 percent of their fruit to other wineries. What they keep and bottle themselves is sold mainly through their mailing list.

BOTTLES TO TRY

○ Martinelli Road Chardonnay / $$$
● Zio Tony Ranch Pinot Noir / $$$$

MATTHIASSON

Many winemakers talk about how "wine is made in the vineyard," but Steve Matthiasson has lived it: He's also a much-sought-after vineyard consultant. Central to his Napa winemaking efforts are the Red Wine, a Merlot-based Bordeaux blend that emphasizes finesse as much as power, and the White Wine, a kitchen-sink blend based on Sauvignon Blanc, whose array of grapes merge into a flavorful harmony. Don't overlook the Refosco—like the rest, it's made with Matthiasson's trademark intense flavor profile at moderate alcohol levels.

BOTTLES TO TRY

○ White Wine / $$$
● Red Wine / $$$$

MAYACAMAS VINEYARDS

This venerable Mount Veeder estate produces the kind of old-school Cabernets that made Napa famous: firm reds with moderate alcohol and earthy herb notes. Mayacamas's best wines age beautifully for decades. One example: The winery's 1971 Cabernet finished seventh in the famous 1976 Judgment of Paris tasting, but second—ahead of all French entrants—in the 1986 retaste. Former Screaming Eagle co-owner Charles Banks (see Qupé, p. 194) and his partners bought Mayacamas in 2013.

BOTTLES TO TRY

○ Chardonnay / $$$
● Cabernet Sauvignon / $$$$

MERRY EDWARDS WINERY

As her business card proclaims, Merry Edwards is the *Reine de Pinot* ("Queen of Pinot"). A pioneer of clone-specific winegrowing, Edwards has been perfecting her sure-handed style of lush, nuanced Pinot Noir and Chardonnay for more than 40 years. Her namesake winery settled into its beautiful Sebastopol facility in 2008. One secret: She produces a creamy, stylish, estate-grown sparkling wine that fans wish she'd make more often than every seven to 10 years or so.

BOTTLES TO TRY

○ **Olivet Lane Chardonnay** / $$$
● **Olivet Lane Pinot Noir** / $$$$

MOUNT EDEN VINEYARDS

This 1940s Santa Cruz Mountains estate, perched above what is now Silicon Valley, has been run by brilliant winemaker Jeffrey Patterson since 1981. Mount Eden's long-respected wines are gaining new cachet as buyers seek out the more restrained styles of the wines Patterson crafts from the cool-climate estate vineyards, some 2,000 feet up. Patterson's Cabernet Sauvignons are superb, but his record with the winery's legacy grapes—Pinot Noir and Chardonnay—often overshadows them. The Domaine Eden label offers the estate's style at a lower price.

BOTTLES TO TRY

○ **Estate Bottled Chardonnay** / $$$$
● **Estate Bottled Pinot Noir** / $$$$

NAVARRO VINEYARDS

Laid-back Navarro is a familiar stop for Mendocino County tourists on Anderson Valley's main wine road, Route 128. Most of its small production is sold directly, either out of the tasting room or via its website. The family-run winery is perhaps best known for its dry Gewürztraminers—often among California's finest—and Méthode à l'Ancienne Pinot Noirs. But Navarro also offers a broad selection of other drinks, from Alsace-style Edelzwicker (see p. 21) to a Roussanne-Marsanne blend to various nonalcoholic grape juices. The gently priced wines are typically made in a lighter, elegant style that suits the table well.

BOTTLES TO TRY

○ **Gewürztraminer** / $$
● **Méthode à l'Ancienne Pinot Noir** / $$

THE OJAI VINEYARD

Ojai's owner-winemaker Adam Tolmach is a pioneer in combining *terroir*-driven vineyard scouting, low-intervention cellar work and minimal artifice in order to allow distinctive grapes and vineyards to shine through. And he has plenty of opportunities to practice his craft: Ojai produces only about 6,000 cases a year, but they are divided among some 24 different wines. Though its roster includes Rieslings and Viognier ice wines, fans identify Ojai with stylish, not overly rich Pinot Noir, Syrah and Chardonnay sourced from top Central Coast vineyards.

BOTTLES TO TRY
- ○ Bien Nacido Vineyard Chardonnay / $$
- ● Santa Barbara County Syrah / $$

OPUS ONE

This groundbreaking Napa Valley joint venture between the late Robert Mondavi and Château Mouton Rothschild was modeled on a *grand cru* Bordeaux, with the focus squarely on its high-end Cabernet-based Opus One blend, one of California's iconic reds. The second wine, the still-pricey, multivintage Overture, is crafted to be softer on the palate and more readily approachable in its youth. Today, the operation is co-owned by the Rothschilds and Constellation Brands (which bought Mondavi), with the Rothschilds taking the lead in vineyard management.

BOTTLES TO TRY
- ● Opus One / $$$$
- ● Overture / $$$$

PATZ & HALL

While working together at Napa's Flora Springs winery in the 1980s, Donald Patz and James Hall hatched a plan to create this Burgundy-centric brand. Thanks in part to an all-star collection of vineyard sources, ranging from Mendocino County in the north down to the Santa Lucia Highlands, Patz & Hall has become one of the country's most reliable sources for Chardonnay and Pinot Noir. The focus on top fruit from single vineyards gives the winery's lineup a diversity that showcases an array of flavor and aroma profiles.

BOTTLES TO TRY
- ○ Dutton Ranch Chardonnay / $$$
- ● Sonoma Coast Pinot Noir / $$$

PAUL HOBBS WINERY / CROSSBARN WINERY

Paul Hobbs's winemaking projects range from Argentina to New York's Finger Lakes, but his home base is Sebastopol in Sonoma County. Even here, his reach extends across boundaries, to Napa's iconic Beckstoffer To Kalon Vineyard and other Beckstoffer properties, from which Hobbs makes his stunning, ultra-luxury-priced Cabs. Closer to home, he creates firm-structured and polished Pinot Noirs and Chardonnays from top Russian River and Carneros vineyards. The second-label CrossBarn wines offer a taste of Hobbs's style at a gentler price.

BOTTLES TO TRY

○ **CrossBarn Chardonnay** / $$
● **Pinot Noir** / $$$

PETER MICHAEL WINERY

A Briton, Sir Peter Michael, founded this highly praised winery in Sonoma's Knights Valley in 1982. Limited production and a strong following make its expensive, French-named wines (e.g., Les Pavots, Point Rouge, Cuvée Indigène) hard to find, but persistence (or getting on the mailing list) will reward Chardonnay and red Bordeaux lovers with expressive, full-flavored, palate-saturating wines. Most of the acclaimed Pinot Noirs hail from Seaview Estate Vineyard on the windy Sonoma Coast.

BOTTLES TO TRY

○ **L'Après-Midi Sauvignon Blanc** / $$$
● **Les Pavots** / $$$$

PINE RIDGE VINEYARDS

Part of the Crimson Wine Group (Seghesio, Archery Summit), Pine Ridge produces wine from 200 acres spread across 12 estate vineyards in five major Napa Valley appellations. Winemaker Michael Beaulac combines fruit from these varied locations into several blends, including the top-of-the-line Fortis and Cave 7. Even the generally excellent Stags Leap District Cabernet is blended from four estate vineyards within that one subregion. Pine Ridge wines are made at a variety of price points. For an affordable introduction to the winery's style with whites, try the vibrant Chenin Blanc–Viognier.

BOTTLES TO TRY

○ **Chenin Blanc–Viognier** / $
● **Napa Valley Cabernet Sauvignon** / $$$

PISONI VINEYARDS & WINERY / LULI WINES

Did Gary Pisoni really hop the wall at Domaine de la Romanée-Conti to snare the cuttings that became the "Pisoni clone"? We may never know, but he is a determined man, planting grape-vines on his father's challenging Santa Lucia Highlands cattle ranch in 1982, and creating one of California's most famous sources of Pinot Noir grapes. The Pisoni label turns out a single coveted estate Pinot Noir each year. Gary Pisoni also bottles an array of highly regarded wines under the Lucia label, and the affordable Luli wines in partnership with sommelier Sara Floyd.

BOTTLES TO TRY

○ **Luli Chardonnay** / $$
● **Pisoni Estate Pinot Noir** / $$$$

QUINTESSA

A stylish Napa winery, Quintessa was established by the Huneeus family, who brought with them from Chile a cosmo-politan flair and a bedrock belief in natural agriculture. This 280-acre property has been farmed biodynamically or sustain-ably from the time it was planted in 1989, and its production is devoted to a single red wine. Composed of aged-barrel selec-tions from the estate's various microclimate blocks, the subtle, refined, luxury-priced Quintessa is a multigrape Bordeaux-style blend that includes the sometimes forgotten (in Bordeaux) Carmenère, a mainstay in the Huneeuses' native Chile.

BOTTLE TO TRY

● **Quintessa** / $$$$

QUPÉ

This "modern stone-age winery" founded by Bob Lindquist, and sold to wine entrepreneur Charles Banks (see Mayacamas, p. 190) in 2013, is one of the Central Coast's original Rhône Rangers, crafting extraordinary Syrah, for starters. Lindquist remains at the winery and continues to make his small-lot, single-vineyard bottlings from plantings he has worked with for years. Qupé's affordable Central Coast Syrah provides a fine sampling of his spicy, vibrant style. At times overshadowed by his reds, Lindquist's whites also offer incredible quality for the price.

BOTTLES TO TRY

○ **Roussanne** / $$$
● **Central Coast Syrah** / $$

RAMEY WINE CELLARS

One of California's most respected trendsetting winemakers, David Ramey worked with the legendary Moueix family in Bordeaux and at prestigious producers like Chalk Hill, Dominus and Rudd, gaining along the way a reputation for groundbreaking Chardonnays and Cabernets. In 1996, Ramey and his wife, Carla, created their own Sonoma-based label. Longstanding personal connections with growers allow Ramey to source grapes from a dazzling collection of top sites, including Sonoma's Woolsey Road Vineyard and Napa's Hyde Vineyard.

BOTTLES TO TRY

○ **Russian River Valley Chardonnay** / $$$
● **Napa Valley Cabernet Sauvignon** / $$$

RAVENSWOOD

When Ravenswood founder Joel Peterson started making Zinfandel in the 1970s, he championed bold, deeply purple Zins that were as far from the prevailing White Zinfandel blush wines as you could get. Though the Sonoma County winery is now part of giant Constellation Brands, Peterson's "no wimpy wines" credo remains operative. Ravenswood's offerings range from the entry-level Vintners Blend series to the top-of-the-line Icon red blend. Its single-vineyard bottlings include the wonderful Dickerson and Belloni Zins.

BOTTLES TO TRY

● **Lodi Old Vine Zinfandel** / $
● **Dickerson Zinfandel** / $$$

REALM CELLARS

With neither capital nor an enology degree, Juan Mercado all but willed Realm into being, succeeding despite skeptics, near-bankruptcy and a warehouse fire that destroyed his entire 2003 vintage. Mercado makes ethereal small lots of wines from some of Napa's greatest vineyards. With partner Scott Becker to handle the business end, and Michel Rolland protégé Benoit Touquette as winemaker, the tiny cult winery is entering a more stable phase of its existence. Fortunately for its mostly mailing-list fans, it still has the same superb grape sources.

BOTTLES TO TRY

● **Beckstoffer To Kalon Vineyard Cabernet Sauvignon** / $$$$
● **The Tempest** / $$$$

RIDGE VINEYARDS

One of California's most celebrated and reliable fine-wine labels, Ridge began commercial production high up on the Monte Bello Ridge in 1962. Its renown is based on Monte Bello, the profound, world-class Cabernet blend sourced from the winery's hilltop home vineyard, and on its premier old-vine Zinfandels, notably the bottlings from Sonoma's Geyserville and Lytton Springs vineyards. But presiding guru Paul Draper turns out a plethora of exciting wines at a range of prices. Much under-appreciated: his remarkable hand with silky Chardonnays.

BOTTLES TO TRY

○ Estate Chardonnay / $$$

● Three Valleys Zinfandel / $$

ROBERT CRAIG WINERY

At the end of a winding road, 2,300 feet up on Napa Valley's Howell Mountain, sits Robert Craig's eponymous winery. It's a perch that suits Craig well—he cut his teeth as general manager of the Hess Collection on Mount Veeder and developed a passion for concentrated, firmly structured mountain-grown grapes. With nearly 25 vintages under his belt, Craig has become known for bottling outstanding Cabernet Sauvignon at gentle prices (e.g., the Mt. George Cuvée). He also makes small quantities of single-vineyard Chardonnay and Zinfandel.

BOTTLES TO TRY

○ Durell Vineyard Chardonnay / $$$

● Mt. George Cuvée / $$$

ROBERT MONDAVI WINERY

To an impressive extent, the Mondavi ship seems to have righted after the rocky years that preceded the family's loss of this iconic winery in a 2004 merger with Constellation Brands. With the cellar in the hands of Geneviève Janssens, Mondavi wines continue to compete with Napa's best at the high end and offer terrific values on less expensive bottlings. Mondavi retains some of Napa's most prized Cabernet Sauvignon sources, and is also known for its fine Fumé Blanc—no surprise there, given that the winery came up with this Sauvignon Blanc alias in the first place.

BOTTLES TO TRY

○ Napa Valley Fumé Blanc / $$

● Napa Valley Cabernet Sauvignon / $$

ROBERT SINSKEY VINEYARDS

Free-spirited Robert Sinskey has remained true to his convictions as his vineyard holdings have expanded to 200 acres. One of California's pioneer biodynamic farmers and winemakers, Sinskey operates much of his Napa winery with solar power and his vehicles with biodiesel. He also has a very graceful hand with his wines, producing a small group of vineyard-based, fancifully named blends (like the Abraxas Vin de Terroir white) and some lovely, food-friendly Pinot Noirs.

BOTTLES TO TRY

● Vin Gris of Pinot Noir / $$$

● Pinot Noir / $$$

ROCHIOLI VINEYARDS & WINERY

The Rochiolis were pioneering vintners in Sonoma's now-prized Russian River Valley, and third-generation winemaker Tom has long made this a name to reckon with in Pinot Noir, both for his estate-based bottlings and for the Rochioli vineyard designates of other top producers. Unusual for a Pinot specialist, Rochioli's Sauvignon Blanc has developed its own avid following, but it is still the estate's Burgundy-inspired, single-vineyard Pinots and Chardonnays that cause collectors to salivate. It can take years to get on the winery's mailing list for those bottles, but fortunately, Rochioli's other offerings are more widely available.

BOTTLES TO TRY

○ Sauvignon Blanc / $$$

● Pinot Noir / $$$$

RODNEY STRONG VINEYARDS

Rodney Strong helped develop Sonoma's fine-wine niche when he retired from a Broadway dancing career and founded his winery in 1959. Owned by the Klein family since 1989, this is a substantial, 800,000-plus-case operation. Longtime winemaker Rick Sayre, with an assist from super-consultant David Ramey (see Ramey Wine Cellars, p. 195), has helped build the brand's well-deserved reputation for putting value in the bottle at entry-level prices and for top-notch single-vineyard bottlings like the signature Alexander's Crown Cabernet Sauvignon.

BOTTLES TO TRY

○ Charlotte's Home Sauvignon Blanc / $

● Estate Vineyards Cabernet Sauvignon / $$

THE SCHOLIUM PROJECT

Former philosophy professor Abe Schoener defies the conventional wisdom of "Never let the public taste your experiments." Seemingly every one of the quirkily named wines he bottles in small quantities has an envelope-pushing intent. Ideal for the wine-curious with a sophisticated palate, Scholium is the cutting edge in action. One of its best-known bottlings is the Prince in His Caves Sauvignon Blanc. Upon request, the Suisun Valley winery sells custom large-format bottles of some of its wines.

BOTTLES TO TRY

○ The Prince in His Caves Sauvignon Blanc / $$$
● The Gardens of Babylon / $$$

SEGHESIO FAMILY VINEYARDS

The Seghesios were one of the first names in Zinfandel, farming the grape in Sonoma County in 1895 and accumulating prime vineyard land over the decades since. This affords certain luxuries: The vines that produce Seghesio's spicy, briary Old Vine Zinfandel, for example, are on average 70 years old. A part of the Crimson Wine Group (Pine Ridge, Archery Summit) since 2011, the winery also turns out notable bottlings of heritage field-blend grapes, as well as small lots of Italian specialties, such as Arneis and the Venom Sangiovese, from the intimidating Rattlesnake Hill Vineyard.

BOTTLES TO TRY

● Sonoma County Zinfandel / $$
● Venom Sangiovese / $$$

SHAFER VINEYARDS

Former publishing executive John Shafer founded his Stags Leap District winery in the late 1970s. Its longtime winemaker Elias Fernandez has a talent for fashioning formidable wines that maintain balance despite their power. That quality is best displayed in the estate's cellar-worthy flagship, Hillside Select, an iconic Stags Leap District Cabernet. Easier to find are Shafer's other reds: the One Point Five Cabernet, an inky Merlot and a full-throttle Syrah blend, Relentless. The winery is also known for its super-juicy Red Shoulder Ranch Chardonnay.

BOTTLES TO TRY

○ Red Shoulder Ranch Chardonnay / $$$
● One Point Five Cabernet Sauvignon / $$$$

BEST OF THE BEST PRODUCERS / PINOT NOIR

1. CALERA WINE COMPANY **2.** FLOWERS VINEYARDS **3.** HIRSCH VINEYARDS **4.** LITTORAI WINES **5.** PISONI VINEYARDS

SIDURI WINES / NOVY FAMILY WINES

This 20-year-old producer rose to cult heights on Adam and Dianna Lee's talent for vineyard scouting. The Siduri label's rich, expressive single-vineyard Pinot Noirs come from prestige growers like Pisoni, Rosella's and Hirsch. The Novy brand concentrates on *terroir*-focused, single-vineyard Syrahs. The Lees sold their operations to Jackson Family Wines in 2015, but Adam signed on to craft wines there for at least three more years.

BOTTLES TO TRY

- Novy Santa Lucia Highlands Syrah / $$
- Siduri Pisoni Vineyard Pinot Noir / $$$

SILVER OAK CELLARS

This venerable winery catapulted to fame in the 1980s and '90s. Its co-founder and guiding light Justin Meyer retired in 2001, but noted winemaker Daniel Baron continues to turn out two of California's most palate-flattering Cabernets—one from Silver Oak's Alexander Valley winery, the other from its Napa Valley facility. Both retain the brand's trademark lusciousness, derived partly from extended cellar aging.

BOTTLES TO TRY

- Alexander Valley Cabernet Sauvignon / $$$$
- Napa Valley Cabernet Sauvignon / $$$$

SMITH-MADRONE

Spring Mountain is one of Napa's prime Cabernet zones, and brothers Stuart and Charles Smith were among the first in the modern era to fall for its charms, founding their winery, with its scenically spectacular vineyard, in the early 1970s. The brothers produce 4,000 cases of distinctive wine—Cabernets that typically eschew big extraction and massive alcohol levels, and minerally Rieslings and Chardonnays crafted for the long haul.

BOTTLES TO TRY

- ○ Riesling / $$
- ● Cabernet Sauvignon / $$$

SPOTTSWOODE ESTATE VINEYARD & WINERY

This family-run estate, now led by Napa mover and shaker Beth Novak Milliken, has been making classically structured Napa Valley Cabernet Sauvignon since 1982, but its house and grounds in St. Helena date to more than 100 years earlier. Its wines come chiefly from the estate vineyard, which has been farmed organically for 30 years. Both the signature Cabernet and the acclaimed Napa-Sonoma Sauvignon Blanc are notable for their balance and elegance. The lovely Lyndenhurst Cabernet, made partly from purchased fruit, is a little easier on the wallet.

BOTTLES TO TRY

○ Sauvignon Blanc / $$$

● Lyndenhurst Cabernet Sauvignon / $$$$

STAGLIN FAMILY VINEYARD

The estate founded by Shari and Garen Staglin in 1985 has since become a cornerstone of Napa's Rutherford District. Managed by the talented team of Fredrik Johansson (winemaker), David Abreu (vineyard manager) and Michel Rolland (consultant), Staglin's organically farmed vineyards yield some of Napa's most sought-after Cabs. Offerings range from pricey (the Salus Chardonnay) to extremely pricey (the INEO blend), and availability can be limited. Profits from the three Salus wines—the Chardonnay and two Cabs—are donated to mental health research.

BOTTLES TO TRY

○ Salus Chardonnay / $$$

● Cabernet Sauvignon / $$$$

STAG'S LEAP WINE CELLARS

Warren Winiarski sold his landmark Napa Valley winery in 2007 to Ste. Michelle Wine Estates and Tuscan giant Antinori (see p. 84). Quality, already good, is up: It's easy to imagine current vintages competing with marquee Bordeaux, as a Stag's Leap Cabernet did at the legendary 1976 Judgment of Paris tasting. With its superbly situated vineyards, the opportunity is there for the winery to reclaim iconic status, especially with its top-notch estate- and single-vineyard Cabs: Cask 23, S.L.V. and Fay. The less pricey Artemis and Karia bottlings are terrific, too.

BOTTLES TO TRY

○ Karia Chardonnay / $$

● Artemis Cabernet Sauvignon / $$$

STAGS' LEAP WINERY

Known for its top bottlings of old-vine Petite Sirah, Stags' Leap is also famous for the feud between former owner, Carl Doumani, and his neighbor, Warren Winiarski, of Stag's Leap Wine Cellars, who couldn't agree on anything (note the apostrophes in the wineries' names). Bought in 1997 by Beringer, which invested significantly in it, the 1890s property is now owned by Treasury Wine Estates. Petite Sirah and decades-old field-blend grapes still shape its two best wines: the Ne Cede Malis Petite Sirah and Audentia, an unusual Cab–Petite Sirah blend.

BOTTLES TO TRY

○ Chardonnay / $$

● Petite Sirah / $$$

STONY HILL VINEYARD

Fred and Eleanor McCrea came upon this rocky, unforgiving patch of land—it was a goat ranch—high on Spring Mountain in the early 1940s. They were determined to plant Chardonnay, a variety largely unknown to US drinkers at the time. With the second and third generations of McCreas now running Stony Hill, the winery's devoted fans can rest easy: Longtime winemaker Mike Chelini still crafts the Chablis-style flagship Chardonnay to keep the original fruit, vibrancy and acidity at the fore.

BOTTLES TO TRY

○ Chardonnay / $$$

● Cabernet Sauvignon / $$$$

TALLEY VINEYARDS

Brian Talley's family has been farming the Central Coast since 1948, and the family's deep familiarity with the local *terroir* is one secret to the winery's success. Today the Talleys work 177 acres in six vineyards in the Arroyo Grande and Edna Valleys, none better known than Rosemary's Vineyard, which grows like a garden plot around the home of matriarch Rosemary and which yields lively, floral Pinot Noirs and Chardonnays. The 36,000-case operation reserves its Talley Vineyards label for estate-produced Pinot and Chardonnay; the under-$30 Bishop's Peak wines are sourced from outside growers.

BOTTLES TO TRY

○ Arroyo Grande Valley Chardonnay / $$

● Rosemary's Vineyard Pinot Noir / $$$$

TREFETHEN FAMILY VINEYARDS

The third generation of Trefethens is putting its stamp on this historic Oak Knoll District property—600 acres centered on the 19th-century Eschol estate. The Trefethens have never bought an outside grape, meaning that microclimates on the property have had to be matched to grapes with varied demands, such as late-ripening Cabernet Sauvignon and aromatic whites like Riesling (with which they have great success). Though its understated, food-complementing Chardonnays put the winery on the map, Trefethen also produces elegant Merlot and Cabernet.

BOTTLES TO TRY

○ Dry Riesling / $$
● Merlot / $$$

TRICYCLE WINE PARTNERS

The Molnar brothers, who grew up on their father's Poseidon Vineyard in Napa's Carneros region, and pal Michael Terrien joined forces in this two-label, small-batch wine company. The Poseidon Vineyard wines are cool-climate Chardonnays and Pinot Noirs with an emphasis on pure fruit rather than oak or jam. The Obsidian Ridge label is for Cabernet Sauvignon and Syrah from a namesake vineyard in the Red Hill Lake County AVA. The Molnars' Hungarian roots show in the barrels, which they import from their own cooperage in Hungary.

BOTTLES TO TRY

○ Poseidon Vineyard Chardonnay / $$
● Obsidian Ridge Cabernet Sauvignon / $$

TRINCHERO NAPA VALLEY

Like other famous California wine families, the Trincheros made a fortune in popularly priced wine (they invented White Zinfandel at their Sutter Home Winery). Bob Trinchero plowed a chunk of those profits into the creation of an ambitious, high-end estate, amassing an impressive collection of vineyards across Napa's subregions, then buying the old Folie à Deux winery in 2004. Winemaker Mario Monticelli uses the different vineyards to create an array of concentrated reds and juicy whites, chiefly from Bordeaux grapes.

BOTTLES TO TRY

○ Mary's Vineyard Sauvignon Blanc / $$
● Meritage / $$$

VARNER WINE / FOXGLOVE

Twins Jim and Bob Varner have raised the profile of their tiny winery in the Santa Cruz Mountains by becoming Chardonnay specialists. Their deft hand with the grape lends their wines a structured European finesse that puts them in a different league. Their fans also appreciate their touch with Pinot Noir, which Bob bottles for the affiliated Neely brand, and the often remarkable value of their Foxglove second label.

BOTTLES TO TRY

○ Varner Bee Block Chardonnay / $$$
● Foxglove Zinfandel / $

WILLIAMS SELYEM

One of America's premier small wineries, Sonoma County's Williams Selyem has kept its artisan cred despite immense consumer demand, making Pinot Noir, Zinfandel and Chardonnay with an attention to detail that lets its minimal-interference approach actually work. Only the most determined fans will be able to acquire one of the single-vineyard wines, but fortunately, there are more-accessible multivineyard bottlings.

BOTTLES TO TRY

○ Unoaked Chardonnay / $$$$
● Russian River Valley Pinot Noir / $$$$

OREGON

CLAIM TO FAME

That Oregon, with its wet weather and short summers, could ever produce world-class wine was in doubt until the 1970s, when pioneer producers like David Lett, David Adelsheim and Dick Ponzi began to receive international acclaim. Today the Willamette Valley is the epicenter of an ambitious, thriving wine region famous for some of the country's most refined Pinot Noir.

REGIONS TO KNOW

COLUMBIA GORGE & WALLA WALLA VALLEY Northeast of the Willamette Valley, these regions run along (and across) the Washington state border (the Walla Walla Valley AVA lies mostly in Washington). Warm, dry summers favor reds: Cabernet dominates, while Syrah and Merlot are made in lesser amounts.

ROGUE VALLEY Southern Oregon's Rogue Valley region includes the valleys of the Rogue River and three tributaries: the Illinois and Applegate rivers and Bear Creek. **Applegate Valley,** with vineyards up to 1,500 feet in elevation, has its own AVA. Bordeaux and Rhône varieties are grown throughout the region.

UMPQUA VALLEY Warmer than the Willamette Valley and cooler than Rogue, Umpqua produces small amounts of Pinot Noir and Pinot Gris, among others.

WILLAMETTE VALLEY Stretching virtually from Portland's suburbs in the north to Eugene in the south, this broad valley is home to most of the state's population as well as most of its wine production. Protected from Pacific winds by the Coast Range, the Valley is divided into six subregions, each with its own AVA: **Chehalem Mountains, Dundee Hills, Eola-Amity Hills, McMinnville, Ribbon Ridge** and the **Yamhill-Carlton District.**

KEY GRAPES: WHITE

CHARDONNAY Not much Chardonnay is crushed in Oregon compared with Pinot Noir and Pinot Gris, but as in Burgundy, the cool-climate conditions that work to create top Pinot Noirs also tend to favor graceful renditions of Chardonnay, with subtle fruit flavors and lively acidity.

PINOT BLANC & RIESLING These aromatic varieties are making headway in Oregon, with a handful of small vintners achieving notable success in the Willamette Valley.

PINOT GRIS Oregon's principal white grape is Pinot Gris. Its expression in the state varies in style but typically leans toward the generous and full-bodied Alsace profile, with refreshing acidity, as opposed to the leaner Pinot Grigio style.

KEY GRAPES: RED

PINOT NOIR Representing more than half of Oregon's wine output, this is the state's image-maker. Oregon Pinot Noir is typically silky smooth, with delicate berry flavors and firm acidity. Somewhere between the earthy, astringent style of Burgundy and the robust offerings characteristic of California, Oregon Pinot Noir has established itself as a true connoisseur's alternative.

Producers/ Oregon

ADELSHEIM VINEYARD

David and Ginny Adelsheim's winery helped put Oregon on the wine world's map in 1972. From the original 15 acres in the Quarter Mile Lane Vineyard, the Adelsheims and their partners now farm more than 200 acres in the northern Willamette Valley. The winery is known for small-lot and single-vineyard Pinot Noirs, but its reputation for vibrant, graceful wines extends to its whites as well.

BOTTLES TO TRY

○ Pinot Gris / $$

● Willamette Valley Pinot Noir / $$

ANTICA TERRA

Oregon aficionados have discovered this remarkable label, which produces wines with unusual depth of character and a finely tuned tension between richness and acidity. Winemaker Maggie Harrison has a knack for making wines that are immediately palate-appealing, yet reveal distinctive layer after layer. Though Pinot Noirs are the calling card, Harrison also produces gorgeous Chardonnay and one of America's finest rosés, Angelicall.

BOTTLES TO TRY

● Angelicall / $$$$

● Botanica Pinot Noir / $$$$

ARGYLE WINERY

Winemaker Nate Klostermann took over for Argyle's co-founder Rollin Soles in 2013, and he has plenty to build on at this top-notch winery. Argyle has long been a producer of some of the state's finest Pinot Noirs, as well as top Rieslings and Chardonnays, much of it from 415 acres of estate vines. Nevertheless, for many fans, Argyle is preeminently a maker of vibrant, world-class sparkling wines (see p. 286).

BOTTLES TO TRY

○ Riesling / $$

● Pinot Noir / $$

BENTON-LANE WINERY

It may be Benton-Lane's eye-catching postage stamp labels that first attract shoppers, but the well-made wines keep them coming back. Steve and Carol Girard produce all of their signature Pinot Noirs from their 138-acre Sunnymount Vineyard. The basic Willamette Valley Pinot Noir is a popular, go-to value red, while the high-end First Class Pinot, which receives full-on traditional Burgundian winemaking treatment, competes with Oregon's best. Made from estate and purchased grapes, Benton-Lane's vibrant Pinot Gris is worth seeking out.

BOTTLES TO TRY

○ Pinot Gris / $$

● Pinot Noir / $$

BERGSTRÖM WINES

Founded by Portland surgeon John Bergström and his wife, Karen, in 1999, Bergström Wines is now led by their son Josh with his wife, Caroline, whom he met while studying winemaking in Burgundy. The five estate vineyards—encompassing 84 biodynamically farmed acres around the Willamette Valley— yield Pinot Noirs of great poise, energy and depth. The winery's much-sought-after single-vineyard bottlings include those from the steep Gregory Ranch in the Pacific Coast Range and from Bergström's Temperance Hill block.

BOTTLES TO TRY

○ Old Stones Chardonnay / $$$

● Cumberland Reserve Pinot Noir / $$$

BIG TABLE FARM

Napa Valley winemaker Brian Marcy and artist-farmer Clare Carver moved to Oregon in 2006 to pursue a comprehensive vision of natural land cultivation and stewardship that includes crops, farm animals and winemaking. Their small-production lots of native-yeast-fermented, unfined, unfiltered wines are headlined by Marcy's sure-handed, complex Pinots and Chardonnays. Keep an eye on the Big Table Farm website for a chance to secure super-small lots like the Edelzwicker white, made from an Alsace-style field blend.

BOTTLES TO TRY

○ Chardonnay / $$$

● Willamette Valley Pinot Noir / $$$

CHEHALEM

A pioneering planter on Ribbon Ridge back in 1980, Willamette Valley stalwart Harry Peterson-Nedry founded Chehalem in 1990, and with his partners, Bill and Cathy Stoller, has added to his vineyard holdings in the Chehalem Mountains and Dundee Hills AVAs. From the INOX Unoaked Chardonnay to the elegant Pinot Noirs and wildly aromatic Pinot Gris and Rieslings, Chehalem wines reflect Peterson-Nedry's obsession with purity, freshness and crisp acidity, sometimes at the expense of palate-flattering fleshiness and fruit. These are not market-driven wines, but distinctive products of a consistent style.

BOTTLES TO TRY
○ INOX Unoaked Chardonnay / $$
● Three Vineyard Pinot Noir / $$$

CRISTOM VINEYARDS

Cristom has a remarkable story of continuity: Winemaker Steve Doerner and vineyard manager Mark Feltz have been in place since Paul Gerrie bought the property in 1992. Why mess with success? Cristom's Pinot Noirs—whole-cluster-fermented with native yeasts and bottled unfiltered—have been some of Washington's most celebrated wines. The four estate-sourced, single-vineyard bottlings named for family matriarchs are relatively rare, but the three more accessible multivineyard blends, including the lovely Mt. Jefferson Cuvée, can also be outstanding.

BOTTLES TO TRY
○ Pinot Gris / $$
● Mt. Jefferson Cuvée Pinot Noir / $$

DOMAINE DROUHIN OREGON

Established in the late 1980s, this US outpost of Burgundy's Maison Joseph Drouhin winery (see p. 41) has deftly blended things French with things Oregonian. At the heart of the efforts are the vines on Drouhin's hilltop vineyard in the Dundee Hills AVA. Pinot Noir is the focus here (124 acres, with only 11 planted to Chardonnay). The entry-level Dundee Hills bottling can be a steal; the pricier and rarer Laurène and Louise cuvées are among America's benchmarks for the wine.

BOTTLES TO TRY
○ Arthur Chardonnay / $$$
● Pinot Noir / $$$

ELK COVE VINEYARDS

This has been a sturdy source for fine Pinot Noir since Pat and Joe Campbell bought their first small vineyard plot in the foothills of the Coast Range in 1974. Today, Elk Cove is at the top of its game under their youngest son, Adam, who sources his prized single-vineyard and limited-release Pinot Noir offerings from six estate vineyards covering 350 acres. The winery also places great emphasis on its whites—Pinot Blanc, Pinot Gris, Riesling and the luscious dessert wine blend Ultima.

BOTTLES TO TRY

○ Pinot Gris / $$

● Pinor Noir / $$

THE EYRIE VINEYARDS

This is the winery that started it all in Oregon. Its founder, the stubborn visionary David Lett, came up from California in 1965 with 3,000 vine cuttings to test out Pinot Noir in rainy Willamette Valley. Along the way, he also bottled America's first Pinot Gris. Now run by his son Jason, Eyrie sources grapes from four venerable estate vineyards (the Reserve Pinot and Chardonnay plots are nearly 50 years old), all essentially organically farmed and unirrigated. Jason continues his late father's emphasis on small-lot fermentation and on wines of grace and balanced proportion rather than power and high alcohol.

BOTTLES TO TRY

○ Pinot Gris / $$

● Pinot Noir Reserve / $$$$

PONZI VINEYARDS

Richard Ponzi and his wife, Nancy, helped jump-start Oregon's commercial wine industry when they established their Willamette Valley winery in 1970. Ponzi's reputation for making top-flight Pinot Noir, Chardonnay and Pinot Gris has only been burnished over the years. Several family members are involved in the enterprise, but what goes into the bottle rests with winemaker daughter Luisa, who brought her years of study in Burgundy back to the family's 130 acres of sustainably farmed vineyards, most of them in the Chehalem Mountains AVA.

BOTTLES TO TRY

○ Chardonnay / $$

● Tavola Pinot Noir / $$

ROCO WINERY

The co-founder (and current consulting winemaker) of Argyle Winery (see p. 205), Rollin Soles and his wife, Corby, began making small lots of Pinot Noir from their Wits' End Vineyard in the Chehalem Mountains in 2003. Early efforts from the 6,000-case ROCO project have met with great acclaim, particularly the Private Stash Pinot Noir from the Wits' End Vineyard. Soles also has a very deft hand with Chardonnay.

BOTTLES TO TRY

○ Chardonnay / $$$
● Willamette Valley Pinot Noir / $$

SOKOL BLOSSER WINERY

This trailblazing Dundee Hills winery is now guided by the second generation of the founding Sokol Blosser family: winemaker Alex and his CEO sister Alison. The most visible sign of the brand's rejuvenation and ongoing vitality under their leadership is the strikingly designed cedar-lined tasting room that opened in 2013. The Sokol Blosser portfolio includes the image-making Pinot Noir bottlings and the affordable Evolution line, consisting of the popular Evolution White, a surprisingly seamless blend of up to nine varieties; a Syrah-based red; and a dry *méthode traditionnelle* sparkler.

BOTTLES TO TRY

○ Evolution / $
● Pinot Noir / $$$

ST. INNOCENT WINERY

Although this highly regarded winery produces a small amount of white wine, its hallmark is Pinot Noir—specifically, the small-lot Pinots made by owner-winemaker Mark Vlossak from an all-star roster of Willamette Valley sites, including his own Zenith Vineyard in the Eola–Amity Hills AVA. The wines' small production (8,000 to 10,000 cases total, divided into numerous cuvées), consistent quality and strong following can make them hard to find (some even sell out as futures). Fortunately, Vlossak also makes the delicious, larger-production Villages Cuvée, which blends fruit from several vineyards.

BOTTLES TO TRY

○ Freedom Hill Vineyard Pinot Blanc / $$
● Villages Cuvée Pinot Noir / $$

TRISAETUM

It is a testimony to James Frey's sophisticated facility that Trisaetum was chosen as the interim site for Burgundy's Louis Jadot to launch its first American venture in 2013. Trisaetum itself produces much-praised Pinot Noir and Riesling, with core offerings from three sustainably farmed estate vineyards: its home plantings in Ribbon Ridge; a rocky slope in the foothills of the Coast Range; and a small plot in the Dundee Hills.

BOTTLES TO TRY

○ **Ribbon Ridge Estate Riesling** / $$

● **Pinot Noir** / $$

WILLAMETTE VALLEY VINEYARDS

From the run-down plum orchard bought by founder Jim Bernau in 1983, Willamette Valley Vineyards has grown into one of Oregon's largest producers. Although winemaker Don Crank III's single-vineyard Pinot Noir bottlings are expensive, the sweet spot for reds here is in the midrange, where you'll find many of the estate-vineyard bottlings. WVV is also a prime source for well-priced whites that overdeliver.

BOTTLES TO TRY

○ **Estate Chardonnay** / $$

● **Estate Pinot Noir** / $$

WASHINGTON STATE

CLAIM TO FAME

Centered in eastern Washington's high desert, which the Cascade Range shields from Pacific rains, the state's wine industry turns out complex reds that rival top California bottlings. Cheaper land and a lower profile mean that these impressive wines often sell for much less than their California counterparts. Washington's growing wine industry now numbers nearly 900 wineries and 13 AVAs with more than 50,000 vineyard acres.

REGIONS TO KNOW

COLUMBIA GORGE This scenic south-central region encompasses both sides of the Columbia River. Its climate shifts dramatically from hot and dry in the east to cool and rainy in the west: No wonder so many grape varieties are planted here.

COLUMBIA VALLEY This huge southeastern region covers a third of the state and encompasses 99 percent of its wine grapes; most other famous Washington AVAs (including Horse Heaven Hills and Walla Walla and Yakima Valleys) are Columbia Valley subregions. The newest of its 10 AVAs is **Ancient Lakes,** a chilly, dry subregion northeast of Yakima.

HORSE HEAVEN HILLS These well-drained slopes with cooling winds off the Columbia River grow some of the state's premier Bordeaux-style reds and earthy, elegant Syrahs.

RED MOUNTAIN This small AVA within Yakima Valley makes some of the state's—and the nation's—very finest reds, notably concentrated Cabernets with plentiful but elegant tannins.

WAHLUKE SLOPE Warm and dry, this up-and-coming district in south-central Washington is planted chiefly with heat-loving red grapes like Merlot, Cabernet and Syrah.

WALLA WALLA VALLEY Many of Washington's finest Cabernets come from this remote southeastern region, which extends into Oregon. Merlot, Syrah and Chardonnay excel here as well.

YAKIMA VALLEY Established in 1983, the Yakima Valley AVA is the oldest in the state. This important district is a major source of Washington Chardonnay and also has highly regarded plantings of Merlot and Cabernet Sauvignon.

❦ KEY GRAPES: WHITE

CHARDONNAY Washington turns out noteworthy Chardonnays at the affordable end of the market and some very fine luxury-priced versions from top producers.

GEWÜRZTRAMINER, SAUVIGNON BLANC & VIOGNIER Accounting for just over 10 percent of Washington's white grape production, these aromatic varieties do well in the state's northern climate. Gewürztraminer tends to yield ripe, floral, usually off-dry wines.

PINOT GRIS This white variety is on the rise—there is actually more Pinot Gris here than in Oregon. Most of it goes into straightforward, fruit-driven wines made in a fresh, appley style.

RIESLING Washington growers produce slightly more Riesling—the state's signature white grape—than they do Cabernet. Cool nights and ideal growing conditions allow the grapes to be crafted into a range of styles from dry to sweet.

🍇 KEY GRAPES: RED

CABERNET SAUVIGNON Washington's most planted red variety makes terrific wines up and down the price scale; its high-end cuvées compete with the world's best. Smooth-textured and bold, Washington Cabernets are more restrained than California's dense, riper-style offerings.

MERLOT Washington is arguably America's premier source for delicious Merlot; its top bottles have a distinctive, spicy complexity and seductive depth.

SYRAH Columbia Valley's Walla Walla Valley, Wahluke Slope, Yakima Valley and Red Mountain subregions provide ideal growing conditions for Syrah. At their best, Washington Syrahs offer peppery, earthy flavors and a firm structure in the Rhône variety's classic style, though they're typically riper than Old World versions.

Producers/ Washington State

ANDREW WILL WINERY

Winemaker-owner Chris Camarda's artisan winery on Vashon Island near Seattle turns out some of the state's most coveted Bordeaux-style reds. His silky, site-specific cuvées are sourced from top Washington vineyards, such as Ciel du Cheval and Champoux. Tiny quantities and high prices make these wines inaccessible to most. Luckily, Camarda also makes a series of excellent, affordable wines that give a taste of his impressive talent (look for the black-labeled bottles).

BOTTLES TO TRY
- Cabernet Sauvignon / $$$
- Ciel du Cheval Vineyard / $$$

BUTY WINERY

Nina Buty (pronounced "beauty") co-founded this Walla Walla boutique winery in 2000, and soon brought on board top-notch California-based consultant Zelma Long (see Vilafonté, p. 273). The headliner among Buty's multivariety reds is the sought-after Rediviva of the Stones, an unusual (outside of Australia) combination of Cabernet Sauvignon and Syrah. The whites include an appealing Sémillon–Sauvignon Blanc–Muscadelle blend. Winemaker Chris Dowsett's emphasis on supple tannins and moderate alcohol levels lends his wines a particular finesse. A second label, Beast, with many one-time bottlings, allows Dowsett to follow his curiosity and push his talent.

BOTTLES TO TRY

○ Sémillon-Sauvignon-Muscadelle / $$
● Rediviva of the Stones / $$$

CADENCE

Benjamin Smith and Gaye McNutt ditched engineering and legal careers, respectively, to establish this small-scale but stellar winemaking venture. Cadence winery may be located in a South Seattle warehouse, but its grapes come from some of Washington's finest Red Mountain area vineyards, such as Tapteil and Ciel du Cheval, as well as the couple's own Cara Mia Vineyard. Graceful Bordeaux-style reds are the ticket here, with all the flavor intensity of Red Mountain grapes shining through.

BOTTLES TO TRY

● Tapteil Vineyard / $$$
● Bel Canto / $$$$

CAYUSE VINEYARDS

Christophe Baron, whose family has tended vines in the Marne Valley of Champagne, France, since 1677, was visiting Walla Walla in 1996, when he had a *coup de foudre*—a revelation—over a stone-covered field. The Châteauneuf-like sight rooted Baron to the spot (it's now his Cailloux Vineyard), and he stayed on to produce exuberant Rhône-style wines and much more from his biodynamically farmed, low-yielding vineyards. Most of his wines are sold out through his mailing list as futures.

BOTTLES TO TRY

● Edith Grenache Rosé / $$$$
● Cailloux Vineyard Syrah / $$$$

CHARLES SMITH WINES

Charles Smith moved to Walla Walla after a stint overseas as a rock band manager. For all his flamboyance, Smith is a meticulous winemaker who insists on low yields and intense fruit that he doesn't bury under planks of oak. His top wines are typically exotic, full-throttle, ultra-complex and very rich; they're made in tiny lots and sold at stiff prices. His namesake brand (he owns several others, such as K Vintners) includes affordable wines with names like Kung Fu Girl Riesling and The Velvet Devil Merlot.

BOTTLES TO TRY

○ **Kung Fu Girl Riesling** / **$**
● **The Velvet Devil Merlot** / **$**

CHATEAU STE. MICHELLE

Chateau Ste. Michelle, one of the many Ste. Michelle Wine Estates brands, is Washington's largest producer, and thanks to its visitors' facilities in suburban Seattle, the one most familiar to wine tourists. The titan brand has also been an innovator, a talent incubator and a highly reliable source for good wine at fair prices. (At under $20, for example, the Indian Wells Red Blend is hard to beat.) Among the winery's many important projects is the collaboration with the Mosel's Ernst Loosen (see Dr. Loosen, p. 140) to create one of America's best Rieslings, Eroica.

BOTTLES TO TRY

○ **Eroica Riesling** / **$$**
● **Indian Wells Red Blend** / **$$**

COLUMBIA CREST WINERY

If Chateau Ste. Michelle's even more price-conscious alter ego seems to be ubiquitous, there's a good reason: Very few large-production wineries anywhere make better wine consistently at such reasonable prices. Under longtime winemaker Ray Einberger and, as of 2011, his Argentinean successor, Juan Muñoz-Oca, Columbia Crest has established a record of punching above its weight, especially with supple, aromatic Cabs and Merlots and lovely, well-proportioned Chardonnays. Made in the winery's Petit Chai ("little barrel room"), the impressive Reserve wines can be revelatory examples of the label's potential.

BOTTLES TO TRY

○ **Grand Estates Chardonnay** / **$**
● **H3 Merlot** / **$**

DELILLE CELLARS

This Woodinville-based operation has been one of Washington's top wineries since the 1990s. Francophile winemaker Chris Upchurch turns out refined, multilayered, ageworthy Bordeaux-style wines under the DeLille Cellars label, and an equally stunning group of Rhône-inspired wines (the Signature Syrah, especially) under the Doyenne label. The Grand Ciel line features a Cab and a Syrah, both sourced entirely from DeLille's estate vineyard. Other grape sources include Harrison Hill's Cabernet blocks, among the oldest in the state.

BOTTLES TO TRY

○ **Chaleur Estate** / $$$
● **Doyenne Syrah** / $$$

GRAMERCY CELLARS

Founded in 2005 by Master Sommelier Greg Harrington and his wife, Pam, this Walla Walla winery created a sensation two years later with its very first offerings, including Syrahs notable not only for their quality, but for their distinctive character: complex, refined reds that boast modest alcohol, bright acidity and subtle oak. Harrington's carefully chosen vineyard sites—firmer grapes for the Lagniappe Syrah from Red Willow, softer ones for the Walla Walla Syrah from Les Collines—yield wines that are ideal for fans of top Rhône- and Bordeaux-style reds.

BOTTLES TO TRY

● **Cabernet Sauvignon** / $$$
● **Lagniappe Syrah** / $$$

HEDGES FAMILY ESTATE

Tom and Anne-Marie Hedges (he's a Washington native; she was born in Champagne, France) broke ground on their Red Mountain estate in 1989. The winery today is a true family affair: Daughter Sarah is the winemaker; son Christophe, the general manager. From their biodynamically farmed estate vineyards come the intensely flavored Bordeaux-style Red Mountain blend and the superb DLD Syrah. Look also for the more affordable CMS blends and the House of Independent Producers (HIP) line, which showcases prime Columbia Valley vineyards.

BOTTLES TO TRY

○ **CMS** / $
● **DLD Syrah** / $$

LEONETTI CELLAR

The handoff from founding father (in this case, Gary Figgins) to son (Chris Figgins) is potentially fraught in any family business, but when the firm in question is a reference-point winery for the US, fans start to worry. The best news: As talented as Gary is, Chris (head of the umbrella Figgins Family Wine Estates) is a truly worthy successor. Deep-pocketed wine lovers who want to taste some of the most deftly layered red wines in the New World should sign up immediately—there is a three- to four-year waiting list to get *on* the purchase list.

BOTTLES TO TRY

- Cabernet Sauvignon / $$$$
- Sangiovese / $$$$

NORTHSTAR WINERY

Part of the Ste. Michelle Wine Estates portfolio, this Walla Walla winery was founded in the early 1990s with talented winemaker Jed Steele at the helm. Northstar's focus was on Merlot, which looked to be Washington's up-and-coming grape back then. Fashion has since moved on to Cabernet and Syrah, but Steele's successor, David Merfeld, continues to craft some of the state's very best Merlots—a reminder of how wonderful the grape can be when given the star treatment usually accorded to Cabernet Sauvignon (which Northstar also handles very well).

BOTTLES TO TRY

- Stella Maris / $$
- Columbia Valley Merlot / $$$

OWEN ROE

This well-regarded bi-state brand opened a new winery in the Yakima Valley in 2013 after 14 years of hauling Washington grapes to Oregon (the Pinot Noirs are still made in Oregon). North of the state line, the category-defying operation turns out Syrahs, Cabs, Bordeaux- and Rhône-style blends, the unique Abbot's Table blend (Zinfandel, Sangiovese, Malbec, Lemberger and more) and whites from the DuBrul Vineyard. The quality level is generally strong across the diverse lineup, which also includes the Sharecropper's and value-oriented Corvidae lines.

BOTTLES TO TRY

- Abbot's Table / $$
- Ex Umbris Syrah / $$

BEST VALUE PRODUCERS / WASHINGTON STATE

1. CHARLES SMITH WINES 2. CHATEAU STE. MICHELLE
3. COLUMBIA CREST 4. HEDGES FAMILY ESTATE / HIP 5. OWEN ROE

PURSUED BY BEAR

TV and film star Kyle MacLachlan, a Yakima native, returned to his roots with this label, a collaboration with Walla Walla's Dunham Cellars. The name refers to the famous Shakespearean stage direction from *The Winter's Tale* (see the goofy rendition on pursuedbybearwine.com), but the project's high-end, mostly Cabernet Sauvignon blend is more refined and supple than theatrically flamboyant. There is also a Syrah, called Baby Bear.

BOTTLES TO TRY
- Baby Bear Syrah / $$$
- Pursued by Bear Cabernet Sauvignon / $$$$

QUILCEDA CREEK VINTNERS

One of the world's great Cabernet winemakers, Paul Golitzin is a scion of both Russian and wine aristocracy. His father, Alex, founded Quilceda Creek in 1979 in their Snohomish home with the guidance of Alex's uncle, the legendary André Tchelistcheff. With Paul as winemaker since 1992, this extraordinary small winery produces a densely layered flagship Cabernet, a Bordeaux-style blend and the somewhat more affordable CVR blend.

BOTTLES TO TRY
- Cabernet Sauvignon / $$$$
- CVR / $$$$

SPRING VALLEY VINEYARD

Spring Valley's silky, sophisticated Uriah, a Merlot-based blend, is a showstopper, but it's only one entry in a strong lineup of pricey reds that are typically massively scaled and super-ripe. The winery's founding Corkrum Derby family partnered with Ste. Michelle Wine Estates in the mid-2000s, but continue to run their operation and kept on talented winemaker Serge Laville (as well as the labels featuring Corkrum ancestors).

BOTTLES TO TRY
- Frederick / $$$
- Uriah / $$$

WOODWARD CANYON

Though its fame has grown in the years since Rick Small founded this benchmark Walla Walla winery in 1981, its output is still modest (about 15,000 cases). The winery's approach is old school, opting for tiny-lot fermentations and traditionally styled, balanced wines made to age gracefully. Small's signature wines are the astonishingly textured Cabernets—the best seem to vanish into collectors' cellars almost as soon as they're bottled—and superlative Chardonnays, but this fantastic winery also turns out a trove of other, more accessible pleasures.

BOTTLES TO TRY
○ Washington State Chardonnay / $$$
● Artist Series Cabernet Sauvignon / $$$

OTHER US STATES

REGIONS TO KNOW

MICHIGAN Savvy Midwestern sommeliers have known for years what the rest of the country is just finding out: Michigan's Rieslings are some of the country's best. Centered around two side-by-side peninsulas jutting into Lake Michigan—**Leelanau** and **Old Mission**—this is a small but energized wine region whose plantings of European-style grapes have doubled to more than 2,600 acres over the past 10 years. European-descended *Vitis vinifera* grapes now account for two-thirds of all vineyard plantings in the state.

NEW YORK Though long since overshadowed by West Coast competition, New York, with nearly 400 wineries and more than 1,400 vineyards, nearly all of them boutique-size and family-owned, vies with Washington for the rank of America's second-largest wine-producing state. The two major growing regions, **Long Island** and the **Finger Lakes,** are located at opposite ends of the state, but both produce high-quality wine. Long Island, with its **North Fork** and **Hamptons** AVAs, has several advantages as a winegrowing region, not the least of which are its built-in audience of Hamptons vacationers and many deep-pocketed winery owners. The area was a latecomer to commercial New York viticulture, but the past 40 years have seen the establishment of scores of high-quality vineyards. Long Island's relatively temperate climate and the mood of the times meant that its vintners concentrated on *vinifera* varieties, such as Cabernet Sauvignon, Chardonnay, Merlot and Cabernet Franc, from the start. Upstate, the historic Finger Lakes region is now gaining acclaim for sophisticated dry Rieslings, Gewürztraminers and Pinot Noirs and ice wine–style bottlings.

THE SOUTHWEST Thanks to cooler temperatures in its high deserts, **Arizona** has emerged as a fine-wine producer boasting 63 wineries and climbing. Full-bodied reds such as Syrah, Cabernet Sauvignon and Sangiovese are succeeding in high-altitude vineyards. **Texas** is the fifth-largest wine-producing state in the US, home to some 275 wineries. Many of the most prominent are in the sprawling Hill Country AVA north of San Antonio and west of Austin, with the Texas wine-tourism capital of Fredericksburg (with its own sub-AVA) at its epicenter. The semiarid High Plains, with vineyards at altitudes of about 3,000 to 4,000 feet, account for about 80 percent of the state's wine grapes, including a wealth of European-style *vinifera* vines. But Texas is also a stronghold of hybrid and native grapes, which are better suited to more strenuous growing conditions. **Colorado**'s rugged vineyards are some of the highest in the world. Bordeaux-inspired reds have become the state's signature pour, most of them produced in the Grand Valley AVA, while the West Elks region is gaining a solid reputation for cool-climate whites and reds. The best-known of **New Mexico**'s 40-plus wineries is Gruet, a family-owned producer of Champagne-style sparkling wine in North Albuquerque (see p. 288). Gruet's tasty and low-priced wines have made it an increasingly available alternative to the big-name sparkling brands.

VIRGINIA Diligent, close-to-the-soil homegrown winemakers, wealthy outside investors and a dose of Old World expertise are all coming together to produce notable wines from classic Bordeaux varieties (Cabernet Sauvignon, Merlot and Cabernet Franc), from Viognier and Chardonnay, and from America's often very fine native Norton grape. It doesn't hurt that the state has a number of high-profile figures, such as Dave Matthews, Donald Trump and AOL's Steve Case, raising consumer interest with their wine projects here. There are already plenty of well-made Virginia wines to discover, and the future looks bright indeed.

Producers/
Other US States

BARBOURSVILLE VINEYARDS / Virginia

Gianni Zonin, of the prominent Veneto wine-producing family, bought this 19th-century estate near Charlottesville and accomplished what onetime neighbor Thomas Jefferson could not: produce fine wine. Vintner Luca Paschina has helped make Barboursville a leader in Virginia's wine industry. Most notable among his galaxy of bottlings from French- and Italian-descended grapes is the high-end red Bordeaux blend, Octagon.

BOTTLES TO TRY

○ Viognier / $$
● Nebbiolo / $$$

BENDING BRANCH WINERY / Texas

Physician Robert Young and son-in-law John Rivenburgh sank their first vine roots into the ground near Comfort, in the Texas Hill Country, in 2009. Focused on vinifera grapes, the operation now has 20 acres, planted to 16 varieties. The emerging star has been Tannat, a tannic red with lively wild berry aromatics. The ambitions of this well-regarded winery are evident in its relatively stiff prices, which range up to $75 for the flagship Chloe Cuvée.

BOTTLES TO TRY

● Thinkers / $$
● Chloe Cuvée / $$$$

BLACK STAR FARMS / Michigan

Black Star Farms bills itself as "An Agricultural Destination," featuring two wineries, three tasting rooms, a distillery and an inn in the Grand Traverse Bay region. Winemaker Lee Lutes sources grapes for the 25,000-case operation from the estate partners' own vineyards, and from a group of growers who act as a sort of cooperative. Riesling and Chardonnay are its mainstays, but Black Star has scored successes with reds as well.

BOTTLES TO TRY

○ Arcturos Dry Riesling / $$
● Arcturos Pinot Noir / $$

DOS CABEZAS WINEWORKS / Arizona

Todd Bostock saw the potential of Arizona wine firsthand while
working at the original incarnation of Dos Cabezas, founded in
the 1990s by Arizona wine pioneer Al Buhl. In 2006, Bostock,
with his wife, Kelly, and his parents, bought the winery and
relocated it to Sonoita, near the family's 15-acre Pronghorn
Vineyard, planted at 4,800 feet to an evolving array of varieties.
The winery's spicy El Campo Tempranillo-Mourvèdre blend is
made from Pronghorn grapes. Dos Cabezas also sources quality
fruit from the Cimarron Vineyard near Willcox, Arizona, owned
by Oregon wine trailblazer Dick Erath.

BOTTLES TO TRY

- Toscano / $$
- El Campo / $$$

MICHAEL SHAPS WINEWORKS / Virginia

An alumnus of Virginia's Jefferson Vineyards and King Family
Vineyards, Michael Shaps founded his own winery in 2007
outside Charlottesville. The Burgundy-trained winemaker
(Shaps is also the owner-winemaker of Maison Shaps in Meursault, France) brings an Old World artisan-wine approach to the
small-lot wines he bottles under the Michael Shaps and Virginia
Wineworks labels. The Petit Verdot and Viognier bottlings have
been especially well received.

BOTTLES TO TRY

- ○ Michael Shaps Viognier / $$
- Petit Verdot / $$

RAVINES WINE CELLARS / New York

A former chief winemaker at the Finger Lakes' foundational Dr.
Konstantin Frank winery, Morten Hallgren also holds an
advanced degree in enology and viticulture from France's elite
Montpellier SupAgro school of agriculture. In 2000, Hallgren
founded Ravines on a slope above Keuka Lake, and built it into
one of the Finger Lakes' top wineries. Ravines has scored suc-
cesses with Bordeaux-style reds and Pinot Noir, but it's the two
dry Rieslings—including a single-vineyard bottling from Argetsinger Vineyard's old vines—that have most captivated its fans.

BOTTLES TO TRY

- ○ Argetsinger Vineyard Dry Riesling / $$
- ○ Dry Riesling / $$

Australia

Why do people assume that a wine-producing country nearly *12 times* the size of France can produce only one type of wine–affordable, juicy, jammy Shiraz? The truth is that Australian wine is as varied as the continent itself. There are the Clare Valley's laser-sharp dry Rieslings and the great Cabernets of Coonawarra; lemony Sémillons from the Hunter Valley and a growing number of impressive, spicy Pinot Noirs from cool-climate regions like the Mornington Peninsula and the Yarra Valley; and many more besides. Then there's Shiraz, the country's No. 1 grape: Australia's dozens of widely varying regions all produce distinctive versions of this wine, from the world-class to the humble. Now is the time to try them.

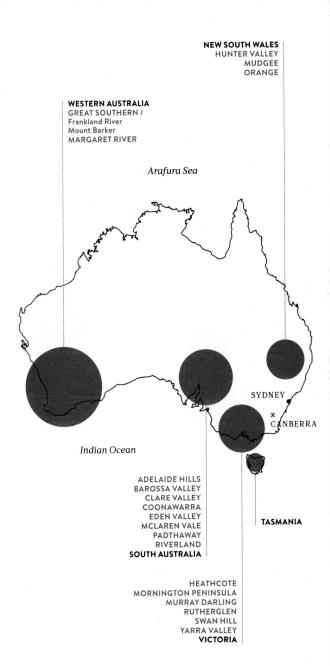

NEW SOUTH WALES
HUNTER VALLEY
MUDGEE
ORANGE

WESTERN AUSTRALIA
GREAT SOUTHERN /
Frankland River
Mount Barker
MARGARET RIVER

Arafura Sea

Indian Ocean

SYDNEY

x
CANBERRA

ADELAIDE HILLS
BAROSSA VALLEY
CLARE VALLEY
COONAWARRA
EDEN VALLEY
MCLAREN VALE
PADTHAWAY
RIVERLAND
SOUTH AUSTRALIA

TASMANIA

HEATHCOTE
MORNINGTON PENINSULA
MURRAY DARLING
RUTHERGLEN
SWAN HILL
YARRA VALLEY
VICTORIA

REGIONS TO KNOW

NEW SOUTH WALES Proximity to Sydney has made this state's **Hunter Valley** one of Australia's best-known wine zones, with its ageworthy Sémillon and juicy Shiraz, as well as Cabernet and Chardonnay. The **Mudgee** district produces richly fruited reds.

SOUTH AUSTRALIA This is the home of Australia's most acclaimed wine districts, among them the **Barossa Valley** and **McLaren Vale,** whose versions of the French Syrah grape (called Shiraz here) set an alternate world standard; and the cooler **Clare** and **Eden Valleys,** which make some of the country's finest Rieslings. **Coonawarra**'s iron-rich *terra rossa* soils yield stellar Cabernet Sauvignon. The cool **Adelaide Hills** produce crisp whites; so does **Padthaway** on the limestone coast (along with quality Shiraz). Much of Australia's affordable, easy-drinking wine comes from **Riverland,** its largest wine-producing region.

TASMANIA The island state of Tasmania is an up-and-coming source of vivacious, cool-climate Riesling, Chardonnay, Sauvignon Blanc and Pinot Noir, as well as sparkling wine.

VICTORIA This southeast state's most exciting wines are from coastal zones like the **Yarra Valley** and the **Mornington Peninsula,** which are turning out refined Pinot Noir and Chardonnay. Warm northwestern districts such as **Murray Darling** and **Swan Hill** have long yielded plump, fruity reds and whites. **Rutherglen** is a major source for high-quality fortified wine.

WESTERN AUSTRALIA On the continent's isolated western coast, the **Margaret River** subregion produces stunning Chardonnays and Cabernets, along with Sauvignon Blanc–Sémillon blends.

The much larger **Great Southern** area makes a vast amount of wine, the best of which display a crisp, focused liveliness. **Frankland River** and **Mount Barker,** both part of Great Southern, are known for racy, lime-inflected Rieslings and spicy Shiraz.

🍇 KEY GRAPES: WHITE

CHARDONNAY The country's dominant white grape is most easily found in multiregion blends made in a full-bodied, often lightly sweet style. But aside from these industrial bottlings, Australian Chardonnays are generally fresher and less sweet these days, and made with less oak. Look for examples from cooler regions, such as South Australia's Adelaide Hills, Victoria's Mornington Peninsula, Tasmania and especially Western Australia's Margaret River, which turns out minerally, complex bottlings that can rival fine Burgundies.

RIESLING Australia's second-most-important high-quality white grape, Riesling here produces refreshing, dry wines, some notable for sharp, Old World–style acidity. There are ageworthy offerings from Clare and Eden Valleys, Tasmania and Western Australia; Barossa Valley Rieslings are riper and rounder.

SAUVIGNON BLANC Increasingly popular Sauvignon Blanc grows best in Australia's coastal zones, where it retains its citrusy acidity. Styles range from grassy and tart to ripe and tropical. In Margaret River, it's commonly combined with Sémillon to create that region's Bordeaux-style blends.

SÉMILLON One reason wines made with this Bordeaux white grape are so underappreciated in the US is that Australians keep most of the best bottles for themselves. Those from the Hunter Valley are bright when they are young and take on honeyed, nutty flavors as they age. Examples from the Barossa are oak-aged and more opulent. Margaret River Sémillon hews to a style roughly between these extremes.

🍇 KEY GRAPES: RED

CABERNET SAUVIGNON Australia is a great source of well-priced, varietally true, straightforward Cabernets. But there are also a considerable number of complex, high-quality bottlings, the finest of which are capable of extensive aging. Warmer areas tend to bring out plush berry and chocolate, whereas cooler-climate places, such as the Margaret River region, produce more streamlined versions, with fresher, juicier flavors. Tiny Coonawarra yields some of the country's greatest Cabernets, which often show a eucalyptus note. Barossa Valley versions are bold, rich and ripe, and sometimes contain a touch of Shiraz.

GRENACHE & MOURVÈDRE (MATARO) These grapes—famous in France's Rhône Valley—thrive in many Australian regions. Grenache displays many of the same fruit-forward characteristics as Shiraz, while Mourvèdre shows a smokier, spicier personality. A number of vintners combine the two grapes with Shiraz in blends labeled *GSM* (Grenache, Shiraz, Mourvèdre).

MERLOT Most Merlot in Australia is used either in blends or to make soft, simple wines. Yet at the high end there are small quantities of firmer, herb-inflected Merlots coming out of coastal areas like the Yarra Valley and Margaret River, and denser, riper versions from warmer inland regions like the Barossa Valley.

PINOT NOIR Planted in several wine regions throughout Australia, Pinot Noir has succeeded mainly on the island of Tasmania and in Victoria's Yarra Valley and Mornington Peninsula, where cooler temperatures preserve the grape's delicate fruit flavors, soft tannins and vibrant aromatics.

SHIRAZ (SYRAH) The red grape behind Australia's signature wine, Shiraz is grown throughout the country, but famously reaches peaks in the Barossa Valley and McLaren Vale, with notable versions from the Hunter Valley and from several Victoria regions as well. Australian Shiraz is typically riper, more fruit-forward and more explosively flavorful than French Syrah, though it is hard to stereotype a wine grown by so many producers with differing ambitions. Shiraz is traditionally aged in American oak, which complements its jammy, ripe fruit.

WINE TERMINOLOGY
Most Australian wine labels specify producer, region, vintage and grape. Blends tend to be named with the dominant grape variety listed first.

Producers/ Australia

BINDI WINES

Michael Dhillon served a wandering wine apprenticeship in Tuscany and California before returning in 1988 to plant vines on his family's sprawling farm, some 1,600 feet up in the wind-swept Macedon Ranges near Gisborne. Bindi's estate wines—four Pinot Noirs and two Chardonnays (there's also a Shiraz, from purchased fruit)—owe their complexity and purity to Dhillon's hands-on farming and hands-off winemaking.

BOTTLES TO TRY

○ Kostas Rind Chardonnay / $$$$
● Original Vineyard Pinot Noir / $$$$

BROKENWOOD WINES

Brokenwood is known for its Cricket Pitch red and white wines, but to connoisseurs, winemaker Iain Riggs is the king of Hunter Valley Shiraz, thanks to his iconic Graveyard Vineyard Shiraz (he's arguably king of Sémillon, too, with his ILR Reserve). The winery is not small, and produces numerous worthy, multi-regional blends using grapes purchased from across New South Wales and beyond.

BOTTLES TO TRY

○ Cricket Pitch / $$
● Hunter Valley Shiraz / $$$

CAPE MENTELLE

David Hohnen, who would go on to found New Zealand's Cloudy Bay (see p. 243), established Cape Mentelle with his brothers in the then-undiscovered Margaret River region in 1970. Now owned by French luxury giant LVMH, the winery uses grapes from the gravelly soils of the Hohnens' original Wallcliffe vineyard to make some of its best wines, including the calling card Cabernet Sauvignon.

BOTTLES TO TRY

○ Sauvignon Blanc–Sémillon / $$
● Cabernet Sauvignon / $$$$

CHARLES CIMICKY

Charles Cimicky's very fine Barossa reds have flown somewhat under the radar in the US, which may explain why prices have remained generally reasonable. Cimicky grew up in the shadow of the vines—his father, Karl, a Czech immigrant to Australia, founded Karlsburg Wines in the early 1970s. Cimicky is determined to make his own mark by showcasing Barossa's native character—restricting irrigation, despite the region's dry conditions, and eschewing chemical fertilizers. His focus is on estate-grown reds, including limited amounts of full-flavored, boldly styled Shiraz, Grenache, Petite Sirah and blends.

BOTTLES TO TRY
- Trumps Shiraz / $$
- The Autograph Shiraz / $$$

CLARENDON HILLS

Roman Bratasiuk is obsessed with the signature imprinted on a wine by its environment. At any given moment, this *terroir*-driven winemaker may have 20 different cuvées from a single harvest aging in French oak in his cellar. With the assistance of his son Adam, Bratasiuk creates only single-variety wines, all from small plots of old vines in McLaren Vale's Clarendon Hills district. Top wines, like the benchmark Astralis Syrah, are famous for their hedonistic flavors (and astronomical cost).

BOTTLES TO TRY
- Blewitt Springs Grenache / $$$
- Brookman Merlot / $$$

CULLEN WINES

The vineyard that Kevin and Diana Cullen planted in the Margaret River region in 1971 helped put this western outpost on the map. Today their daughter Vanya cultivates the dry-farmed, 69-acre, mature-vine estate biodynamically. Cullen made its mark with refined versions of Bordeaux varieties, both red and white. Highly coveted bottlings like the Cabernet-based Diana Madeline and the Sauvignon Blanc–Sémillon Ephraim Clarke display Vanya's skill at fashioning intensely flavored wines at relatively moderate alcohol levels.

BOTTLES TO TRY
- ○ Ephraim Clarke / $$$
- ● Diana Madeline / $$$$

D'ARENBERG

Chester Osborn's teetotaler great-grandfather founded the McLaren Vale winery that Osborn now runs in time-honored fashion (grapes are basket-pressed and foot-trodden here). This vital and inventive producer fields more than 50 wines, many with offbeat names like the Broken Fishplate or the Wild Pixie. But there's a serious method behind the whimsy: The portfolio includes a slew of good values, and the top-tier bottlings, like the Ironstone Pressings GSM and the Dead Arm Shiraz, are among Australia's finest.

BOTTLES TO TRY

○ The Broken Fishplate Sauvignon Blanc / $$

● The Custodian Grenache / $$

GIACONDA

Established in the 1980s by Rick Kinzbrunner, and now run with his son Nathan, this Beechworth, Victoria, estate has world-class ambitions, formed, perhaps, by Kinzbrunner's 10-year, international apprenticeship in winemaking. Giaconda is one of Australia's most exclusive luxury producers: Its output is tiny and its prices are for the deep-pocketed only. Though the winery turns out well-regarded Pinot Noir, Shiraz and Rhône-style whites, its flagship is the Estate Vineyard Chardonnay—often compared to luscious, complex top Burgundies.

BOTTLES TO TRY

○ Estate Vineyard Chardonnay / $$$$

● Warner Vineyard Shiraz / $$$$

GIANT STEPS / INNOCENT BYSTANDER

Vintner and jazz enthusiast Phil Sexton, one of Australia's leading cool-climate specialists, moved to Victoria's Yarra Valley after selling his successful Margaret River winery, Devil's Lair. He named his flagship venture Giant Steps, after a John Coltrane album and as a reference to his leap from Western Australia to a cool part of the country's southeast coast. The Giant Steps label concentrates on mainstream varieties such as Pinot Noir and Chardonnay. Its affordable sister label, Innocent Bystander, offers terrific takes on Pinot Gris and Moscato.

BOTTLES TO TRY

○ Innocent Bystander Pinot Gris / $$

● Giant Steps Sexton Vineyard Pinot Noir / $$$

GLAETZER WINES

The Glaetzer family's roots in Barossa Valley viticulture date to the 1800s, but it took Colin Glaetzer (creator of the famous E&E Black Pepper Shiraz at Barossa Valley Estate) to establish an eponymous label for the family, in 1995. His son Ben took over winemaking in 2004 and is now a star in his own right, most famously for the full-throttle Amon-Ra Shiraz he bottles from very low-yielding, very old vines (up to 130 years old) in the Barossa's top Ebenezer subdistrict. Glaetzer bottles three other small-production reds, all paragons of Barossa's brawny style.

BOTTLES TO TRY
- Bishop Shiraz / $$$
- Amon-Ra Shiraz / $$$$

GROSSET WINES

This is the winery that, perhaps more than any other, brought Australian Riesling international attention. Jeffrey Grosset apprenticed under legendary Riesling pioneer John Vickery before starting his own estate in 1981, with high-altitude vineyards planted in the Clare Valley. The headliner among Grosset's dry, racy, full-flavored Rieslings is the famous Polish Hill bottling, with the Springvale a close second. The German-style, off-dry Alea was added in 2012. Grosset's non-Riesling offerings, such as the Gaia Bordeaux-style blend, are notable, too.

BOTTLES TO TRY
- ○ Polish Hill Riesling / $$$
- Gaia / $$$$

HENSCHKE

One of the world's great wineries, this 148-year-old Eden Valley operation is still family-run: Fifth-generation owner-winemaker Stephen Henschke shares duties with his viticulturist wife, Prue. Although best known for its monumental, and famously expensive, Hill of Grace Shiraz, Henschke offers many wines that are less stratospherically priced, yet still exceptionally well made. Henry's Seven is a supple, rich, Rhône-inspired red blend; Keyneton Euphonium, a Shiraz-based blend, provides an accessible taste of the winery's polished, powerful style.

BOTTLES TO TRY
- Henry's Seven / $$$
- Keyneton Euphonium / $$$

JACOB'S CREEK

Starting with a single red blend in 1976, Barossa Valley's Jacob's Creek went on to become Australia's first international megabrand. It's now gone international in a different vein, launching the Two Lands label, a collaboration between Napa Valley's esteemed Ehren Jordan (see Failla, p. 180) and Jacob's Creek vintner Bernard Hickin. Tapping Jacob's Creek's wealth of vineyards, the Two Lands wines, priced under $15, join the winery's ubiquitous entry-level bottlings, made with grapes sourced from across southeast Australia, and its single-region reserve tier in providing plenty of affordable drinking pleasure.

BOTTLES TO TRY

○ Reserve Chardonnay / $

● Two Lands Cabernet Sauvignon / $

JIM BARRY WINES

This family-owned Clare Valley producer is a go-to name for all three of the region's signature varieties: Riesling, Shiraz and Cabernet Sauvignon. The late Jim Barry helped pioneer modern Clare Valley winemaking in the 1960s, planting what are now some of the region's best-known vineyards. Among these is the Armagh Vineyard, source of an acclaimed Shiraz that's monumentally full-bodied (and pricey). Beautifully crafted Rieslings, three Cabernets and the stunning Lodge Hill Shiraz are other highlights of the generally affordably priced lineup.

BOTTLES TO TRY

○ The Lodge Hill Riesling / $$

● The Cover Drive Cabernet Sauvignon / $$

JOHN DUVAL WINES

After 29 years with giant Penfolds (see p. 233), star winemaker John Duval left in 2002 to pursue his own projects. Instead of the sprawling portfolio he oversaw at Penfolds, Duval focuses on just five limited-production cuvées at his boutique Barossa winery: two Shirazes (Entity and the reserve, Eligo), the Annexus Grenache and two Plexus Rhône-style blends (a white and a red). The wines' rich, concentrated flavors are true to Barossa type, but their finesse separates them from their supersized peers.

BOTTLES TO TRY

○ Plexus MRV / $$$

● Entity Shiraz / $$$

KAY BROTHERS

Founded by brothers Herbert and Frederick Kay in 1890 and still owned by the family, this McLaren Vale winery showcases the rich tradition of early Australian winemaking with its not-inexpensive lineup of full-bodied, fruit-driven reds. The broodingly dark Block 6 Shiraz comes from the property's original, nearly 125-year-old vines, and is made, like all Kay Brothers reds, the old-fashioned way, with basket-pressing, the original open-top fermentors and very little filtration.

BOTTLES TO TRY

- ● Basket Pressed Shiraz / $$$
- ● Cuthbert Cabernet Sauvignon / $$$

KILIKANOON

This Clare Valley–based winery built a formidable reputation on the steely, mineral-rich Rieslings and polished reds made by its founder, Kevin Mitchell. Kilikanoon got its start in 1997, when Mitchell purchased the property, including vineyards planted by his father, Mort, in the 1960s. Among the midsize winery's most acclaimed bottlings are the Mort's Block Riesling and powerhouse Shirazes from the Clare Valley, Barossa Valley and McLaren Vale. Also worth looking for is Kilikanoon's affordable Killerman's Run label.

BOTTLES TO TRY

- ○ Mort's Block Riesling / $$
- ● Killerman's Run Shiraz / $$

LEEUWIN ESTATE

In 1972, Robert Mondavi zeroed in on a cattle ranch in the remote Margaret River region of Western Australia and concluded that it could produce world-class wines. His analysis proved astute: On his advice, Leeuwin Estate's founders Denis and Tricia Horgan planted vines on their land in 1974 and went on to become one of Australia's most revered Chardonnay producers. The balanced but muscled-up Burgundian complexity of Leeuwin's Art Series cuvées sets the standard for Margaret River; the Siblings bottlings can be impressively elegant, and are available at decidedly more wallet-friendly prices.

BOTTLES TO TRY

- ○ Art Series Chardonnay / $$$$
- ● Siblings Shiraz / $$

MAC FORBES

Former Mount Mary winemaker Mac Forbes has risen to fame with his own Yarra Valley winery, thanks to his insistence on throttling back the richness of Australian Pinots, Chardonnays and Rieslings in favor of Burgundian finesse. Influenced by his time with Portugal's new-wave wine guru Dirk Niepoort (see p. 132), Forbes practices winemaking that is non-interventionist and expressive of grape, vintage and a range of specific sites, with memorable names like Gruyere and Woori Yallock.

BOTTLES TO TRY
○ Chardonnay / $$$
● Pinot Noir / $$$

MOSS WOOD

This is one of the handful of pioneering wineries that set the stage for Margaret River's emergence as a high-quality wine region. Established in 1969 by Bill Pannell in the northern Wilyabrup subregion, Moss Wood soon earned a reputation for refined medium- to full-bodied Cabernets. The estate's wine-maker since 1979, and its full owner, with his wife, Clare, since 1985, Keith Mugford has expanded the winery's esteemed portfolio, bringing Sauvignon Blanc into the mix with the addition of the nearby Ribbon Vale Vineyard in 2000.

BOTTLES TO TRY
○ Ribbon Vale Sauvignon Blanc–Sémillon / $$
● Cabernet Sauvignon / $$$$

PENFOLDS

Few wineries in the world succeed as brilliantly as Penfolds in turning out both large-production everyday bottlings and rarefied cuvées built for cellaring. The super-luxury-priced, Shiraz-based Grange has established itself since the 1950s as Australia's most famous wine, with an international cult following. At the same time, Penfolds's affordable wines, like the inexpensive Koonunga Hill Shiraz-Cabernet, are reliable overachievers. That emphasis on quality comes from an illustrious history (Penfolds has been in the Barossa since 1844) and the talent of chief winemaker Peter Gago.

BOTTLES TO TRY
● Koonunga Hill Shiraz-Cabernet / $
● Bin 138 Grenache-Shiraz-Mourvèdre / $$$

ROBERT OATLEY VINEYARDS

Sailor and entrepreneur Bob Oatley made his first fortune in coffee trading before founding the wildly successful Rosemount Estate brand in the late 1960s. After selling Rosemount in 2001, Oatley doubled down with his son Sandy on his namesake wine company, now a mini empire with a multiplicity of brands, such as Montrose, Wild Oats and Four in Hand. The three well-priced Robert Oatley brands concentrate on regional specialties, among them three silky, bright Margaret River Chardonnays and two Pinot Noirs from Victoria's Mornington Peninsula.

BOTTLES TO TRY

○ Robert Oatley "Signature Series" Chardonnay / $$
● Wild Oats Shiraz / $

SHAW & SMITH

A member of Australia's Hill-Smith wine dynasty (see Yalumba, p. 237) and the first Australian to achieve the Master of Wine qualification, Michael Hill Smith founded this Adelaide Hills label with his vintner cousin Martin Shaw in 1989. The duo quickly established a reputation for superb Sauvignon Blanc. Their rendition of that variety has become an Adelaide Hills benchmark, as has their M3 Chardonnay. But it's Shaw & Smith's coolly styled Shiraz and Pinot Noir that are revelatory, especially for those who equate Australia with jammy fruit bombs.

BOTTLES TO TRY

○ Sauvignon Blanc / $$
● Shiraz / $$$

THE STANDISH WINE COMPANY

Star winemaker Dan Standish's five tiny-production, old-vine Barossa Shirazes attract a cultish following. The headliners are the Standish Shiraz and the Shiraz-Viognier blend, The Relic, both sourced from his parents' 100-year-old, dry-farmed, organic vineyard in the Vine Vale subdistrict. The small, super-concentrated grapes from these elderly vines yield intense, complex wines with a kaleidoscopic mix of floral, mineral, fruit and savory flavors. Standish's minimalist approach in the winery lets the power and purity of the vineyard sources shine through.

BOTTLES TO TRY

● The Relic / $$$$
● The Standish Shiraz / $$$$

TAHBILK

An iconic, pagoda-like white lookout tower greets visitors to this historic Central Victoria winery, founded in 1860 and owned by the Purbrick family since 1925. Tahbilk is famous for its rare, very-old-vine wines, like the 1927 Vines Marsanne and 1860 Vines Shiraz. Fortunately, the winery also turns out a range of compelling wines in greater abundance, all from estate vineyards in the lush Nagambie Lakes subregion. The basic Marsanne—Tahbilk claims to have the world's largest plantings of the Rhône white grape—is both affordable and ageworthy, while its reds are beautifully refined.

BOTTLES TO TRY

○ Marsanne / $

● Cabernet Sauvignon / $$

TORBRECK

Legendary winemaker David Powell founded his celebrated Barossa Valley winery in 1994, naming it for the Scottish forest where he once worked as a lumberjack. Chief winemaker Craig Isbel has overseen production of Torbreck's brooding, phenomenally layered Barossa reds, such as the famous RunRig Shiraz-Viognier, since 2006; he is also providing continuity as the winery, owned since 2008 by US businessman Peter Kight, enters a new era without its founder, who departed in 2013.

BOTTLES TO TRY

● Woodcutter's Shiraz / $$

● RunRig / $$$$

TWO HANDS WINES

The "two hands" behind this high-end, Barossa-based *négociant* label are its founders, Michael Twelftree and Richard Mintz. The label has become known for its showy, polished wines—chiefly Shiraz, Grenache and Cabernet, with a few oddballs like Moscato—made from grapes sourced from top vineyards in South Australia and Victoria. The goofily named Picture Series wines are the most affordable; Garden Series and Single Vineyard bottlings are a step up in price. The expensive Flagship series cuvées are named after Greek mythological figures.

BOTTLES TO TRY

● Sexy Beast Cabernet Sauvignon / $$$

● Aerope Grenache / $$$$

TYRRELL'S WINES

English immigrant Edward Tyrrell founded this trailblazing Hunter Valley winery more than 150 years ago, and his descendants still own and run it. Now led by fourth-generation Bruce Tyrrell (his son Chris is assistant winemaker), this is a big operation with many labels, grape varieties, styles and price points. The Winemaker's Selection and Sacred Sites ranges are at the top end; the basic, widely available Old Winery tier provides high-value, solid drinking. (The bargain-priced Long Flat brand most familiar to US drinkers has been sold off.)

BOTTLES TO TRY

○ Vat 1 Hunter Sémillon / $$$
● Old Winery Shiraz / $

VASSE FELIX

This is the foundational Margaret River wine estate. Perth cardiologist Tom Cullity planted the original Vasse Felix vineyard, the region's first, in 1967, and released the first Margaret River wines in 1972. Since coming on board in 2006, winemaker Virginia Willcock has dialed back the power of Vasse Felix wines to gain brighter, more minerally flavors. Today the estate is producing its best bottles yet: three tiers of top-notch Chardonnay and Cabernet Sauvignon, plus a Shiraz and red and white blends. Its signature Chardonnay is crisp yet creamy; the Cabernet, generous and herb-edged.

BOTTLES TO TRY

○ Chardonnay / $$
● Cabernet Sauvignon / $$$

WYNNS COONAWARRA ESTATE

Wynns has floated like a cork above the financial vicissitudes of its parent company (like Penfolds, it is now part of the huge Treasury Wine Estates portfolio spun off by Foster's Group in 2011). Its stability is due in part to the continuing presence of talented winemaker Sue Hodder and to the wealth of vineyard holdings at her disposal, including those planted in the famous *terra rossa* ("red earth") soils of Coonawarra. A prime beneficiary is the estate's Black Label Cabernet Sauvignon, rich and redolent of crushed dark fruit but with a firm underlying structure.

BOTTLE TO TRY

● Black Label Cabernet Sauvignon / $$$

BEST VALUE PRODUCERS / AUSTRALIA
1. D'ARENBERG **2.** INNOCENT BYSTANDER **3.** JACOB'S CREEK
4. PENFOLDS **5.** ROBERT OATLEY VINEYARDS

YALUMBA

At 167 years of age, Barossa-based Yalumba is as old as the Australian wine industry itself and is still owned by the Hill-Smith family, descendants of founder Samuel Smith. Although Shiraz and Cabernet remain the foundation of Yalumba's lineup, chief winemaker Louisa Rose has been acclaimed for her work with Viognier. Portfolio highlights include the benchmark Octavius Shiraz; The Signature, a powerful Cabernet-Shiraz blend that competes with cult bottlings twice its price; and the affordable Y Series Viognier, which is reliably silky, aromatic and succulent. Not to be overlooked: Yalumba's barrel-aged ports.

BOTTLES TO TRY
○ **Eden Valley Viognier** / $$
● **Old Bush Vine Grenache** / $$

YANGARRA ESTATE VINEYARD

California's Jackson Family Wines acquired this McLaren Vale estate in 2001 and brought in Peter Fraser as winemaker. Prizing finesse over power, Fraser crafts vibrant, well-balanced wines from a biodynamically farmed, 247-acre estate vineyard, planted chiefly to Rhône varieties. The property includes a prized plot of nearly 70-year-old Grenache vines that yield Yangarra's consistently great High Sands bottling. The basic cuvées, like the herb-inflected Shiraz, are also worthy buys, with a subtlety and moderated weight that make them especially food-friendly.

BOTTLES TO TRY
○ **Roussanne** / $$
● **GSM** / $$

New Zealand

This island country essentially redefined people's idea of Sauvignon Blanc back in the 1980s. Since then, the grape has become New Zealand's signature variety, producing over 70 percent of the country's wine. It's the engine that powers New Zealand's entire wine business–but an unlooked-for consequence is that wine buyers often don't realize the scope and ambition of the country's wineries. The South Island's sea-chilled breezes, lush green valleys and mostly long, cool summers make it a great source for Pinot Noir, Riesling and Chardonnay; the North Island also produces good Pinot, as well as impressive Syrahs and Cabernets. If you love New Zealand Sauvignon Blanc, check out what else this extraordinary wine region has to offer.

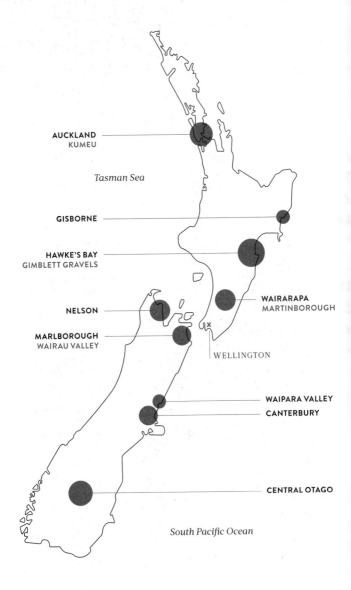

AUCKLAND
KUMEU

Tasman Sea

GISBORNE

HAWKE'S BAY
GIMBLETT GRAVELS

NELSON

MARLBOROUGH
WAIRAU VALLEY

WAIRARAPA
MARTINBOROUGH

WELLINGTON

WAIPARA VALLEY
CANTERBURY

CENTRAL OTAGO

South Pacific Ocean

REGIONS TO KNOW

CENTRAL OTAGO New Zealand's southernmost and highest vineyards provide a unique wine-growing *terroir*. In a rain-soaked country, this sheltered inland region's hot summers, cold winters and dry autumns make it perfect for growing the voluptuous Pinot Noir it's known for. Central Otago Pinot is typically deeper in color and richer than classic Burgundy versions.

GISBORNE A white-wine zone on the North Island's east coast, Gisborne produces mostly creamy Chardonnay and a smattering of Pinot Gris, Gewürztraminer, Viognier and Sauvignon Blanc.

HAWKE'S BAY One of the few spots warm enough to properly ripen heat-loving red grapes, the North Island's Hawke's Bay is is the go-to region for Merlot, Cabernet Sauvignon and Syrah, with the finest examples coming from **Gimblett Gravels**.

MARLBOROUGH Located on the South Island's northeast coast, Marlborough is New Zealand's most important wine region, with almost 90 percent of the country's Sauvignon Blanc vineyards, nearly half of its Pinot Noir and a third of its Chardonnay. Most of Marlborough's vineyards are in the **Wairau Valley**.

WAIPARA VALLEY & CANTERBURY These neighboring districts on the South Island both specialize in Pinot Noir. Canterbury's main white is Chardonnay, while Waipara grows aromatic varieties like Riesling, Sauvignon Blanc and Pinot Gris.

WAIRARAPA The region whose **Martinborough** subzone helped stake New Zealand's claim to Pinot Noir greatness also turns out noteworthy Chardonnay and Pinot Gris.

❧ KEY GRAPES: WHITE

CHARDONNAY A trend toward less oak aging has improved New Zealand Chardonnays, with their apple and citrus notes. Riper, oaked versions now share shelf space with leaner, crisper styles.

GEWÜRZTRAMINER, PINOT GRIS & RIESLING Increasingly fashionable alternatives to the ubiquitous Sauvignon Blanc and Chardonnay, these Alsace grapes thrive in Waipara Valley and Gisborne. New Zealand Rieslings tend to be made in an off-dry—i.e., lightly sweet—style, balanced by zesty acidity. Most of the country's Pinot Gris comes from the South Island, whose bottlings are leaner than those from North Island zones.

SAUVIGNON BLANC Few countries are as identified with a single grape as New Zealand is with its showy, often exotic Sauvignon Blancs. While the traditional style here is zingy and unoaked, with herb, lime and grapefruit notes, warmer vintages and a move toward fruitier wines have resulted in a wider array of styles. North Island Sauvignon Blancs tend to be riper and fruitier than those from Marlborough, the most prolific region for the grape.

❧ KEY GRAPES: RED

CABERNET SAUVIGNON & MERLOT One of the few spots in New Zealand warm enough for these red grapes is Hawke's Bay, on the North Island. Look for examples from its Gimblett Gravels subregion, where vintners make fine Bordeaux-style blends.

PINOT NOIR Vibrant acidity is a hallmark of New Zealand's most popular red. Cool regions like Marlborough offer tangy, berry-flavored versions, whereas Central Otago yields richer examples. Martinborough produces the North Island's best Pinots.

SYRAH Most of New Zealand is too cold for Syrah, but examples from Hawke's Bay's Gimblett Gravels subzone can be excellent, with seductive floral, spice and black-fruit notes.

WINE TERMINOLOGY

New Zealand labels generally list region, grape, vintage and, in some cases, vineyard name. The term *reserve* may be used to designate higher-quality wines but has no legal meaning.

Producers/
New Zealand

ASTROLABE WINES

In an odd accident, 4,000 cases of Astrolabe's Sauvignon Blanc were lost in a 2011 shipwreck on New Zealand's Astrolabe reef. The incident focused international attention on the label, co-founded by winemaker Simon Waghorn. His vibrant, layered, cool-climate wines took it from there. The overachieving Province wines are 100 percent single-grape bottlings, but sourced from multiple vineyards around the Marlborough region.

BOTTLES TO TRY

○ **Province Sauvignon Blanc** / $$
● **Province Pinot Noir** / $$

BRANCOTT ESTATE

With its vast vineyard holdings on the South Island and beyond, Pernod Ricard–owned Brancott has a geographical reach—and a sales volume—that help make it one of New Zealand's most successful producers. Sauvignon Blanc is the brand's signature wine, but Brancott's solid lineup of accessible bottlings also includes a cross section of popular varietals at multiple price tiers, including some notable Pinot Noirs.

BOTTLES TO TRY

○ **Sauvignon Blanc** / $
● **Letter Series T Pinot Noir** / $$

CLOS HENRI VINEYARD

Henri Bourgeois founded his well-known domaine in Sancerre in the 1950s; a desire for new frontiers led his sons Rémi and Jean-Marie to venture (way) out. They bought more than 240 acres in Marlborough in 2000, and began releasing Sauvignon Blancs and Pinot Noirs in 2003. Clos Henri's Sauvignon Blanc eschews some of the local flamboyance in favor of a more classical dry and pure Loire style.

BOTTLES TO TRY

○ **Sauvignon Blanc** / $$
● **Petit Clos Pinot Noir** / $$

CLOUDY BAY

It's rare that a single wine becomes so iconic that it defines both a style and a country, but that's exactly what Cloudy Bay's Marlborough Sauvignon Blanc did in the 1980s and '90s. Crisp, peppery and intense, it gave New Zealand a near-instant wine identity. Tim Heath, the LVMH-owned winery's senior winemaker since 2012, has toned down Cloudy Bay's herbaceousness in recent vintages. He barrel-ferments the famously full-bodied Te Koko to provide an alternative to the house style.

BOTTLES TO TRY

○ Te Koko Sauvignon Blanc / $$$

● Pinot Noir / $$$

CRAGGY RANGE

No winery better illustrates New Zealand's potential for world-class wines beyond Sauvignon Blanc than this Hawke's Bay estate. Founded by Australian-American magnate Terry Peabody with acclaimed Kiwi wine guru Steve Smith (after 17 years at the helm, Smith relinquished his management role in 2015 to pursue other projects), Craggy Range produces one of New Zealand's greatest Syrahs, Le Sol, as well as some of its best examples of Chardonnay, Pinot Noir and Bordeaux-inspired reds. And, of course, chief winemaker Matt Stafford also turns out wonderful Sauvignon Blanc.

BOTTLES TO TRY

○ Te Muna Road Vineyard Sauvignon Blanc / $$

● Le Sol Syrah / $$$$

DOG POINT VINEYARDS

Dog Point debuted in 2002 after much anticipation, thanks to the fame of winemaker James Healy and viticulturist Ivan Sutherland, two Cloudy Bay alumni (see above). Making the most of the long, mellow growing season in Marlborough's Wairau Plains, they produce racy but concentrated Sauvignon Blancs, Chardonnays and Pinot Noirs that have found international favor. The calling card is the Section 94 Sauvignon Blanc, which emerges from 18 months in oak with its vibrancy intact, but the whole range is worthy of attention.

BOTTLES TO TRY

○ Sauvignon Blanc / $$

● Pinot Noir / $$$

FELTON ROAD

Felton Road's minerally, dark-fruited, much-sought-after Pinot Noirs have become standard-bearers for the New Zealand version of this grape. Complex and impeccably—biodynamically—made, they're definitive expressions of Central Otago *terroir*, with their effortless balance of lush New World fruit and savory strength. No other place produces Pinot Noir exactly like this. In fact, no two parcels on the Felton Road estate yield exactly the same wine, either. That's why winemaker Blair Walter bottles his best plots, like the famed Block 3 and Block 5 Pinots, separately.

BOTTLES TO TRY

○ **Bannockburn Riesling** / $$$
● **Block 5 Pinot Noir** / $$$$

GREYWACKE

To Sauvignon Blanc fanatics, Kevin Judd's name is as well known as that of Cloudy Bay, the Marlborough winery he helped make famous. Judd left Cloudy Bay to create this boutique label in 2009. (Pronounced "gray-wacky," it's named for the river stones found in the soils of Judd's first vineyard). Made at the Dog Point winery (see p. 243), Judd's Greywacke wines include Pinot Noir and small lots of Chardonnay, Riesling, Pinot Gris and Gewürztraminer. But it's the creamy, barrel-fermented, let-it-rip Wild Sauvignon that really sets fans' hearts beating.

BOTTLES TO TRY

○ **Wild Sauvignon** / $$
● **Pinot Noir** / $$$

KIM CRAWFORD WINES

Kim Crawford launched this brand in 1996 as a "virtual" winery: He crushed Marlborough grapes in a rented facility while his wife, Erica, managed marketing out of their Auckland cottage. Acquired first by Canada's Vincor in 2003, then by Constellation Brands in 2006, the winery has grown exponentially. Under winemaker Anthony Walkenhorst, it continues to turn out the unoaked Chardonnay that put it on the map. Other offerings include the US's top-selling New Zealand Sauvignon Blanc, a ripe, bright and zesty wine that is quintessential Marlborough.

BOTTLES TO TRY

○ **Sauvignon Blanc** / $
○ **Unoaked Chardonnay** / $

KUMEU RIVER

The Brajkovich brothers—Milan, Paul and winemaker Michael—run this much-lauded Chardonnay specialist. Their Croatian-immigrant grandfather Mick founded what would become known as San Marino Vineyards in 1944; the name was changed to Kumeu River in 1986. Poised between the Pacific Ocean and the Tasman Sea north of Auckland, the vineyards are cool, cloud-covered and dry-farmed. The Chardonnays, like the famed Maté's Vineyard bottling, benefit from handpicked grapes, barrel fermentation and *sur lie* aging.

BOTTLES TO TRY
○ Pinot Gris / $$
○ Maté's Vineyard Chardonnay / $$$

MAHI WINES

Globetrotting wine consultant Brian Bicknell founded Mahi (Maori for "work" or "craft") with his wife, Nicola, in 2001, finally buying his own winery in Marlborough in 2006. The focus is on single-vineyard wines from his own organic plots and on partnerships with top growers. Bicknell puts his flagship Sauvignon Blancs, Ballot Block and Boundary Farm, through Burgundy-like paces, including partially fermenting them in French barrels and stirring the lees to create complexity and a silky palate texture. Mahi's Pinot Noirs are elegant and refined.

BOTTLES TO TRY
○ Ballot Block Sauvignon Blanc / $$
● Marlborough Pinot Noir / $$

NAUTILUS ESTATE

The Hill-Smith family, owners of Australia's venerable Yalumba winery (see p. 237), also own this Wairau Valley estate, the first in New Zealand to build a facility customized entirely to Pinot Noir. Thanks to the pains Nautilus takes with its flagship grape (e.g., using only handpicked fruit and aging in French oak), its estate Pinot Noir regularly ranks among Marlborough's best. Just one other Nautilus bottling is widely available in the US: the tangy, grapefruit-scented Sauvignon Blanc. For wines like the rare Nautilus Grüner Veltliner, you'll have to go to the source.

BOTTLES TO TRY
○ Sauvignon Blanc / $$
● Pinot Noir / $$

PALLISER ESTATE

Founded in 1984, Palliser was one of the pioneering wineries in what is now the Pinot Noir hotbed of Martinborough. Although Pinot Noir has been a focus for the winery from the start, winemaker Allan Johnson also crafts outstanding Sauvignon Blancs from Palliser's 227 ISO- and CEMARS-certified organic acres on the Martinborough Terrace, along with a beautiful Riesling and *méthode traditionnelle* sparkler. Palliser wines are very well priced in the US given their quality; the second-label Pencarrow bottlings are an even better buy, when you can find them.

BOTTLES TO TRY

○ Sauvignon Blanc / $$
● Pinot Noir / $$

PEGASUS BAY

Neurologist and wine writer Ivan Donaldson moonlighted as a *garagiste* winemaker for years until he and his wife, Christine, founded Pegasus Bay in the Waipara Valley in 1985. Their boutique winery quickly became one of New Zealand's finest estates. Today their son Matthew and his wife, Lynnette Hudson, make seductive Pinot Noirs, as well as elegant Rieslings and a fine Sauvignon Blanc–Sémillon blend. Their winemaking—including native-yeast fermentations and bottling without filtration—delivers the full range of their vineyards' flavors.

BOTTLES TO TRY

○ Sauvignon-Sémillon / $$
● Pinot Noir / $$$

PYRAMID VALLEY VINEYARDS

What causes a new boutique winery in a remote location to be suddenly taken up by wine critics around the world? Burgundy-trained winemaker Mike Weersing and his wife, Claudia, moved to North Canterbury in 2000 because they felt the clay-limestone soils were perfect for Pinot Noir and Chardonnay, and their unique talents have done the rest. Unswerving true believers in all things natural and biodynamic, the Weersings make wines like the Angel Flower Pinot Noir, whose linger-awhile, layered complexity comes from the vine, not the winery.

BOTTLES TO TRY

○ Moteo Ridge Vineyard Chenin Blanc / $$
● Angel Flower Pinot Noir / $$$$

RIPPON

Situated on the picturesque shores of Otago's Lake Wanaka, Rippon produces graceful, richly textured wines, chiefly Pinot Noir. Founded by Lois and the late Rolfe Mills, the winery is now in the hands of son Nick, who honed his winemaking skills in Burgundy before bringing that region's traditionalist techniques back home. The operation remains small, and Nick does things the hard way, applying hands-on biodynamic farming techniques to his nonirrigated, mostly ungrafted vines.

BOTTLES TO TRY

○ **Mature Vine Riesling / $$$**

● **Mature Vine Pinot Noir / $$$$**

SPY VALLEY WINES

Spy Valley grows Sauvignon Blanc (few Marlborough wineries don't), and its version is perfectly delicious. But this substantially sized winery also offers a wealth of worthy alternatives from its 400 sustainably farmed acres, including bright, richly styled Chardonnays, lithe Pinot Noirs and aromatic whites such as Gewürztraminer, Pinot Gris and Riesling. The three tiers—Satellite, Spy Valley and Envoy—are reasonably priced for their quality. Grapes for the Envoy series are cherry-picked from small, single plots on the property. Owners Bryan and Jan Johnson named the winery for a nearby government spy station.

BOTTLES TO TRY

○ **Sauvignon Blanc / $$**

● **Pinot Noir / $$**

VILLA MARIA

A son of Croatian immigrants, George Fistonich sold his car to help fund Villa Maria's first vintage in 1962. Now a knight, Sir George runs one of the country's largest wine companies, comprising five separate wineries on the North and South Islands: Vidal, Esk Valley, Thornbury, Te Awa and Villa Maria (the best-known brand, especially in the US). Villa Maria turns out four tiers, with offerings that range from reliable, everyday wines to often outstanding cuvées produced from a range of grapes, including some of the country's most notable Syrahs.

BOTTLES TO TRY

○ **Wairau Valley Sauvignon Blanc Reserve / $$$**

● **Cellar Selection Syrah / $$**

Argentina

Argentineans are among the most beef-loving people in the world, eating over 120 pounds per person per year. Given that, it's no surprise that the country's most famous grape variety is Malbec, whose rich blackberry fruit and peppery spice notes go excellently with a rare steak. But consider how much more this South American country has to offer: Its top Chardonnays and Cabernets have the polish and poise to compete internationally, while floral-edged Torrontés is a largely undiscovered gem. Meanwhile, the remote Patagonian wilderness has become the most unlikely source of impressive Pinot Noir—yet another good reason to start exploring the world of Argentinean wine.

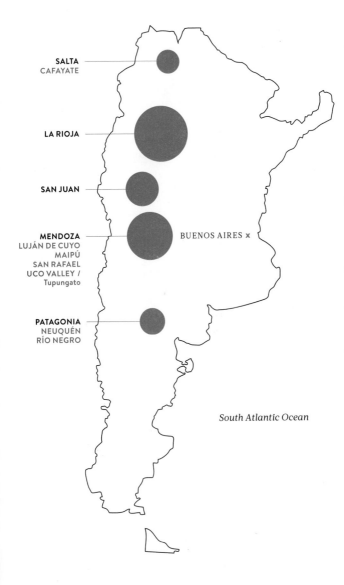

SALTA
CAFAYATE

LA RIOJA

SAN JUAN

MENDOZA
LUJÁN DE CUYO
MAIPÚ
SAN RAFAEL
UCO VALLEY /
Tupungato

BUENOS AIRES x

PATAGONIA
NEUQUÉN
RÍO NEGRO

South Atlantic Ocean

REGIONS TO KNOW

LA RIOJA & SAN JUAN These traditional wine regions have been moving gradually from bulk production to high-quality wine-making, especially in San Juan's cooler corners, which are acquiring a reputation for Syrah.

MENDOZA Three-quarters of Argentina's wine production comes from this vast west-central region in the foothills of the Andes. Its near-desert climate makes for a long, dry growing season, while snowmelt rivers and elaborate irrigation systems provide the necessary water. **Maipú, Luján de Cuyo** and **San Rafael** are the oldest and best-known growing regions. Newer, higher-altitude subregions such as the **Uco Valley** and its **Tupungato** subzone, which lie at elevations of more than 3,200 feet, are gaining fame for their refined, cooler-climate reds and whites.

PATAGONIA Ambitious winemakers are learning how to harness this southernmost region's assets and cope with its challenges. Patagonia is becoming known for impressive and graceful Pinot Noir, as well as standbys like Malbec.

SALTA This mountainous province in northwestern Argentina boasts some of the world's highest-altitude vineyards. Its **Cafayate** district is a source of refreshing whites, such as Torrontés.

🍇 KEY GRAPES: WHITE

CHARDONNAY Argentinean Chardonnay ranges in style from crisp, light-bodied and lightly oaked to rich, full-bodied and creamy. Top wines have grown increasingly sophisticated. Many of the finest examples come from high-altitude vines and can be impressive bargains.

PINOT GRIS (PINOT GRIGIO), SÉMILLON & VIOGNIER Small amounts of these aromatic whites are finding a foothold in Argentina's cooler regions.

SAUVIGNON BLANC This crisp variety ripens easily in Argentina's sunny climate, yielding medium-bodied, melony whites. The best versions come from cooler climates, such as the Uco Valley and other high-altitude zones.

TORRONTÉS The country's signature white grape, Torrontés makes distinctive, refreshing wines that showcase crisp citrus flavors and exuberant floral aromas. For the best examples, look to Salta, a high-altitude region that is ideally suited to the grape.

KEY GRAPES: RED

BONARDA Not related to the Italian grape of the same name, Bonarda (a.k.a. Douce Noir and Charbono) was Argentina's most widely planted wine grape before Malbec's resurgence. It has typically been made into deeply colored, everyday wines but is now being taken more seriously by top winemakers. Polished single-variety bottlings are joining rustic, cherry-inflected blends.

CABERNET SAUVIGNON Look for Cabernets from Mendoza, where sunny, arid days and cool nights result in wines packed with powerful cassis and a hint of bell pepper.

MALBEC An also-ran blending grape in Bordeaux (its major Old World claim to fame is in Cahors in southwestern France; see p. 61), Malbec was cultivated for a century in Argentina without creating much of a stir—or indeed without always being identified correctly. Over the past generation, it has become the country's signature variety, made in styles ranging from clean, fruity and agreeable to impressively complex in the right hands.

PINOT NOIR Most of Argentina's wine regions are too warm to grow thin-skinned Pinot Noir, but remote Patagonia has turned out to be ideal for it, producing velvety, aromatic examples.

SYRAH Argentinean vintners often blend Syrah with other red grapes, typically Malbec. But on its own, Syrah can yield great wines full of dark, brooding fruit and spice.

WINE TERMINOLOGY

Most Argentinean wine labels identify grape variety, the region where the grapes were grown, the producer's name and the vintage. *Bodega* is the term for a winery; the word *finca* refers to a vineyard or estate. The designation *reserva* is applied to red wines with a year of aging in oak barrels before release (six months for whites). *Gran reserva* wines require two years of aging for reds and a year for whites.

Producers/ Argentina

ACHAVAL FERRER

Fans of this superstar winery held their collective breath when it was sold to SPI Group, owner of Stolichnaya vodka, in 2011. So far, so good, but the concern is understandable: Achaval Ferrer has been devoted to the kind of high-cost-for-high-quality winemaking that doesn't generate easy profits. Under the guidance of Italian winemaker Roberto Cipresso, the winery thins grape clusters for low yields and employs French oak barrels. The famous single-vineyard Malbecs are among the world's finest; look to the basic tier for a more affordable taste.

BOTTLES TO TRY
- Cabernet Sauvignon / $$
- Finca Bella Vista Malbec / $$$$

BODEGA CATENA ZAPATA

This onetime bulk-wine producer underwent a radical change when Nicolás Catena took it over in 1989. During his stint teaching economics at Berkeley in the 1980s, Catena had witnessed Napa Valley's great transformation and returned to Mendoza with big ambitions. Today he and his physician daughter, Laura, preside over one of Argentina's iconic estates. Notable wines include those from the Catena, Catena Zapata and Catena Alta tiers, plus the entry-level Alamos line.

BOTTLES TO TRY
- ○ Catena Chardonnay / $$
- ● Catena Cabernet Sauvignon / $$

BEST VALUE PRODUCERS / ARGENTINA

1. BODEGA CATENA ZAPATA **2.** CLOS DE LOS SIETE **3.** FAMILIA ZUCCARDI **4.** TERRAZAS DE LOS ANDES **5.** TRAPICHE

BODEGA Y VIÑEDOS O. FOURNIER

José Manuel Ortega Gil-Fournier became a passionate wine collector during his days as a high-rolling investment banker. The hobby turned into a mission when the Spanish-born Ortega bought the first of his three Argentinean estates, a 650-acre property in the Uco Valley, in 2000. What's remarkable, given Ortega's relatively recent entry into the business, is how fantastic the wines are. Winemaker José Spisso fashions reds and whites that compete with the country's best across a range of prices.

BOTTLES TO TRY

○ Urban Uco Torrontés / $

● B Crux / $$

CHEVAL DES ANDES

Argentina's most high-profile (and costliest) wine comes from this joint venture between Mendoza's Terrazas de los Andes (see p. 254) and Bordeaux's Château Cheval Blanc. The oft-stated aim at Cheval des Andes is to produce the *grand cru* of the Andes, pairing top Bordeaux expertise with exceptional Argentinean vineyards. The refined, sometimes flamboyantly ripe Bordeaux-style blend features Malbec and Cabernet Sauvignon.

BOTTLE TO TRY

● Cheval des Andes / $$$$

CLOS DE LOS SIETE

France's superstar wine consultant Michel Rolland brought together seven Bordelais partners to create an ambitious group of wineries in the rugged foothills of the Andes. Clos de los Siete is the crown jewel of the group, and also the name of Rolland's signature bottling, drawn from the partnership's 2,100 acres in the cool, desert-like Uco Valley. A Malbec-based blend of Bordeaux varieties crafted in a velvety, luscious style, the Clos de los Siete bottling is a striking world-class bargain.

BOTTLE TO TRY

● Clos de los Siete / $$

FAMILIA ZUCCARDI

This is one of Argentina's largest family-owned wineries, now headed by third-generation Sebastian Zuccardi. Though the budget-priced Santa Julia brand accounts for much of the volume, the various Zuccardi-label lines are mostly premium wines from Uco Valley vineyards (the entry-level Serie A line is sourced more widely). Sebastian Zuccardi is a restless experimenter: He embarked on an ambitious micro-mapping of the soils and built a new winery equipped with all-cement fermenters, which he believes offer the purest translation of *terroir*.

BOTTLES TO TRY

○ Zuccardi Q Chardonnay / $$

● Zuccardi Serie A Malbec / $

TERRAZAS DE LOS ANDES

Moët & Chandon's (see p. 279) scouting efforts in Argentina for its Bodegas Chandon sparkling wines also led to the 1999 opening of this Mendoza still wine producer. It has superb vineyard locations across the region, with grape varieties tailored to *terroir* and elevation. Under former Bodegas Chandon winemaker Hervé Birnie-Scott, Terrazas's offerings range from the very well-priced Altos del Plata line to the more refined *reserva* and single-vineyard cuvées. The stellar Cheval des Andes (see p. 253) is a Terrazas joint venture with Bordeaux's Château Cheval Blanc.

BOTTLES TO TRY

○ Torrontés Reserva / $

● Altos del Plata Malbec / $

TIKAL

International bon vivant, intellectual and sportsman Ernesto Catena—son of Nicolás and brother of Laura (see Bodega Catena Zapata, p. 252)—has been determined since 2002 to make his own mark on the wine world, one boutique label at a time. His brands include Siesta, Animal, Alma Negra, Padrillos and Tikal, named for his son. Juicy, flavorful and accessible yet very well made, Tikal's premium-priced Malbecs and Malbec blends are meant for current enjoyment, with names like Amorío ("love affair") and Júbilo ("rejoice").

BOTTLES TO TRY

● Amorío / $$

● Júbilo / $$$

TRAPICHE

This Mendoza giant has become one of Argentina's most ambitious wineries. Soon after Daniel Pi took over as chief winemaker more than a decade ago, Trapiche released an impressive collection of single-vineyard Malbecs that helped restore luster to the brand, which had been increasingly focused on value-driven wines. While its top bottlings compete with boutique labels, Trapiche remains a source of everyday, affordable wines. Two great examples are the peppery Oak Cask Malbec and, at a small step up in price, the ebulliently fruity Broquel Bonarda.

BOTTLES TO TRY

○ **Chardonnay** / $
● **Broquel Bonarda** / $

VALENTÍN BIANCHI

Many quality-focused producers handpick their grapes and sort them twice to select only pristine fruit, but very few lavish that kind of care on wines that sell for around $10 a bottle, as this winery does for its Valentín Bianchi and Elsa Bianchi lines. Needless to say, higher-priced tiers, like Famiglia and Particular and top-end Enzo Bianchi, receive even closer attention. Founded in 1928, this large-scale pillar of Argentinean winemaking is currently run by the family's third generation, with consulting help from Robert Pepi of California's Eponymous Winery.

BOTTLES TO TRY

● **Valentín Bianchi Cabernet Sauvignon** / $
● **Famiglia Bianchi Malbec** / $$

VIÑA COBOS

Celebrated California winemaker Paul Hobbs has been working in Argentina as a consultant since 1989. In the late '90s, he founded Viña Cobos in Mendoza with two Argentinean enologists. This is one of Argentina's surest bets for a delicious bottle across all price tiers. Hobbs's classic style—rich, indulgent, crowd-pleasing, with impressive poise and balance—is evident even in the entry-level single-variety Felino wines. The pricey Bramare Vineyard Designates and collectors' Cobos bottlings are simply some of South America's very finest wines.

BOTTLES TO TRY

○ **Felino Chardonnay** / $$
● **Felino Malbec** / $$

Chile

This narrow toothpick of a country–
it's only 217 miles across at its widest
point–somehow has a seemingly
inexhaustible number of impressive
wine regions. The vineyards near
Santiago have long been known for
inexpensive, appealing reds as well
as ambitious Cabernets. But not that
long ago, vivid, minerally Sauvignon
Blancs started appearing from areas
like San Antonio and Leyda, hard
up against the cold Pacific Ocean.
And in the past couple of years,
Chilean winemakers have started
producing impressive wines in
even more far-flung regions, like
Bío Bío and Elqui. All of this
exploration has revealed a much
more complex country than wine
lovers may expect.

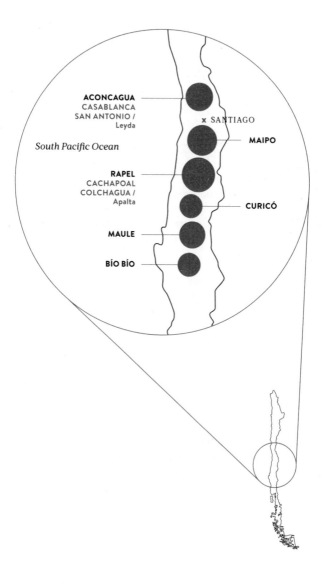

ACONCAGUA
CASABLANCA
SAN ANTONIO /
Leyda

x SANTIAGO

MAIPO

South Pacific Ocean

RAPEL
CACHAPOAL
COLCHAGUA /
Apalta

CURICÓ

MAULE

BÍO BÍO

REGIONS TO KNOW

ACONCAGUA Just about an hour's drive from Chile's capital, Santiago, the Aconcagua region includes a cluster of valleys that have achieved phenomenal success with crisp, cool-climate red and white grape varieties, chiefly Pinot Noir and Sauvignon Blanc. Look for wines from the **Casablanca** and coastal **San Antonio** subregions, as well as **Leyda,** San Antonio's best-known zone.

BÍO BÍO This rainy southern district is a stronghold of basic table wine. Recently, forward-looking vintners here have been creating exciting Pinot Noirs and aromatic whites, such as Riesling and Gewürztraminer.

COSTA, ENTRE CORDILLERAS & ANDES An attempt to simplify and rationalize Chile's appellation system, these new geographic designations identify three broad north–south viticultural areas: coastal (Costa), central (Entre Cordilleras) and Andean (Andes). Most of Chile's wines come from the Entre Cordilleras ("between ranges") area, between the Coastal Range and the Andes.

CURICÓ The vineyards of this region north of Maule are planted with a wide diversity of grape varieties. Curicó is best known as a producer of everyday-drinking, big-bodied Cabernet Sauvignon and Carmenère and fresh Sauvignon Blanc.

ELQUI & LIMARÍ These two far northern districts burst out of obscurity over the past decade with stunning renditions of Sauvignon Blanc and savory, elegant Syrah. The latter has become a specialty of Elqui, one of the country's northernmost wine-producing regions.

MAIPO Chile's most famous wine region is also (perhaps not coincidentally) the one closest to Santiago. Its herb-tinged Cabernets, particularly those from the high Andean foothills to the east, in **Alto Maipo,** are some of the country's best.

MAULE Most of the wines coming from this relatively warm zone in south-central Chile are unremarkable, though exceptions are becoming more common, including some terrific old-vine Carignane and fruity, straightforward Merlot.

RAPEL About one Chilean wine out of four comes from the central Rapel Valley, which encompasses the **Colchagua** and **Cachapoal** subregions. Warm temperatures help red wine grapes flourish in Colchagua, where Cabernet Sauvignon vines dominate; other heat-loving grapes such as Carmenère, Merlot and Syrah thrive here as well. Some of Colchagua's most acclaimed cuvées come from its small, sheltered **Apalta** area. The Cachapoal subregion is also making increasingly ambitious reds.

KEY GRAPES: WHITE

CHARDONNAY The cooler, ocean-influenced zones near the coast produce Chile's best Chardonnays.

SAUVIGNON BLANC This Bordeaux variety has become Chile's flagship white. Bright, fragrant Sauvignons come from regions up and down the coast, where cool breezes help develop its tangy citrus and grass flavors.

KEY GRAPES: RED

CABERNET SAUVIGNON Chile is supremely well-suited to the grape, which is why it's the most widely planted variety here and why a disproportionate number of the planet's top Cabernet bargains come from Chile. Offering savory notes and firm structure, in addition to exuberant fruit, the best Chilean Cabernets can challenge premier California bottlings in quality.

CARMENÈRE Like Merlot, the grape for which it was long mistaken, Carmenère came to Chile from France's Bordeaux region. The confusion is understandable: Both varieties possess plummy fruit and fine-grained tannins, but Carmenère expresses an alluring spicy accent that's distinctively Chilean.

MERLOT Often combined with Cabernet Sauvignon or Carmenère grapes in blends, Chilean Merlot is typically juicy, supple and loaded with layers of ripe plum and black cherry.

PINOT NOIR Chilean Pinots have improved dramatically in recent years, though quality can be inconsistent. This finicky grape grows best in marginal climates with cooler temperatures, which in Chile means coastal zones like Casablanca, San Antonio and the latter's Leyda subzone, as well as remote Bío Bío.

SYRAH The Chilean wine industry's Francophile bent shows in its Syrahs, which at their best combine powerful dark fruit with notes of pepper and violets. Young plantings in districts like Elqui and Limarí are turning out impressive new wines from cool-climate vineyards.

WINE TERMINOLOGY

Chilean labels list the name of the winery (*viña*) or brand, grape variety and often a proprietary name for blends. Producers are increasingly using single-vineyard designations and adding the term *reserva* to top-quality wines. Introduced in 2011, the Costa, Andes and Entre Cordilleras geographical designations (see p. 258) are now appearing on wine labels.

Producers/ Chile

ALMAVIVA

Chilean powerhouse Concha y Toro and Baron Philippe de Rothschild SA teamed up to create the Almaviva label. First released in 1996 and sourced in part from the Maipo Valley's legendary Puente Alto vineyard, the single Almaviva bottling is a powerful, velvety red blend based on Cabernet, with smaller amounts of Carmenère and other Bordeaux varieties. With such resources and expertise behind it, it's no surprise that Almaviva consistently ranks among Chile's greatest (and priciest) reds.

BOTTLE TO TRY
● Almaviva / $$$$

CARMEN

A large, well-funded winery that's part of the Claro Group (a broad-based conglomerate), Carmen has two major historical claims to fame: It was Chile's first commercial winery back in 1850; and it was where, more than 160 years later, Carmenère was "rediscovered" in its vineyards (it had been mistaken for Merlot). Carmenère is now Chile's signature grape variety. Winemaker Sebastián Labbé has extraordinary fruit sources available to him, since Carmen owns prime vineyard land around the country, and it shows in the top wines. The clean-styled entry-level wines can also be attractive for the price.

BOTTLES TO TRY

○ Gran Reserva Sauvignon Blanc / $
● Gran Reserva Carmenère / $

CONCHA Y TORO

Chile's largest producer, Concha y Toro makes wine from every major grape in every major region of the country. Of its dizzying lineup (there are 12 sub-brands), the affordable Casillero del Diablo and midpriced Marques de Casa Concha lines can offer great value. The more expensive Terrunyo wines highlight specific vineyard blocks. Two world-class reds top off the portfolio: the voluptuous Carmín de Peumo Carmenère and the ageworthy, Bordeaux-influenced Don Melchor Cabernet Sauvignon.

BOTTLES TO TRY

○ Casillero del Diablo Chardonnay / $
● Marques de Casa Concha Cabernet Sauvignon / $$

CONO SUR

Among the world's largest Pinot Noir producers, Cono Sur—the name refers to South America's Southern Cone region—is a huge, Burgundy-inspired part of the Concha y Toro group. With 2,200 acres of grapes across 40 vineyards, the winery offers an extensive, generally strong-value portfolio, ranging from the bargain-priced Bicicleta label on up to the Silencio Cabernet Sauvignon. Cono Sur's Pinots (which received the long-term ministrations of consultant Martin Prieur from Burgundy's Jacques Prieur) and Chardonnays deserve special attention.

BOTTLES TO TRY

○ Reserva Especial Chardonnay / $
● Visión Pinot Noir / $$

DE MARTINO

The family-owned De Martino winery is certified organic, and in 2009 it launched Chile's first carbon-neutral wine program. But the main reason to seek out this Maipo-based label is its terrific wines. De Martino helped pioneer Carmenère grapes, and remains one of the most reliable producers of the variety. Under winemaker Marcelo Retamal, De Martino has also ventured into emerging zones: The ripe, juicy Legado Chardonnay Reserva, for example, comes from the Limarí Valley, where cooler temperatures temper the grape's lushness.

BOTTLES TO TRY

○ **Legado Chardonnay Reserva** / **$**
● **Estate Carmenère Reserva** / **$**

KINGSTON FAMILY VINEYARDS

Though Michigan-born mining engineer Carl John Kingston failed to find gold in early 1900s Chile, his ranch on the chilly Casablanca coast is yielding vinous gold these days. Putting their chips on cool-climate red grapes, Kingston's descendants began planting vines in 1998 and released their first wines in 2003. Growing Syrah and Pinot Noir on windblown hills best known for whites isn't easy, but the results have been taut wines of subtle elegance at realistic prices. California Pinot specialist Byron Kosuge and local talent Evelyn Vidal share winemaking duties.

BOTTLES TO TRY

○ **Cariblanco Sauvignon Blanc** / **$$**
● **Tobiano Pinot Noir** / **$$**

LAPOSTOLLE

Alexandra Marnier Lapostolle (of the family that owns Grand Marnier) co-founded this stylish, deep-pocketed Colchagua estate, whose image-making factors include 900-plus acres of organically and biodynamically farmed vineyards and the French expertise of such luminaries as consultant Michel Rolland and winemaker Jacques Begarie. Lapostolle wines are reliable across the portfolio, from the bargain-priced Casa Sauvignon Blanc to the midpriced Cuvée Alexandre and up to Clos Apalta, the much-celebrated Carmenère-based, Bordeaux-style blend.

BOTTLES TO TRY

○ **Casa Sauvignon Blanc** / **$**
● **Cuvée Alexandre Cabernet Sauvignon** / **$$**

LUIS FELIPE EDWARDS

This winery has come a long way since Luis Felipe, Sr., bought 148 acres in 1976 and released the first wine under his name in 1994—it now has nearly 4,600 acres and produces 2.5 million cases of wine a year. The operation is still family-owned and -run, and headquartered at the original (much-transformed) Colchagua estate. The extensive lineup stretches from rock-bottom-priced supermarket quenchers to the connoisseur-quality LFE wines, like the taut, structured LFE 900 reds, sourced from Chile's highest vineyards.

BOTTLES TO TRY

○ Family Selection Sauvignon Blanc / $

● LFE 900 Single Vineyard / $$$

MATETIC VINEYARDS

Founded in 1999 in the scenic Rosario Valley, the Matetic family's thriving operation is well known, both for the wines made under the Corralillo and EQ labels and as a center of upscale tourism, thanks to its restaurant and boutique hotel. From the beginning, Matetic has had a posse of consultants from California, including Truchard alum Ken Bernards, Shake Ridge's Ann Kraemer and the late biodynamics guru Alan York (all 395 acres are certified biodynamic). The region's cool climate and clay-granite soils result in racy wines, like the flagship Syrah, as well as graceful Pinot Noirs and Chardonnays.

BOTTLES TO TRY

○ EQ Chardonnay / $$

● Corralillo Syrah / $$

MIGUEL TORRES

The Chilean arm of Spain's Torres wine empire lays claim to being the first foreign winery to open in Chile (in 1979). During his wine studies in Dijon, Burgundy, Miguel A. Torres (see p. 120) was tipped off by a Chilean classmate to the country's possibilities. In true Torres style, the company's ambitions have escalated: It now has some 865 vineyard acres in six properties throughout Chile. Of special interest are its efforts to showcase the underrated País grape, long associated with bulk wine.

BOTTLES TO TRY

○ Santa Digna Sauvignon Blanc Reserva / $

● Cordillera Vigno Carignan / $$

MONTES

One of the top names in Chilean wine, Montes is also one of the most dependable. The visionary founding partner, winemaker Aurelio Montes, was among the first to recognize the potential of Chile's hillside terrain in 1988, and to exploit the Colchagua Valley for Syrah and heat-loving Bordeaux red varieties. While most of Montes's wines are affordable bottlings designed for near-term drinking, his top cuvées—like the Cabernet-based Alpha M, the Purple Angel Carmenère and the Folly Syrah—have expanded the definition of "Chile's best." Montes continues to push the envelope with its new Outer Limits series.

BOTTLES TO TRY

○ Alpha Chardonnay / $$
● Classic Series Cabernet Sauvignon / $

SANTA RITA

Although headquartered near the city limits of Santiago, this giant winery (and wine-tourist magnet) owns vineyards all over Chile. Founded in 1880, Santa Rita was a pioneer in promoting European grape varieties and became one of the country's largest brands under the Claro Group's umbrella. Best known for value bottlings, the winery also makes one of Chile's great Cabernets, Casa Real. Vineyards in emerging zones, such as Limarí and Leyda, are paying off with crisp whites and elegant reds.

BOTTLES TO TRY

○ 120 Sauvignon Blanc / $
● Casa Real Cabernet Sauvignon / $$$$

VERAMONTE

Chile's Huneeus family, which also owns Quintessa in Napa (see p. 194) and the Primus, Ritual and Cruz Andina brands in Chile and Argentina, created this trailblazing estate in 1998, where they pioneered cool-climate wines from the Casablanca Valley. A veteran of Sonoma's Benziger (see p. 170), Veramonte's head winemaker, Rodrigo Soto, brings a boutique touch to one of Chile's most reliable producers of crisp, affordable Sauvignon Blanc and Chardonnay. The winery's Pinot Noir has caught up to its whites with a string of fragrant, gracefully fruity vintages.

BOTTLES TO TRY

○ Sauvignon Blanc / $
● Pinot Noir / $

VIÑA ERRÁZURIZ

Eduardo Chadwick, a fifth-generation descendant of Errázuriz's founder, has transformed this historic Aconcagua winery into one of Chile's most cutting-edge producers, boldly pitting his top wines against Bordeaux first growths in blind tastings. This is another of Chile's large-scale producers, but across the board—from under-$15 varietals to the triple-digit-priced Viñedo Chadwick Cabernet Sauvignon and Seña Bordeaux blend—Errázuriz is among the country's best bets for getting a solid bottle of wine. Its more affordable offerings include the estimable Single Vineyard Carmenère and the wild-fermented cuvées.

BOTTLES TO TRY

○ Wild Ferment Chardonnay / $$
● Single Vineyard Carmenère / $$

VIÑA LEYDA

Few wineries better demonstrate the tremendous potential of the breezy, misty coastal Leyda zone (and the larger San Antonio subregion) than this namesake label. Overcoming the lack of water for irrigation (now delivered via a five-mile pipeline) and a cool season that makes grape-growing risky, Viña Leyda proved that the region could yield terrific wines. In the hands of winemaker Viviana Navarrete, one of the impressive cadre of younger female winemakers in Chile, Leyda's 568 acres of vineyards yield refreshing, elegant Pinot Noir, spicy Syrah and some of Chile's most exciting and vibrant whites.

BOTTLES TO TRY

○ Single Vineyard Garuma Sauvignon Blanc / $$
● Single Vineyard Las Brisas Pinot Noir / $$

South Africa

South Africa is the only African wine-producing country of any note, with wines that walk a line between the ripe generosity of the New World and the more austere elegance of the Old World. Value hunters will find that South Africa abounds in overachieving white varietals, including fantastic old-vine Chenin Blancs and zippy Sauvignons, while at the high end, collectors can look for Stellenbosch's Bordeaux-inspired reds. *Terroir*-driven idealists will discover a new generation of ambitious, minimalist young winemakers, most of them in the up-and-coming Swartland region. They're a great example of the potential of South Africa, and a fine reason to start drinking its varied, impressive wines right now.

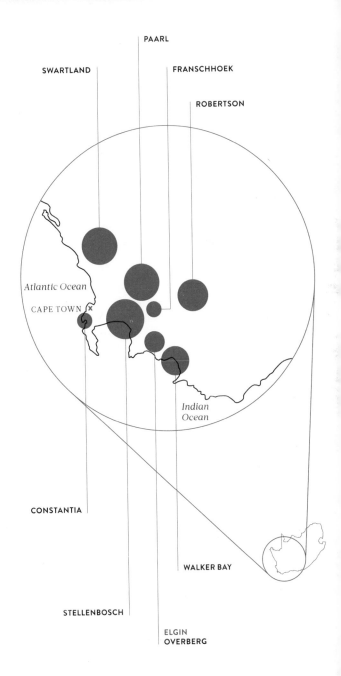

SWARTLAND

PAARL

FRANSCHHOEK

ROBERTSON

Atlantic Ocean

CAPE TOWN ✕

Indian Ocean

CONSTANTIA

WALKER BAY

STELLENBOSCH

ELGIN
OVERBERG

REGIONS TO KNOW

CONSTANTIA Breezy, coastal Constantia started providing wines for thirsty Cape Towners centuries ago. Today its vineyards specialize in cool-climate renditions of Sauvignon Blanc, Chardonnay and Pinot Noir.

FRANSCHHOEK The "French Corner," named for the Huguenots who settled there in the 17th century, is an hour east of Cape Town and a major wine tourism destination. Franschhoek is surrounded by mountains on three sides, which makes for a range of climates. The area's prestigious estates produce a variety of wines, including Cabernet Sauvignon and Chardonnay.

OVERBERG Located where the Atlantic and Indian Oceans meet, Overberg—especially its **Elgin** subzone—is home to talented winemakers styling fresh, cool-climate wines.

PAARL While large cooperative wineries dominate this region north of Stellenbosch, smaller, quality-focused producers are increasing in number. Red grapes—chiefly Cabernet, Shiraz, Pinotage and Merlot—thrive in Paarl's relatively warm climate.

STELLENBOSCH The heart of South African wine country, Stellenbosch produces many acclaimed wines, mostly red (though good whites exist, too). Some of the best-known bottlings are blends based on Cabernet Sauvignon and Merlot.

SWARTLAND Old vines and unirrigated vineyards have made Swartland, once known for rustic red wines, a mecca for South Africa's *terroir*-hunting purists. They're making unusual blends and acclaimed reds and whites, notably Shiraz and Chenin Blanc.

WALKER BAY Burgundy grape varieties—i.e., Pinot Noir and Chardonnay—do well in this sea-cooled region on the Indian Ocean side of the Cape of Good Hope.

♟ KEY GRAPES: WHITE

CHARDONNAY & SAUVIGNON BLANC South African Chardonnays tend to fall between the ripe, fruity style of California bottlings and the leaner, mineral-driven French versions; Sauvignon Blancs range from herbal and tart to exotically fruity.

CHENIN BLANC South Africa's most important white grape (also known here as Steen) yields wines ranging in style from zippy to lush, with more tropical flavors than exhibited by French Chenin Blancs.

♟ KEY GRAPES: RED

CABERNET SAUVIGNON & SHIRAZ (SYRAH) Wines crafted from these powerful grapes make South Africa's most convincing case for greatness. Cabernet Sauvignon is the country's dominant red variety, and plantings of Shiraz (also called Syrah here) have nearly doubled in the past decade. These reds tend to split into two camps: Some South African vintners aim for ripe, plush styles akin to California's and Australia's, while others make earthier, herb-inflected versions that recall French bottlings.

PINOTAGE Once South Africa's preeminent red grape, Pinotage—a cross of Pinot Noir and Cinsaut—now ranks behind Cabernet and Shiraz in plantings. Pinotage's distinctively pungent, funky notes limit its appeal abroad, although a few vintners craft fruitier versions that downplay its varietal funk.

PINOT NOIR With an increase in plantings in cool-climate regions, Pinot Noir production is on the rise in South Africa, though little is currently exported to the US.

WINE TERMINOLOGY

South African wine labels list winery name, variety, region and vintage. Blends may be given proprietary names; the varieties that went into them usually appear on the back label. Regional names are regulated by the Wine of Origin system, which recognizes official winegrowing areas.

Producers/ South Africa

A.A. BADENHORST FAMILY WINES

Cousins Hein and Adi Badenhorst moved to Swartland in 2008 to work 69 acres of old-bush-vine Chenin Blanc, Cinsaut and Grenache, and pressed an old cellar from the 1930s back into service. Adi's winemaking is resolutely natural and traditional, resulting in wines of great individuality. The top tier consists of the Rhône-style red blend and Chenin-based white blend; look to the Secateurs and Curator lines for bargains.

BOTTLES TO TRY

○ Secateurs Chenin Blanc / $

● "Red Blend" / $$$

CAPE POINT VINEYARDS

On a narrow peninsula surrounded by the Atlantic Ocean, Cape Point has established a reputation for layered, luscious, world-class Sauvignon Blanc. Former investment banker Sybrand van der Spuy bought the land in 1996 to mine kaolin but fell under the wine spell. Winemaker Duncan Savage creates individualistic wines like the Isliedh ("ai-lay") Sauvignon Blanc–Sémillon, which is fermented mostly in barrel but with a portion in amphorae.

BOTTLES TO TRY

○ Sauvignon Blanc / $$

○ Isliedh / $$$

DEMORGENZON

In 2003, DeMorgenzon's new owners, investment guru Wendy Appelbaum and her polymath husband, Hylton, began a reset of their Stellenbosch winery. Among other innovations, these passionate music-lovers pipe Baroque pieces through their cellar and vineyards. Does it work? DeMorgenzon does makes one of South Africa's greatest Chenin Blancs, from age-old bush vines. Look for stellar deals under the winery's DMZ label.

BOTTLES TO TRY

○ Reserve Chenin Blanc / $$$

● DMZ Syrah / $

FAIRVIEW / GOATS DO ROAM

Few South African vintners have as much passion for Rhône varieties as Fairview's Charles Back, who introduced Viognier to the country and named his high-quality, value-driven Goats do Roam label in a cheeky homage to Côtes du Rhône. But Back and chief winemaker Anthony de Jager are serious about their craft, and the high-end wines, such as the Caldera Southern Rhône blend, the Shirazes and the dessert wine La Beryl Blanc, compete with the country's best. The entry-level La Capra bottles can be very good deals indeed.

BOTTLES TO TRY
- ○ La Capra Chenin Blanc / $
- ● Goats do Roam / $

HAMILTON RUSSELL VINEYARDS

Hamilton Russell's wines compete with world-class whale watching as a compelling reason to visit the fishing village of Hermanus. Located on breezy Walker Bay, the area is home to some of the continent's southernmost vineyards. Cool-climate pioneer Tim Hamilton Russell gambled astutely on the region in the mid-1970s; today his son Anthony crafts its two benchmark estate-grown cuvées, a Pinot Noir and a Chardonnay. Part of the profits from Anthony's second label, Southern Right (named for a species of whale that frequents the bay), benefit conservation initiatives, some of them whale-related.

BOTTLES TO TRY
- ○ Chardonnay / $$
- ● Pinot Noir / $$$

INDABA WINES

Widely distributed in the US, Indaba wines deliver lively, fresh, straightforward drinking pleasure, often at single-digit prices. The winery's long-term grower contracts on prime vineyards (including parcels of old-vine Chenin Blanc) ensure the consistency of its wines. The juicy Chenin Blanc and Sauvignon Blancs are especially dependable. Another reason to appreciate Indaba: The brand donates a significant portion of its profits to support education initiatives.

BOTTLES TO TRY
- ○ Chenin Blanc / $
- ● Mosaic / $

KEN FORRESTER VINEYARDS

Many of Ken Forrester's labels display the date 1689, the year the first winery was established on the Stellenbosch land that eventually became his flagship vineyard. Forrester didn't jump into winemaking until 1993, after a successful career as a restaurateur, but his brilliant old-vine Chenins have turned him into a poster boy for the variety. His luscious FMC cuvée tops a portfolio that includes multiple Chenin Blancs—all food-friendly and affordable. The juicy Petit line bottlings offer great value, though the layered Reserves are only a few dollars more.

BOTTLES TO TRY

○ Old Vine Reserve Chenin Blanc / $

● Petit Cabernet Sauvignon-Merlot / $

MULDERBOSCH VINEYARDS

Founded in 1989, Mulderbosch was relaunched in 2011 after its acquisition by Terroir Capital, an investment firm led by Charles Banks, the former co-owner of Napa's iconic Screaming Eagle winery. With Adam Mason as its new winemaker, consulting help from Screaming Eagle alum Andy Erickson and bigger facilities, Mulderbosch is aiming to become a major player in the US. Expect to see more of its famous pungent-but-crowd-pleasing Sauvignon Blanc, its lineup of Chenins and the soft, refined Bordeaux-style red, Faithful Hound.

BOTTLES TO TRY

○ Sauvignon Blanc / $$

● Faithful Hound / $$

NEIL ELLIS WINES

One of the foundational names in modern South African wine, Neil Ellis first made his mark as a *negociant*. These days, Ellis and his children, including winemaker Warren, operate out of their own winery in Stellenbosch's Jonkershoek Valley, but the grapes come from Ellis's savvily selected vineyards across the Western Cape, including Chardonnay from Elgin and Sauvignon Blanc from Groenekloof. Well worth looking for are the winery's spicy, *terroir*-driven Vineyard Selection reds and the value-oriented Sincerely bottlings.

BOTTLES TO TRY

○ Elgin Chardonnay / $$

● Pinotage / $$

BEST VALUE PRODUCERS / SOUTH AFRICA
1. DEMORGENZON / DMZ 2. GOATS DO ROAM 3. INDABA WINES
4. KEN FORRESTER VINEYARDS 5. MULDERBOSCH VINEYARDS

THE SADIE FAMILY WINES / SEQUILLO CELLARS

This winery's first vintage in 2000 marked a turning point for the Swartland wine region, not least because it brought the visionary Eben Sadie to bat for the cause. His 59 acres are divided into 53 parcels planted to a prodigious number of varieties. Sadie produces a small quantity (under 4,000 cases a year) of distinctive, very pricey wines, like the layered, cerebral Old Vines series. Far more affordable are his Sequillo-label wines.

BOTTLES TO TRY
○ Skurfberg / $$$
● Sequillo / $$

TOKARA

Tokara enjoys one of the world's most scenic winery locations, at the crest of Stellenbosch's Helshoogte Pass. Its industrial-chic building complex is an upscale tourism center with a serious winery attached. Star winemaker Miles Mossop crafts reasonably priced all-estate wines such as the complex, high-end Director's Reserve series. The entry-level Chardonnays and Shirazes are well worth seeking out for more affordable drinking.

BOTTLES TO TRY
○ Chardonnay / $$
● Director's Reserve / $$$

VILAFONTÉ

Legendary California winemaker Zelma Long and her grape-guru husband, Phil Freese, joined with Warwick Wine Estate's Mike Ratcliffe to create this pioneering label in 1996. From their 40 acres of Bordeaux-variety vines in the Simonsberg-Paarl area, the partners fashion two concentrated and refined boutique cuvées: Series M, based on Malbec and Merlot, and Series C, based on Cabernet Sauvignon and Cabernet Franc.

BOTTLES TO TRY
● Series M / $$$
● Series C / $$$$

Champagne & Other Sparkling Wines

Champagne is without question the world's most famous sparkling wine— so much so that the Champenois launched an ongoing campaign to prevent people from using their region's name as a blanket term. Champagne is indeed wonderful, but there are also affordable Proseccos and elegant Franciacortas from Italy; citrusy, earthy Cavas from Spain; and from the US, impressive Champagne equivalents at half the price. All are worth exploring, and all are worth opening for everyday dinners as well as special occasions and parties.

CHAMPAGNE

CLAIM TO FAME

The word *Champagne* properly (and in most countries, legally) refers only to the sparkling wine made in France's Champagne region, due east of Paris. That Champagne became the global model of refinement for sparkling wines was the result of centuries of winemaking trial and error and the unique limestone soil and ocean-influenced climate of Champagne itself. Two turning points in the long saga were the producers' ability to harness the crucial second fermentation in the bottle, which gives the wine its intensity and persistence, and then to manage the bottle itself (before the mid-17th century, the pressure of the bubbles often caused bottles to explode). Champagne still sets the standard for sparkling wine, and the market has never been stronger, for both the famed *grande marque* houses and the new darlings of aficionados: small, single-grower bottlings.

REGIONS TO KNOW

AUBE Located about 70 miles southeast of central Champagne, the slightly warmer Aube region has traditionally been a major source of fruit—mainly Pinot Noir—for large producers in the more prestigious Marne districts, to the north. But increasingly its top growers—chiefly in the **Côte des Bar** subregion—are vinifying their own wines rather than selling their grapes.

CÔTE DES BLANCS & CÔTE DE SÉZANNE Côte des Blancs lies south of the city of Epernay and produces wines renowned for freshness and delicacy. Chardonnay dominates both this region and its neighbor to the south, Côte de Sézanne.

MONTAGNE DE REIMS This stretch of wooded hills and vineyards follows a mountain ridge between Reims and Epernay and focuses primarily on Pinot Noir. Most of Champagne's *grand cru* vineyards for red grapes are found here.

VALLÉE DE LA MARNE Champagne's largest growing region encompasses the city of Epernay and the land west of it. Vallée de la Marne is home to many acclaimed grower-producers, with the best vineyards located on hillsides above the Marne River.

❦ KEY GRAPES: WHITE

CHARDONNAY Thanks to the Champagne region's cool climate and stony soil, its Chardonnay yields fresh, lively whites. The variety accounts for less than a third of the region's vineyards. Most Champagnes are blends of Chardonnay, Pinot Noir and Pinot Meunier; blends based on Chardonnay typically offer crisp, leaner profiles and mineral notes.

❦ KEY GRAPES: RED

PINOT MEUNIER This grape is prized for its ability to ripen early (a lifesaver for vintners in cooler vintages) and for its fruity, floral flavors, which round out a traditional Champagne blend.

PINOT NOIR Burgundy's great red-wine grape is used in Champagne to make both rosés and whites. The main grape of the Aube and Montagne de Reims subregions, black-skinned Pinot Noir lends body, richness and bright berry tones to Champagne.

WINE TERMINOLOGY

BLANC DE BLANCS Most Champagnes are made from blends of red and white grapes, but Blanc de Blancs ("white from whites") cuvées are crafted entirely from white grapes—Chardonnay— and represent about 5 percent of all Champagne.

BLANC DE NOIRS These white Champagnes are made using red grapes only (Pinot Noir and Pinot Meunier). To create the wine, the clear juice of red grapes is drained from the skins before it gains any color. (Rosé Champagnes are made by blending a bit of red wine into white sparkling wine or by leaving the red grape skins in the pressed juice for a short time to bleed in color.)

DISORGEMENT The second fermentation inside the bottle gives Champagne its fizz but also creates lees, a yeasty sediment. The disgorgement process removes the lees, typically by freezing the sediment in the bottle's neck and removing the "plug" of ice. The disgorgement date is a key indicator of a nonvintage Champagne's age, and of how long a vintage wine has aged on its lees.

DOSAGE The sugary syrup that is added to most Champagne after it is disgorged (see above). Dosage tops up the bottle (some wine is lost during disgorgement) and adds some sweetness.

SWEETNESS LEVELS The most widely produced Champagnes are labeled *brut* ("dry"). Champagne sweetness levels are categorized as follows, from bone-dry to quite sweet: *brut nature* (a.k.a. *brut zéro* or *non* or *pas dosé*), *extra brut*, *brut*, *extra sec* ("extra dry," but actually sweeter than *brut*), *sec* and *demi-sec*.

MÉTHODE CHAMPENOISE/TRADITIONNELLE In this, the most traditional and costly way to make sparkling wine, a second fermentation is induced in the bottle (rather than in vats; other, lesser methods add carbonation). Only wines from Champagne made using this process may be labeled *méthode champenoise*.

PREMIER CRU Champagne ranks wines by their village of origin. Forty-four villages, chiefly in the Montagne de Reims and the Côte des Blancs, have *premier cru* ("first growth") status.

GRAND CRU Seventeen Champagne villages are designated *grand cru*, the highest regional classification level.

GRANDE MARQUE Meaning a great or major brand, this is a term for large, prestigious Champagne houses.

TÊTE DE CUVÉE A Champagne house's top-tier bottling, usually sold under a proprietary name, such as Moët's Dom Pérignon.

GROWER CHAMPAGNE The term for Champagnes made by grape growers who bottle wines from their vineyards, instead of selling their grapes to large producers. Grower-producers highlight the qualities imparted to wine by the plot where it was grown (its *terroir*). These wines carry a code starting with "RM" (*récoltant manipulant*, or "grower-producer") on their labels. An "NM" (*négociant manipulant*, or "buyer-producer") code signifies a wine made in whole or in part from purchased grapes.

NONVINTAGE/NV Most Champagnes are nonvintage, i.e., they are blends of wines from different vintages, a practice designed to maintain a consistent house style from year to year.

VINTAGE Producers make vintage Champagnes only in exceptional years; these wines are typically aged longer and priced higher than their nonvintage counterparts.

Producers/ Champagne

BOLLINGER

Founded in 1829, Bollinger is still family-owned, a rarity today among *grande marque* houses. Made entirely or largely of Pinot Noir in the rich, toasty, full-bodied house style, Bollinger wines, especially top vintage bottlings like Vieilles Vignes Françaises and La Grande Année, develop body and structure from barrel fermentation. Even the nonvintage Special Cuvée, with its high percentage of aged reserve wines, is known for its richness.

BOTTLES TO TRY

○ La Grande Année Brut / $$$$
○ Special Cuvée Brut NV / $$$$

GOSSET

The small, top-quality house of Gosset dates back to 1584, making it one of the Champagne region's oldest producers. The Renaud Cointreau family bought Gosset in 1993 and has wisely preserved the essentials that make the brand stand out. Because they don't undergo the softening of a secondary, malolactic fermentation that's common in Champagne, Gosset's powerful, full-bodied wines have a distinctive freshness and lift.

BOTTLES TO TRY

○ Excellence Brut NV / $$$
○ Celebris Extra Brut / $$$$

KRUG

LVMH-owned Krug produces some of the world's costliest wines—its Clos d'Ambonnay was introduced at over $3,000 per bottle. Scarcity, prestige and marketing drive up the prices, but these wines can be truly thrilling, with extraordinary complexity, endless layers of flavor and great longevity. This results partially from the addition of very high amounts of reserve wines. Fermenting the reserve wines in oak adds a signature richness, too.

BOTTLES TO TRY

○ Grande Cuvée Brut NV / $$$$
● Rosé Brut NV / $$$$

LANSON

Lanson's house style—fresh and taut—is a point of pride for this venerable Champagne producer, established in 1760. Unlike most Champagnes, Lanson's don't go through a malolactic fermentation to soften the wines' acidity. The basic Black Label bottling is a good, affordable choice for fans of uncompromisingly tart, bracing sparklers. A big step up is the Extra Age cuvée: Created to honor the house's 250th anniversary, it gains intensity from long-aged *grand cru* and *premier cru* wines. Lanson's continuity over several ownership changes—it's now owned by the Boizel Chanoine Champagne Group—has been assured by Jean-Paul Gandon, the head winemaker for more than 40 years.

BOTTLES TO TRY
○ Black Label Brut NV / $$$
○ Extra Age Brut NV / $$$$

LOUIS ROEDERER

Louis Roederer sources 70 percent of its grapes from estate-owned vineyards, more by far than most major Champagne houses. That kind of quality control contributes to Roederer's remarkable consistency; another factor is winemaker Jean-Baptiste Lécaillon, who has been with the winery since 1989. Roederer's famed prestige cuvée, Cristal, was created for Czar Alexander II of Russia in 1876. The complex, elegant Brut Premier nonvintage is an excellent introduction to the house style.

BOTTLES TO TRY
○ Brut Premier NV / $$$
○ Cristal Brut / $$$$

MOËT & CHANDON / DOM PÉRIGNON

Moët & Chandon bottled its first vintage Champagne in 1842, and it has been choosy ever since, creating vintage-dated wines in just 70 of the ensuing years. The vintage bottlings—a white and a rosé—make up a tiny portion of its vast output. Moët is best known for its popular Impérial Brut, now drier and crisper than in years past. Moët's legendary *tête de cuvée*, the vintage-dated Dom Pérignon, is today its own brand, crafted by the winemaking genius Richard Geoffroy.

BOTTLES TO TRY
○ Impérial Brut NV / $$$
○ Dom Pérignon Brut / $$$$

PERRIER-JOUËT

Fruity, delicate, floral wines are the hallmark of this Epernay producer, which celebrated its 200th anniversary in 2011. Now part of the Pernod Ricard drinks group, Perrier-Jouët owns top vineyards in the Chardonnay-centric Côte des Blancs subregion. The Chardonnay-based house style is most apparent in Belle Epoque, a.k.a. Fleur de Champagne, Perrier-Jouët's best-known cuvée, instantly recognizable by its flower-strewn enameled bottle, a design dating from the Art Nouveau period.

BOTTLES TO TRY
- Grand Brut NV / $$$
- Belle Epoque Brut / $$$$

PHILIPPONNAT

This small, highly esteemed house has had ups and downs over the years, but since its current owners, the Boizel Chanoine Champagne Group, brought Charles Philipponnat back to his ancestral cellar from Moët in 1999, the trend has been largely up. The house has always made great wine from its signature walled vineyard, the Clos des Goisses, arguably Champagne's finest. Philipponnat's nonvintage Royale Réserve has a special story, too: The three cuvées' reserve wines—up to 30 percent of the blend—are kept in oak barrels that are topped and filled using a version of sherry producers' solera system (see p. 293).

BOTTLES TO TRY
- Royale Réserve Brut NV / $$$
- Clos des Goisses Brut / $$$$

PIERRE PÉTERS

Rodolphe Péters farms his family estate's 63 parcels, most in the Côte des Blancs, and most of those in the Chardonnay Champagne bull's-eye of *grand cru* vineyards centered on the town of Le Mesnil-sur-Oger. This grower-producer's most famous wine is the *tête de cuvée* Les Chétillons, sourced from three parcels of very old vines that express the purity and minerality of Le Mesnil; like most of the subregion's great bottlings, this one can take some time to open up. The Cuvée de Réserve nonvintage bottling shares the same elegance and raciness.

BOTTLES TO TRY
- Cuvée de Réserve Blanc de Blancs Grand Cru Brut NV / $$$$
- Cuvée Spéciale Les Chétillons Blanc de Blancs Grand Cru Brut / $$$$

BEST OF THE BEST PRODUCERS / CHAMPAGNE

1. BOLLINGER **2.** DOM PÉRIGNON **3.** LOUIS ROEDERER
4. POL ROGER **5.** SALON

POL ROGER

Sir Winston Churchill was a friend of the Pol-Roger family and a huge fan of their wines—so much so that the house named its prestige cuvée in his honor. This Epernay producer is still family-owned and makes strong wines at every level. Blended from the three main Champagne grapes, Pol Roger's basic Brut Réserve ("White Foil") is vividly crisp yet creamy, with complex fruit and toast notes and a dosage at the drier end of the brut scale.

BOTTLES TO TRY
○ **Brut Réserve NV** / $$$
○ **Sir Winston Churchill Brut** / $$$$

RUINART

Cloth merchant turned vintner Nicolas Ruinart is credited with kicking off the "modern" Champagne (i.e., sparkling wine) business in 1729. His pioneering house is now part of the expansive LVMH luxury portfolio, and Chardonnay is very much its backbone. The top Dom Ruinart Blanc de Blancs features a roundness and depth from its blend of Montagne de Reims fruit (as opposed to the leaner Côtes des Blancs grapes).

BOTTLES TO TRY
○ **Dom Ruinart Blanc de Blancs Brut** / $$$$
● **Brut Rosé** / $$$$

SALON

The product of Eugène-Aimé Salon's singular vision in the early 1900s, Salon has stayed true to its roots within the Laurent Perrier corporate umbrella. The house releases only one Champagne under its name, and only in exceptional years. Made from *grand cru* Chardonnay grapes grown in the Côte des Blancs around Le Mesnil-sur-Oger, the wines are bottle-aged for 10 years. The supremely elegant and layered wine that emerges is one of most coveted and expensive whites in the world.

BOTTLE TO TRY
○ **Blanc de Blancs Brut** / $$$$

TAITTINGER

With roots dating back to 1734, Reims-based Taittinger is one of the few major family-owned Champagne houses. Its range of elegant yet oddly underrated wines can be first-rate, defined by a sleek, minerally frame enriched by just enough creamy lushness to keep them from tasting austere. The entry-level Brut La Française is delicate and fine-boned. Prélude, a 50-50 blend of Pinot Noir and Chardonnay, has more body and intensity and makes a terrific alternative to Taittinger's pricey prestige cuvées.

BOTTLES TO TRY

○ Brut La Française NV / $$$
○ Prélude Grands Crus Brut NV / $$$$

ULYSSE COLLIN

Like his mentor Anselme Selosse, Olivier Collin is a true believer in natural winemaking—his native yeast fermentations linger and linger, sometimes for months, without artificial prompting, in neutral oak barrels, and are bottled unfined and unfiltered with extremely low dosage. Clearly wanting the *terroir* to shine through with little intervention, Collin works his vineyards closely and uses many organic methods, including manual and horse plowing. His distinctive grower-produced wines have made the former law student a star among the cognoscenti.

BOTTLES TO TRY

○ Blanc de Blancs Extra Brut NV / $$$$
○ Les Maillons Blanc de Noirs Extra Brut NV / $$$$

OTHER SPARKLING WINES

REGIONS TO KNOW

FRANCE Beyond Champagne, France abounds with sparkling wines, most made with grapes typical of each region. Eight of the country's sparkling wine appellations—the largest is the Loire—are able to use the term *crémant* to indicate they are produced by the *méthode traditionnelle*. Wines labeled *mousseux* may or may not have been made this way.

ITALY Italy's northern regions are the main source of the country's *spumante* (sparkling) wines. One of the best is made in Lombardy's Franciacorta zone, using the traditional method (*metodo classico* in Italian). Also noteworthy are Piedmont's flowery Moscato d'Asti and light red, berry-scented Brachetto d'Acqui. The Veneto's affordable and popular Proseccos are made mostly from the Glera variety (see p. 77) using the Charmat method, in which the wine undergoes its second fermentation in tanks rather than bottles. Some of the best Proseccos come from the Conegliano Valdobbiadene area north of Venice.

SPAIN Long marketed as less costly Champagne substitutes, Spain's Cavas by law must be made by the *méthode traditionnelle* (see p. 277). Most Cavas come from the Catalonia region near Barcelona and are based largely on the white Macabeo grape.

UNITED STATES The quality of American sparkling wines has been steadily improving. While the best bottlings still come from the cooler regions of Northern California—such as Carneros, Sonoma and the Anderson and Green Valleys—Washington state, Oregon, New York and New Mexico are making a growing number of complex, vibrant sparklers.

Producers/Other Sparkling Wines

FRANCE
BOUVET-LADUBAY

Dating to 1851, Bouvet is one of the Loire's standard-bearers in the production of *méthode traditionnelle* sparklers, ranging in style from *brut zéro* to extra brut to demi-sec. Its well-known basic brut is made from Chenin Blanc and Chardonnay in a crisp, refreshing style. Justin-Marcel Monmousseau bought Bouvet in 1932, and his descendants have run the winery since then, despite changes in ownership. In 2006, then-owner Taittinger sold Bouvet to Dr. Vijay Mallya, chairman of India's sprawling UB Group, with interests in beer, spirits and much else.

BOTTLES TO TRY
○ Signature Brut NV / $
● Excellence Rosé Brut NV / $

FRANÇOIS PINON

Former child psychologist and seventh-generation vintner François Pinon is best known for his still wines, which are among the benchmark bottlings of the Loire's renowned Vouvray region. It's no wonder then that his *pétillant* (sparkling) cuvées are equally compelling. Typically sourced from younger vines and less-ripe lots within his 33 estate acres, all certified organic, Pinon's sparklers are made in both brut and *brut non dosé* styles.

BOTTLES TO TRY

○ Brut NV / $$

● Brut NV / $$

LANGLOIS-CHATEAU

The Loire Valley produces more sparkling wine than any French region after Champagne, and its top *crémants*—like those of Langlois-Chateau—can offer amazing value. In 1973, Bollinger (see p. 278) acquired this respected producer and has invested significantly in it over the years, allowing the firm to purchase more vineyards and upgrade its facilities, and giving it a higher consumer profile. Langlois-Chateau ages its pear-inflected *crémant* on its lees for 24 months rather than the typical nine months, which helps give it unusual lushness. The rosé is classic Loire: All Cabernet Franc, it offers light, delicate berry flavors.

BOTTLES TO TRY

○ Crémant de Loire Brut NV / $$

● Crémant de Loire Brut NV / $$

ITALY
FERRARI

The first Ferrari to bring the name to prominence wasn't the carmaker's founder, Enzo, but Giulio Ferrari (no relation), who established this winery in Trentino in 1902 based on a radical premise: that sophisticated Italian sparkling wine could be made from Chardonnay. He was the first in Italy to devote his vineyards to the French grape. Ferrari's *metodo classico* sparkling wines, like the brut and Perlé bottlings, are now among the most highly regarded in Italy, and priced accordingly, though they are still notable bargains compared to Champagnes.

BOTTLES TO TRY

○ Brut NV / $$

○ Perlé / $$$

MIONETTO

This well-known label is a source of terrific, gently priced Prosecco (and other sparkling wines). A key to Mionetto's success is its location in Valdobbiadene, the hilly subregion of Veneto, where terraced vines yield the area's best grapes for Prosecco. Another factor is the winery's close ties with growers, many of whom have been supplying it with fruit for decades. In the large lineup, the crisp, zesty brut bottling stands out. For Moscato fans, the graceful *dolce* (lightly sweet) version is a go-to choice.

BOTTLES TO TRY

○ **Moscato Dolce NV / $**
○ **Prosecco Brut NV / $**

MONTE ROSSA

This is one of the producers that have placed Franciacorta on the sparkling wine lover's map of the world. Directed by Emanuele Rabotti, the son of the founders, the far-from-small-scale family concern farms 170-plus acres of vines and produces nearly 42,000 cases a year. Much of that is the base nonvintage brut, Prima Cuvée, made from Chardonnay with a dash of Pinot Noir and Pinot Blanc and bottle-aged for more than two years. The prestige Cabochon cuvée rests for at least three years in bottle, and can be a ringer for fine Champagne at two-thirds the price.

BOTTLES TO TRY

○ **Cabochon Brut / $$$**
○ **Prima Cuvée Brut NV / $$$**

SPAIN
FREIXENET

Propelled by the phenomenal success of its two flagship Cavas, Carta Nevada and Cordon Negro, Catalonia's Freixenet has become an international powerhouse, with wineries all over the world. The union by marriage of the Ferrer and Sala winemaking families resulted in the release in 1914 of the first Freixenet *méthode traditionnelle* sparkling wine. Still family-owned, Freixenet delivers reliably delicious, well-priced Cavas. The pink-hued Elyssia Pinot Noir is berry-driven and elegant; the ubiquitous black-bottled Cordon Negro is fresh, tasty and balanced.

BOTTLES TO TRY

○ **Cordon Negro Brut NV / $**
○ **Elyssia Gran Cuvée Brut NV / $$**

GRAMONA

Independent, family-owned Gramona is one of the benchmark Cava producers in the rugged Penedès region outside Barcelona. Today the fifth generation of the Gramona-Batlle family works from the futuristic underground Celler Batlle winery. Their investments in R&D and land have clearly benefitted the extensive Gramona portfolio of still and sparkling wines. These are high-quality products with *tête de cuvée*-like touches, such as giving the III Lustros Gran Reserva five years of bottle aging.

BOTTLES TO TRY

○ Imperial Gran Reserva Brut / $$

○ III Lustros Gran Reserva Brut Nature / $$$

RAVENTÓS I BLANC

Inspired by his travels in Champagne, Josep Raventós Fatjó made what is widely held to be the first Spanish *méthode traditionnelle* sparkler in 1872, laying the foundation for the successful Codorníu brand (and an entire industry). Raventós i Blanc was founded in 1986 by a branch of the Raventós family to craft fine sparkling wine from estate grapes. In 2012, reacting to what its owners saw as the pursuit of volume over quality, Raventós left the Cava DO and declared a new designation, Conca del Riu Anoia, focused on *terroir*-driven, organic and biodynamic viticulture.

BOTTLES TO TRY

○ L'Hereu / $$

● de Nit / $$

UNITED STATES
ARGYLE WINERY

This pioneering winery released its first sparkling wines in 1987, when the idea of fine Champagne-style wines from Oregon raised more eyebrows than enthusiasm among potential buyers. Argyle's co-founder Rollin Soles persevered, and now the winery's elegant sparklers rank among the country's finest (its still wines can be very fine as well). Made in six styles using traditional Champagne techniques and varieties, they are all vintage-dated. Soles's protégé Nate Klostermann has been in charge of the Argyle cellar since Soles stepped aside in 2013.

BOTTLES TO TRY

○ Vintage Brut / $$

○ Extended Tirage / $$$$

DOMAINE CARNEROS

Domaine Carneros's classic French-style château is a familiar sight to wine tourists on California's Route 12. Founded in 1987 by Taittinger (see p. 282) and directed by Eileen Crane from the start, the winery has established itself as one of the state's top sparkling wine producers, its offerings a viable alternative to French sparklers, especially at the entry-level price. The far costlier flagship Blanc de Blancs bottling, Le Rêve, echoes the graceful power of Taittinger's Champagnes. Nearly all of Domaine Carneros's grapes, including those for its notable still wines, come from four certified-organic estate vineyard sites.

BOTTLES TO TRY

○ Brut / $$
○ Le Rêve / $$$$

DOMAINE CHANDON

Moët & Chandon (see p. 279) doesn't do things in a small way. The Champagne giant's resources allowed Domaine Chandon, its Napa Valley sparkling wine facility, to acquire a massive 1,000 acres in Carneros, for leaner Pinot Noir and Pinot Meunier, as well as vineyards in Yountville (the home ranch), for richer Pinot Noir and Chardonnay, and in Mount Veeder, for a smaller-berried, mountain Chardonnay. Chandon's broad range of offerings—including still wines—is generally fairly priced.

BOTTLES TO TRY

○ Brut Classic NV / $$
○ Étoile Brut NV / $$

GLORIA FERRER CAVES & VINEYARDS

Despite the abundance of still wine makers in California's cool Carneros zone in the mid-1980s, there were no sparkling houses there until José Ferrer (of the Spanish wine family behind Freixenet; see p. 285) founded this estate, named for his wife, Gloria, on land acquired in 1982. Four years later, the winery began turning out well-regarded sparkling whites and rosés. The 335 estate acres are planted mainly to Pinot Noir, which takes the lead role in most Gloria Ferrer wines, from signature sparklers like the creamy, lively Blanc de Noirs to varietal still wines.

BOTTLES TO TRY

○ Royal Cuvée Brut / $$
○ Sonoma Brut NV / $$

GRUET WINERY

In addition to remarkable cacti, central New Mexico's high desert now grows grapes for delicious sparkling wine, thanks to the groundbreaking efforts of the Gruet family. Founders of France's G. Gruet et Fils Champagne house, the Gruets planted an Albuquerque-area vineyard in 1984, and five years later released their first New Mexican sparkling wine. The apple-and-citrus-driven basic brut and toasty Blanc de Noirs in particular are among the best-value sparkling wines made anywhere.

BOTTLES TO TRY
○ Brut NV / $
○ Blanc de Blancs / $$

IRON HORSE VINEYARDS

Audrey and Barry Sterling were wine pioneers in the cool, foggy Green Valley subregion of the Russian River Valley in the 1970s. Since then, the Sterling family has been producing some of California's most refined sparkling wines, as well as noteworthy still wines, from estate Chardonnay and Pinot Noir plantings. Iron Horse sparklers display French-style raciness and leaner-bodied charm, with an extra underpinning of flavor from extended bottle aging on the lees.

BOTTLES TO TRY
○ Classic Vintage Brut / $$$
○ Wedding Cuvée / $$$

ROEDERER ESTATE

When famed Champagne house Louis Roederer (see p. 279) came to America in 1982, it chose not to follow Mumm and Domaine Chandon to Napa Valley. Instead, then-president Jean-Claude Rouzaud went with his own sense of where the best sparkling wine grapes would grow. Today the Roederer winery in Northern California's Anderson Valley crafts some of America's top sparkling wines. Adhering to Champagne tradition, Roederer adds substantial reserve wines, aged in French oak casks, to its cuvées. The older wines lend depth and nuance beyond their price to the nonvintage brut and brut rosé; the vintage white and rosé L'Ermitage wines rival true Champagne in quality.

BOTTLES TO TRY
○ Brut NV / $$
○ L'Ermitage / $$$

SCHARFFENBERGER CELLARS

When John Scharffenberger founded this winery in the then-boondocks of Anderson Valley in the early 1980s, it and nearby Roederer Estate looked set to alter the course of American sparkling wine, with grapes from cooler, more Champagne-like climate conditions infusing the wines with extra vibrancy. In Roederer's case, that's exactly what happened, while Scharffenberger was sold, changed its name and generally lost its way. Now owned by Roederer's parent, Scharffenberger Cellars is staging a comeback. With red-fruit aromatics from Pinot Noir and extra textural richness from base wines put through a secondary, malolactic fermentation, its Brut Excellence offers terrific value.

BOTTLES TO TRY

○ Brut Excellence NV / $$
● Brut Rosé Excellence NV / $$

SCHRAMSBERG VINEYARDS

Venerable Schramsberg—revived by the late Jack and Jamie Davies in 1965 when it was a century old—is making its finest sparkling wines these days. Bottlings like the foundational Blanc de Blancs and the high-end J. Schram and Schramsberg Reserve now show the result of years spent scouting top grape sources. Any given wine may be blended from Napa, Sonoma, Mendocino and Marin County grapes, and vinified in multiple ways to layer in complexity. The Daviess' son Hugh and sparkling wine vintner Keith Hock are leading this top winery to new heights.

BOTTLES TO TRY

○ Blanc de Blancs / $$$
○ J. Schram / $$$$

SOTER VINEYARDS

Tony Soter, a pioneering California winemaker and consultant and founder-owner of Etude Wines (see p. 179), moved from Napa Valley to the Willamette Valley for this venture. Made from very low-yielding Chardonnay and Pinot Noir vines and bottled drier than many French Champagnes, Soter's brut rosé is one of the New World's most impressive sparklers. The winery's still Pinot Noirs from its home Mineral Springs Vineyard are among Oregon's most refined and accomplished wines.

BOTTLE TO TRY

● Brut Rosé / $$$$

Fortified & Dessert Wines

The most exciting news right now in fortified wines is sherry. Long maligned, almost universally (and mistakenly) thought of as always sweet, this complex, beautiful wine from southern Spain has become a favorite of hip sommeliers. Other dessert wines (save for Moscato, which has found odd success with both sorority girls and rap stars) get less press but are no less worth investigating: from Italian vin santos to French Sauternes and Barsacs to the most storied of them all, vintage port from Portugal's Douro Valley.

FORTIFIED WINES

The practice of fortifying wines involves adding a neutral spirit before bottling. Traditional fortified wines include sherry, port, Madeira and Marsala, although variations abound. These wines have a higher alcohol content—usually 16 to 20 percent—than typical unfortified wines. With some exceptions (like fino sherry and vintage port), these wines can be sipped over time; they have the consumer-friendly trait of maintaining their flavors and aromas when repeatedly opened and recorked.

FORTIFIED WINES

SHERRY

CLAIM TO FAME

Made only in southern Spain's Jerez region, sherry is stereotyped in the US as an aperitif, but it is actually a vastly underrated food wine. Dry fino styles complement salty, savory dishes; sweeter olorosos are delicious with desserts. Sherry gains its distinctive taste from the Jerez area's chalky soils and, in most cases, from flor, a yeast that appears on the surface of the wine as it ferments. Flor helps give sherry its nutty, appley tones, while a neutral spirit, added after fermentation, increases its alcohol and body. Except for a handful of rare, vintage-dated wines (called *añadas*), all sherries are blends of wines from different years, combined in a blending system called solera. The blending process and long aging result in consistent, complex wines that come in two basic types, fino and oloroso, and a range of sweetness levels.

KEY GRAPES

The white Palomino grape is the principal variety used to make sherry; sweeter styles of the wine are made with the white Pedro Ximénez or Moscatel (Muscat of Alexandria) grapes.

WINE TERMINOLOGY

FINO Dry, pale and graceful, with notes of green apple, sea salt and straw, fino sherry is a classic pairing for tapas: from almonds to ham to shellfish. Like white table wine, fino sherry tastes best chilled and loses its appeal within a few days of opening.

AMONTILLADO This nutty sherry starts out as fino, then loses its flor and ages in the barrel for many years (at least for high-quality versions). The resulting oxidation is what gives amontillados their darker color. The finest examples are dry; "medium" amontillado is sweeter, though not as sweet as most olorosos.

MANZANILLA Made around the port city of Sanlúcar de Barrameda, this fino sherry is racy and bone-dry. Its lighter alcohol and salty tang make it terrific with seafood or tapas.

OLOROSO Darker than finos and shading from dark gold to amber, olorosos are more highly fortified, which prevents the formation of flor. Exposure to oxygen darkens their color and creates nutty, earthy flavors. Most olorosos are sweet, though dry examples are usually of high quality and worth seeking out.

PALO CORTADO With the freshness of an amontillado and the body and depth of an oloroso, this relatively rare sherry is exposed to oxygen as it ages. Some vintners create inexpensive shortcuts to the style by blending amontillado and oloroso.

PEDRO XIMÉNEZ/PX Made from partially raisined grapes, this rich, viscous and ultra-dark sherry can stand in for dessert.

CREAM SHERRIES These sweet, often simple sherries are typically made from a blend of young sherries—usually oloroso—that are sweetened with partially fermented, fortified Pedro Ximénez wines. "Pale" versions are lighter in color and taste.

VOS This term designates any sherry with an average age of over 20 years. Made in a smooth and complex style, these wines can be dark and intensely nutty. VOS stands for *Vinum Optimum Signatum,* a Latin phrase meaning "certified best wine," but the category is easier to remember as "very old sherry."

VORS Although this designation is reserved for sherries with an average age of over 30 years, some VORS (*Vinum Optimum Rare Signatum,* or "certified best rare wine") bottlings are much older. While they are most often used to boost the complexity of younger wines, VORS wines are increasingly being bottled and sold on their own.

ALMACENISTA This is a small-scale wholesaler that matures young sherries in a solera and sells them on to larger houses for blending, bottling and shipping. Some of the best sherries are released as small-lot bottlings with an *almacenista* family name.

SOLERA In this sherry blending system, a bodega arranges casks into levels according to wine age. Small amounts of the oldest tier of wines are extracted and replaced by younger wines, which in turn get replaced by even younger wines, and so on. There may be four to as many as 20 tiers, with the oldest ones containing a blend of wines from decades of different vintages.

Producers/ Sherry

EL MAESTRO SIERRA

Upstart barrel-maker José Antonio Sierra created his own bodega in 1830. Still in family hands, El Maestro Sierra was long a kind of sleeping giant, with decades of remarkable stocks built up, and viable soleras between 60 and 100 years old. In 2011, Ana Cabestrero became cellarmaster and is reawakening this small-scale, ultra-high-quality producer. Its fame rests on a trickle of aged VORS bottlings, but the basic Fino is worth seeking out.

BOTTLES TO TRY
- Fino / $$$ (375 ml)
- Oloroso 1/14 VORS / $$$$ (375 ml)

LUSTAU

The go-to name for many sherry lovers, Lustau was founded in 1896 as an *almacenista*; today its own Almacenista line, sourced from smaller local producers, is a connoisseur's delight. The extensive portfolio offers some 30 wines, from cream sherry to 30-year-old VORS bottlings. An excellent introduction is Los Arcos Dry Amontillado, with its firm balance of creamy dried fruit and roasted nuts and a fine cut of acidity.

BOTTLES TO TRY
- Los Arcos Dry Amontillado / $$
- Almacenista Vides 1/50 Palo Cortado / $$$ (750 ml)

VALDESPINO

Devotees of this reliable producer appreciate its wide range: from the barrel-fermented fino, Inocente, and amontillado, Tio Diego (both single-vineyard wines from the famed Macharnudo vineyard), to the aged categories, including the revered VORS bottlings. One of the oldest wineries in Jerez, Valdespino was purchased by Grupo Estévez in 1999, and has gone from strength to strength under top winemaker Eduardo Ojeda.

BOTTLES TO TRY

○ **Inocente Fino** / $$ (375 ml)

○ **Tio Diego Amontillado** / $$

FORTIFIED WINES
PORT

CLAIM TO FAME

Portugal's second-largest city, Oporto, gave its name to the country's emblematic wine. With lush fruit and sweetness, and ranging in style from light, juicy rubies to powerful vintage bottlings, port is the quintessential after-dinner drink. Experimental bartenders are discovering its versatility in cocktails, too, and in the process are freshening up port's dusty image.

KEY GRAPES

Port is a blended wine, made chiefly from five major red varieties (although more than 80 are permitted). The most important of these is Touriga Nacional, with Touriga Franca, Tinta Barroca, Tinto Cão and Tinta Roriz (Tempranillo) valued for bringing qualities like fragrance, fruit, spice and tannins to the blend. Port comes in three main styles: ruby, tawny and vintage. There are also white ports, a wonderful summer drink on the rocks.

WINE TERMINOLOGY

COLHEITAS These are fine, aged tawnies produced from a single vintage (not to be confused with vintage port, opposite). They must be aged in wood for a minimum of seven years.

RUBY The most extensively produced and typically the least expensive style of port, ruby is a juicy, fruity blend of young wines. Ruby reserve ports are more complex, often bearing proprietary names such as W. & J. Graham's Six Grapes. Late-bottled vintage (LBV) ports are thick-textured single-vintage rubies that have been aged four to six years in barrel and are drinkable upon release.

TAWNY Ready to drink on release, barrel-aged tawny ports offer delicate, nutty aromas and notes of dried fruit. In theory, a tawny has been aged in wood longer than a ruby and has thus taken on a lighter, tawny hue. In reality, many inexpensive tawnies are the same age as typical rubies; they are just made with lighter wines. Age-designated tawnies are another matter: Seductive and complex, they're made from blends of the highest-quality ports and released in 10-, 20-, 30- and 40-year-old versions (the figures refer to the average age of the blend's component wines).

VINTAGE Vintage ports are produced from grapes harvested in a single year; they spend only two to three years in cask and age primarily in bottle. Producers declare a vintage in only the best years, usually just two or three times a decade. Decadent vintage ports are big, black, densely flavored wines that age effortlessly for decades. Single-quinta (vineyard) vintage ports are made with grapes from one vineyard, usually in nondeclared vintages.

Producers/ Port

DOW'S

One of the great names in wine, Dow's produces benchmark ports across its portfolio, including vintage bottlings that are legendary for their ability to improve with age. Though Dow's is part of the Symington family stable, its style is typically drier and more austere than that of other Symington brands, such as Graham's and Warre's. For the years in which Dow's doesn't declare a vintage, the single-quinta vintage ports from Bomfim or Senhora da Ribeira and the aged tawnies are stellar options.

BOTTLES TO TRY
- Aged 10 Years Old Tawny / $$$
- Quinta do Bomfim Vintage / $$$

FONSECA

This 200-year-old house is now part of the Fladgate Partnership, but its wines continue to be made by a member of the co-founding Guimaraens family. Today's sixth-generation winemaker David Guimaraens took over the cellar in time for the monumental 1994 vintage, and he's maintained Fonseca's reputation as a pinnacle brand for vintage port ever since. But Fonseca's rich, full-bodied wines also cover port's major bases. For a summery alternative to red port, try Fonseca's white Siroco, which makes a refreshing cocktail poured over ice with a splash of tonic.

BOTTLES TO TRY

○ Siroco / $$

● Bin 27 / $$

QUINTA DO CRASTO

Leonor and Jorge Roquette's famed Crasto (from *castrum*, Latin for "fort") estate is one of the Douro's finest vineyards. The winery produces not only fine vintage port (its grapes are still foot-trodden in traditional *lagares*), but also cutting-edge dry wines (see p. 133). The hidden gem in the fortified lineup may be the affordable, full-flavored LBV port, which is bottled unfiltered to retain its character. The Roquettes' sons, Tomás and Miguel, now manage production and marketing.

BOTTLES TO TRY

● Late Bottled Vintage / $$

● Vintage / $$$

QUINTA DO NOVAL

French insurance giant AXA Millésimes, owner of several Bordeaux châteaus, purchased Noval in 1993, becoming only its third owner since 1715. The company embarked on a major program of replanting, upgrading of facilities and generally returning Quinta do Noval to its grape-treading-by-foot roots. Today the winery provides consistently fine, nearly all estate-grown ports, ranging from the late-bottled vintage to the single-vineyard vintage ports. Noval's most sought-after bottling is the costly Nacional, made in minute quantities with grapes from a single five-acre plot of ungrafted vines.

BOTTLES TO TRY

● Late Bottled Vintage / $$

● Vintage / $$$$

TAYLOR, FLADGATE & YEATMAN

Perhaps the best known of the "British" port houses, with a richly fruited, robust style to match, Taylor is among the most highly regarded producers of late-bottled vintage, aged tawny and, of course, vintage ports. The house's prestige begins with its extensive vineyard holdings, including its gem, the Quinta de Vargellas. Run by the eighth generation of Yeatmans, this is a family affair in more ways than one: Longtime winemaker David Guimaraens, who also handles duties at sister property Fonseca (see opposite), took the reins from his father in 1995.

BOTTLES TO TRY
- Late Bottled Vintage / $$
- 20 Year Old Tawny / $$$

W. & J. GRAHAM'S

The Symingtons (see Dow's, p. 295), who acquired W. & J. Graham's in 1970, are the second family of Scottish origin to guide this house. They followed the founding Grahams, who had employed their ancestor A.J. Symington in 1882. Graham's river-facing Quinta dos Malvedos property, the estate's star vineyard, merits its own bottling in years when the wines are not needed to make one of the house's nearly immortal vintage ports. The vineyard also contributes to Six Grapes, the highly popular and accessibly priced reserve ruby.

BOTTLES TO TRY
- Six Grapes / $$
- Quinta dos Malvedos Vintage / $$$

DESSERT WINES

The longest-lived wines in the world are sweet. Legendary bottlings of Bordeaux's Sauternes and Hungary's Tokaji routinely outlive the people who made them, and offer luscious, honeytinged flavors of incredible complexity (with price tags to match their prestige). But great sweet wines are made all over the world, often at affordable prices. Whether from California, Italy, Australia or elsewhere, they're characterized by ample sweet fruit and enough bright acidity to keep them from being cloying. That acidity also explains why *dessert wine* is a bit of a misnomer: Many of them make a terrific match not only for desserts but also for savory foods, including foie gras and blue cheeses.

WINE TERMINOLOGY

BOTRYTIS Botrytized wines owe their unique taste to *Botrytis cinerea*, a mold (called "noble rot") that affects grapes, concentrating their sugars and shriveling them, which causes each berry to yield just a tiny trickle of juice. Because the grapes are left to hang longer (and are exposed to "ignoble rot" as well), this is a risky and costly process. Among the most prized botrytized wines are Bordeaux's Sauternes, made of Sémillon, Sauvignon Blanc and Muscadelle. Superb examples come from the Sauternes subregion of Barsac. Loire Valley vintners make fine botrytized sweet wines with Chenin Blanc; in Alsace, these wines are identified by the *Sélection de Grains Nobles* designation. German and Austrian vintners use mainly Riesling to craft sublime, luxury-priced botrytized wines, labeled *Beerenauslese* (BA) or *Trockenbeerenauslese* (TBA), depending on sugar levels (see p. 138). Hungary's famous botrytized Tokaji wines have undergone a renaissance in recent years: They are graded by *puttonyos* (a sweetness measure), and the lower 3 and 4 *puttonyos* levels have been eliminated; only top-rated 5- and 6-level wines will now be made. California, Australia, South Africa and New Zealand also make botrytized wines, some of them world-class.

LATE-HARVEST These wines rely on grapes harvested very late in the season, when they have developed extremely high sugar levels. The best-known bottlings come from Germany (marked *Auslese* or *Beerenauslese*, indicating progressively greater sweetness) and Alsace (where they're called *Vendanges Tardives*). California, Australia, South Africa, Chile and the Greek island of Samos make good versions, too.

ICE WINE/EISWEIN This wine is made by pressing grapes that have frozen on the vine, a process that yields very small amounts of sweet, concentrated juice. The most famous ice wines are made from Riesling in Germany and Austria; many great examples also come from Canada.

PASSITO An Italian specialty, *passito* wines are made from grapes that have been dried before pressing. Tuscan vintners use Trebbiano and/or Malvasia to make the local version, vin santo, while Sicilian winemakers use the Zibibbo grape (a.k.a. Muscat of Alexandria) for their delicious *passito* wines.

DOUX This term (meaning "sweet" in French) refers to the sweetest wines produced in the Loire region as well as to sweet Champagnes and Vins Doux Naturels, the lightly fortified wines of southern France (see below). Wines labeled *doux* often have an almost syrupy consistency.

MOELLEUX In the Loire Valley, *moelleux* refers, in theory, to the less sweet of the region's two dessert-wine categories (the other being *doux*). Confusingly, though, there is no official sugar level used to define the category, and some producers use the term even on incredibly sweet bottlings. *Moelleux* wines often gain complexity and sweetness from botrytis (see opposite). The term is also used in other French regions to describe medium-sweet wines.

VIN DOUX NATUREL Fortified with spirits during the fermentation process, these wines are produced mainly in southern France. The two most noteworthy white examples are Muscat de Beaumes-de-Venise from the Rhône Valley and Muscat de Rivesaltes from the Roussillon region; Banyuls is the most famous red Vin Doux Naturel.

Producers/ Dessert Wines

BLANDY'S MADEIRA

No other wine in the world can outlast the extraordinary longevity of fine Madeira, which can reach its peak decades—even centuries—after most wines are finished. In fact, five years ago, Blandy's poured a thrilling Bual wine from 1811, the year of its founding, at tastings celebrating its 200th anniversary. Just as impressive, the company is still owned and run by descendants of its founder, John Blandy. Its intense vintage Malmsey is virtually indestructible; the far more affordable 10-year-old is decadent, caramel-inflected and ready to drink now.

BOTTLES TO TRY
○ Alvada 5 Year Old / $$ (500 ml)
○ Aged 10 Years Malmsey / $$$

CHAMBERS ROSEWOOD WINERY

Founded in 1858 in the Rutherglen region of the Australian state of Victoria, this much-lauded winery produces dry, sweet and fortified wines under the leadership of sixth-generation vintner Stephen Chambers. Though the sweet wines (or "stickies," as they're called in Australia) have an avid following among cognoscenti, these exotically layered marvels remain severely underrated. Chambers Rosewood is most celebrated for its upmarket, rich and concentrated Grand- and Rare-tier Muscats and Muscadelles, but its basic Rutherglen bottlings of these varieties are two of Australia's best dessert-wine values.

BOTTLES TO TRY

○ Rutherglen Muscadelle / $$$ (375 ml)

○ Grand Muscat / $$$$ (375 ml)

CHÂTEAU DOISY-DAËNE

Denis Dubourdieu, a famed University of Bordeaux enology professor much in demand as a consultant, has also run his family's five wineries since 2000. This Sauternes estate in the prestigious Barsac subregion showcases his notions of sustainable agriculture as well as his preference for elegance and profundity over sheer power. The Barsac bottling is typically among the finest wines of the vintage, while the botrytized L'Extravagant can be almost otherworldly. There is also a trickle of dry white.

BOTTLES TO TRY

○ Barsac / $$$ (375 ml)

○ L'Extravagant / $$$$ (375 ml)

CHÂTEAU RIEUSSEC

Over the 30-plus years of their stewardship of this prestigious Sauternes estate, the Domaines Barons de Rothschild (as in *the* Lafite Rothschilds) have returned this gem to its rightful glitter, reducing production, building new cellars and raising the bar for grapes that make it into the final blend (there's also a delicious second wine, Carmes de Rieussec). A Sauternes first growth from 1855 in its own right, Rieussec's vineyards border those of Château d'Yquem, and its sublime wines can be ringers for those of its more famous neighbor, at a more forgiving price.

BOTTLES TO TRY

○ Carmes de Rieussec Sauternes / $$$

○ Sauternes Premier Grand Cru / $$$$

DISZNÓKŐ

Disznókő is one of the Tokaj region's traditional crown jewels—its vineyards were classified as a first growth in 1772 and were first noted as far back as 1413. The estate stole a march on its Hungarian rivals when it was acquired in 1992 not long after the fall of Communism by French conglomerate AXA Millésimes, which swooped in with expertise and investment capital. The restored property is a remarkable 250-acre single vineyard, whose glory is in powerful, unctuous, topaz-colored, botrytized Aszú wines ranked at the top 5 and 6 *puttonyos* end of the sweetness scale.

BOTTLES TO TRY

○ **Late Harvest Tokaji** / $$$ (500 ml)

○ **5 Puttonyos Tokaji Aszú** / $$$$ (500 ml)

SARACCO

Sales of Moscato, a light and often sweet white wine, have exploded recently, and a lot of mediocre bottlings are flooding the market. For benchmark Moscatos from a longtime expert, look to Paolo Saracco, whose exceptional touch with the grape earned him the nickname "the maestro of Moscato." His wines come from Italy's Moscato heartland, in Piedmont's Asti district, but the deftness is all his own: He manages to pack whole floral bouquets into nearly weightless wines (about 6 percent alcohol) that are balanced, graceful, lightly sweet and fantastic with light desserts.

BOTTLE TO TRY

○ **Moscato d'Asti** / $

Pairing Guide

These days the adage "White wine with fish and red with meat" seems to have been replaced with "Drink whatever you like with whatever you want." Both approaches have advantages, but neither is an absolute. The truth is that there is no one principle for creating perfect wine matches beyond the fact that you want to bring together dishes and wines that highlight each other's best qualities rather than obscure them. To help make delicious matches at home, the following pages provide five basic strategies for matching and tips for pairing based on the main course and cooking technique. The specific bottle recommendations are all from this guide.

WINE-PAIRING GUIDELINES

THINK ABOUT WEIGHT One simple approach to pairing wine and food is to match lighter dishes with lighter wines and richer dishes with richer wines. We all know that a fillet of sole seems "lighter" than braised beef short ribs. With wine, the best analogy is milk: We know that skim milk feels lighter than whole milk, and wine is similar. So, for instance, Cabernet Sauvignon or Amarone feels richer or heavier than a Beaujolais or a crisp rosé from Provence.

TART GOES WITH TART Acidic foods—like a green salad with a tangy vinaigrette—work best with similarly tart wines: a Sauvignon Blanc, say, or a Muscadet from France. It might seem as though a richer, weightier wine would be the answer, but the acidity in the food will make the wine taste bland.

CONSIDER SALT & FAT Two things to keep in mind about how your palate works: First, salt in food will make wine seem less sour, softening the edge in tart wines; and fat in a dish—whether it's a well-marbled steak or pasta with a cream sauce—will make red wines seem lighter and less tannic.

SPLIT THE DIFFERENCE In restaurants, a group of people will rarely order the same entrées; instead, someone will order fish, another person a steak, a third the pasta with duck ragù, and so on. In instances like this, go for a wine that follows a middle course—not too rich, not too light, not too tannic. For reds, Pinot Noir is a great option; for whites, choose an unoaked wine with good acidity, like a dry Riesling or a Pinot Gris from Oregon.

MOST OF ALL, DON'T WORRY Pairings are meant to be suggestions. Play around with possibilities and don't get caught up in absolutes. After all, Cabernet may go well with a cheeseburger, but if you don't like cheeseburgers, that doesn't matter at all.

Pairing Chart

	DISH	BEST WINE MATCH
CHICKEN	**STEAMED OR POACHED**	Medium white or light red
	ROASTED OR SAUTÉED	Rich white or medium red
	CREAMY OR BUTTERY SAUCES	Rich white
	TANGY SAUCES MADE WITH CITRUS, VINEGAR, TOMATOES	Medium white
	EARTHY FLAVORS LIKE MUSHROOMS	Light or medium red
	HERBS	Light white
PORK	**GRILLED OR SEARED, LEAN**	Medium red
	GRILLED OR SEARED, FATTY	Rich red
	BRAISED OR STEWED	Rich red
	SWEET SAUCES OR DRIED FRUIT	Medium white
	SPICY INGREDIENTS	Medium white or light red
	CURED OR BRINED	Medium white or rosé

GREAT VARIETIES	BOTTLE TO TRY
Chardonnay (unoaked), Riesling, Gamay	Weingut Selbach-Oster Riesling Kabinett / p. 143
Chardonnay, Chenin Blanc, Marsanne, Tempranillo	Domaine Champalou Vouvray / p. 49
Chardonnay, Viognier	Alban Vineyards Central Coast Viognier / p. 169
Sauvignon Blanc, Verdicchio	Domaine Pascal Jolivet Sancerre / p. 50
Cabernet Franc, Pinot Noir	Failla Wines Sonoma Coast Pinot Noir / p. 180
Albariño, Godello, Pinot Grigio, Vermentino	Bodegas Valdesil Montenovo Godello / p. 115
Cabernet Franc, Sangiovese	Castello di Monsanto Chianti Classico / p. 87
Grenache blends, Merlot	Yangarra Estate Vineyard GSM / p. 237
Cabernet Sauvignon, Malbec	Viña Cobos Felino Malbec / p. 255
Pinot Blanc, Pinot Gris (Alsace), Riesling	Domaine Zind-Humbrecht Pinot Blanc / p. 23
Riesling (off-dry), Gamay, Pinot Noir (lighter-bodied)	Château des Jacques Morgon / p. 44
Sauvignon Blanc, Verdicchio, rosé	Bodegas Gran Feudo Rosado / p. 111

DISH	BEST WINE MATCH
BEEF	
GRILLED OR SEARED STEAKS, CHOPS, BURGERS	Rich red
BRAISED OR STEWED	Rich red
SWEET SAUCES LIKE BARBECUE	Rich red
SPICY INGREDIENTS	Medium red
LAMB	
GRILLED OR ROASTED	Rich red
BRAISED OR STEWED	Rich red
SPICY INGREDIENTS	Light or medium red
FISH	
GRILLED	Medium white, rosé or light red
ROASTED, BAKED OR SAUTÉED	Medium white or light red
FRIED	Light white or rosé
STEAMED	Light white
SPICY INGREDIENTS	Medium white
HERB SAUCES	Light or medium white
CITRUS SAUCES	Light or medium white
SHELLFISH, COOKED	Medium or rich white
SHELLFISH, RAW	Light white

GREAT VARIETIES	BOTTLE TO TRY
Cabernet Sauvignon, Malbec, Merlot	Duckhorn Vineyards Napa Valley Merlot / p. 178
Cabernet Sauvignon, Nebbiolo	Giacomo Borgogno & Figli No Name Barolo / p. 74
Grenache, Zinfandel	Bedrock Wine Co. Old Vine Zinfandel / p. 170
Sangiovese, Tempranillo	Bodegas Muga Rioja Reserva / p. 110
Grenache, Syrah, Zinfandel	Domaine Rostaing Les Lézardes Syrah / p. 58
Cabernet Sauvignon, Malbec, Syrah	Buty Winery Rediviva of the Stones / p. 213
Dolcetto, Pinot Noir	Cloudy Bay Pinot Noir / p. 243
Chardonnay, Riesling, rosé, Pinot Noir	Domaine Drouhin Oregon Arthur Chardonnay / p. 207
Pinot Blanc, Pinot Gris (US or Alsace), Gamay	The Eyrie Vineyards Pinot Gris / p. 208
Grüner Veltliner, Riesling, Vermentino, rosé	Schloss Gobelsburg Tradition Grüner Veltliner / p. 150
Riesling, Sauvignon Blanc (Loire-style)	Domaine Weinbach Réserve Personnelle Riesling / p. 22
Chenin Blanc, Riesling (off-dry)	Chateau Ste. Michelle Eroica Riesling / p. 214
Arneis, Grüner Veltliner, Sauvignon Blanc	Weingut Hirsch Veltliner #1 / p. 151
Chenin Blanc, Pinot Grigio	Livio Felluga Pinot Grigio / p. 80
Chardonnay (unoaked), Grenache Blanc	Domaine Christian Moreau Père & Fils Chablis / p. 36
Albariño, Muscadet, Vinho Verde	Pazo de Señoráns Albariño / p. 116

DISH	BEST WINE MATCH
GAME	
VENISON	Rich red
DUCK OR GAME BIRDS, ROASTED OR PAN-ROASTED	Medium red
DUCK OR GAME BIRDS, RAGÙ OR STEW	Medium or rich red
PASTA	
BUTTER OR OIL	Medium white or rosé
CREAMY, CHEESE SAUCES	Medium white or red
TOMATO-BASED SAUCES	Medium red
SPICY SAUCES	Medium white or light red
MEAT SAUCES	Rich red
FISH AND SEAFOOD SAUCES	Medium white
EGGS	
PLAIN OR WITH HERBS	Sparkling
WITH CHEESE (QUICHE)	Sparkling, medium white or rosé
SALADS	
TART DRESSINGS LIKE VINAIGRETTE	Light white
CREAMY DRESSINGS	Medium white
PASTA & OTHER STARCHY SALADS	Rosé or light red

GREAT VARIETIES	BOTTLE TO TRY
Amarone, Grenache, Monastrell, Syrah	Gramercy Cellars Lagniappe Syrah / p. 215
Carmenère, Merlot, Pinot Noir	Patz & Hall Sonoma Coast Pinot Noir / p. 192
Nebbiolo, Sangiovese, Syrah, Teroldego, Touriga Nacional	Foradori Teroldego Rotaliano / p. 79
Fiano di Avellino, Pinot Blanc, Soave, rosé	Terredora di Paolo Terre di Dora Fiano di Avellino / p. 103
Chardonnay, Barbera, Dolcetto	Cantina Bartolo Mascarello Dolcetto d'Alba / p. 71
Sangiovese	Fattoria Selvapiana Chianti Rufina / p. 88
Riesling (off-dry), Sauvignon Blanc, Carmenère, Dolcetto	Viña Errázuriz Single Vineyard Carmenère / p. 265
Aglianico, Corvina, Malbec, Nebbiolo	Clos de los Siete / p. 253
Vermentino	Argiolas Costamolino Vermentino di Sardegna / p. 99
Champagne or other dry sparkling	Roederer Estate Brut NV / p. 288
Champagne or other dry sparkling, Riesling (dry), rosé	Raventós i Blanc de Nit Brut Rosado / p. 286
Sauvignon Blanc, Vinho Verde	Lapostolle Casa Sauvignon Blanc / p. 262
Chenin Blanc, Pinot Gris	Cristom Vineyards Pinot Gris / p. 207
Rosé, Beaujolais	Domaine Tempier Bandol Rosé / p. 65

Recipes

MAHIMAHI WITH HERBED
WHITE WINE SAUCE & SAUVIGNON BLANC

Total **30 min;** Serves **4**

This sauce's intense herbs—thyme and marjoram—pair beautifully with the grassy, lightly herbal flavors in Sauvignon Blanc.

- ¼ **cup pine nuts**
- 1 **cup bottled clam juice**
- ¼ **cup dry white wine**
- 1 **medium shallot, minced**
- 1 **tablespoon finely chopped thyme**
- 1 **tablespoon finely chopped marjoram**
  Salt and freshly ground pepper
  Four 6-ounce skinless mahimahi fillets
  Extra-virgin olive oil, for rubbing
- 2 **tablespoons finely chopped flat-leaf parsley**

1. In a small saucepan, toast the pine nuts over moderate heat, shaking the pan a few times, until the nuts are fragrant, about 1 minute. Transfer to a plate.

2. Add the clam juice to the saucepan and boil over high heat until reduced by half, about 5 minutes. Add the wine and boil until reduced to ¼ cup, about 5 minutes. Add the shallot, thyme and marjoram and season with salt and pepper. Cover the sauce and keep warm.

3. Light a grill. Rub the fish fillets with olive oil and season with salt and pepper. Grill over high heat, turning once, until nicely charred and just cooked through, about 3 minutes per side. Transfer the fish to plates.

4. Stir the parsley into the wine sauce. Coarsely chop the toasted pine nuts. Spoon the sauce over the fish, sprinkle with the pine nuts and serve.

GRILLED TROUT WITH LEMON-CAPER
MAYONNAISE & RIESLING

Total **25 min;** Serves **4**

Riesling's brisk acidity makes it delicious with lush sauces like the lemon-caper mayonnaise here.

- **3 scallions, thinly sliced**
- **2 tablespoons capers**
- **2 tablespoons chopped parsley**
- **1½ tablespoons fresh lemon juice**
- **½ teaspoon finely grated lemon zest**
- **¾ cup mayonnaise**
- **Salt and freshly ground pepper**
- **Four 10-ounce boneless rainbow trout, heads and pin bones removed**

1. In a mini food processor, pulse the scallions, capers, parsley, lemon juice, lemon zest and mayonnaise until the scallions are finely chopped. Season with salt and pepper.

2. Light a grill or heat a grill pan. Spread ½ tablespoon of the lemon-caper mayonnaise on each side of each trout; season with salt and pepper. Grill the fish over high heat, turning once, until lightly charred and cooked through, about 6 minutes. Serve the trout with the remaining lemon-caper mayonnaise.

SERVE WITH Grilled fennel wedges and grilled scallions.

SIZZLING SHRIMP SCAMPI & CHARDONNAY

Total **30 min;** Serves **8**

Silky whites, such as Chardonnays from California, Chile or Australia, pair well with rich seafood like salmon or these buttery shrimp.

- **2 sticks unsalted butter, softened**
- **3 large garlic cloves, very finely chopped**
- **1 tablespoon plus 2 teaspoons chopped flat-leaf parsley**
- **1½ teaspoons finely grated lemon zest**
- **1 teaspoon fresh lemon juice**
- **½ teaspoon chopped thyme leaves**
- **Kosher salt and freshly ground black pepper**
- **3 pounds large shrimp, shelled and deveined, tails left on**
- **1 tablespoon thinly sliced basil leaves**
- **Crusty bread, for serving**

1. Preheat the oven to 450°. In a medium bowl, mix the butter with the garlic, 2 teaspoons of the parsley, the lemon zest, lemon juice and thyme and season with salt and pepper.

2. In a large gratin dish, arrange the shrimp, tails up, in a circular pattern. Dot the shrimp with the flavored butter and roast for about 10 minutes, until the shrimp are pink and the butter is bubbling. Sprinkle the shrimp with the remaining 1 tablespoon of chopped parsley and the basil leaves. Serve hot, with bread.

MAKE AHEAD The flavored butter can be refrigerated for up to 1 week or frozen for up to 1 month.

OVEN-FRIED CHICKEN & PINOT NOIR

Total **35 min;** Serves **4**

Chicken can easily go with white or red, but for this dish, the light
tannins in Pinot Noir work terrifically with the crisp panko crust.

- **2 large eggs, beaten**
- **2 cups panko**
- **½ cup all-purpose flour**
- **½ teaspoon celery salt**
- **½ teaspoon garlic salt**
- **½ teaspoon cayenne pepper**
- **4 large skinless, boneless chicken thighs, lightly pounded**
- **½ cup canola oil**
- **Lemon wedges, for serving**

1. Place a rimmed nonstick baking sheet on the lower rack in the
oven and preheat the oven to 450°. Put the beaten eggs, panko
and flour in 3 shallow bowls. Season the flour with the celery
salt, garlic salt and cayenne. Dust the chicken with the seasoned
flour, then dip it in the egg, and finally in the panko, pressing to
help the breadcrumbs adhere.

2. Pour the canola oil onto the baking sheet. Carefully dip the
chicken thighs in the oil, being sure to coat both sides evenly, and
arrange them on the baking sheet. Bake the chicken thighs for
about 25 minutes, until they're golden and crispy, turning halfway
through. Drain on paper towels and serve with lemon wedges.

LAMB CHOPS WITH FRIZZLED HERBS & SYRAH

Total **40 min;** Serves **8**

Lamb and Syrah are a classic match, as both can have a lightly gamey character; look to wines from California's Central Coast or France's Rhône Valley.

- ½ **cup extra-virgin olive oil**
- ¼ **cup red wine vinegar**
- 8 **large garlic cloves, chopped**
- ¼ **cup plus 2 tablespoons rosemary leaves**
- 24 **frenched lamb chops (about 5½ pounds)**
- **Vegetable oil, for frying**
- 16 **sage leaves**
- ¼ **cup flat-leaf parsley leaves**
- **Kosher salt and freshly ground pepper**

1. In a large glass baking dish, whisk the olive oil, vinegar, garlic and 2 tablespoons of the rosemary. Add the chops to the marinade and turn to coat. Let stand for 30 minutes.

2. Meanwhile, in a small saucepan, heat ½ inch of vegetable oil until shimmering. Add the remaining ¼ cup of rosemary leaves to the hot oil and fry for 15 seconds. Using a slotted spoon, transfer the rosemary to paper towels to drain. Fry the sage leaves until the bubbles in the oil subside, about 45 seconds; transfer to the paper towels. Add the parsley leaves to the hot oil and cover the pan immediately to avoid splattering; fry for 15 seconds, then add to the other herbs. Season the herbs with salt.

3. Heat a grill pan. Scrape the marinade off the lamb chops and season the chops with salt and pepper. Working in batches, grill the chops over moderately high heat, turning once, just until pink in the center, about 6 minutes total. Transfer the lamb chops to plates, sprinkle with the frizzled herbs and serve.

GRILLED HANGER STEAK WITH
GARLIC-BRANDY BUTTER & CABERNET

Active **30 min;** Total **50 min;** Serves **4**

One reason steak pairs so well with Cabernet is that the wine's firm tannins refresh the palate after each bite. Anything from Napa Cabernet to a classic Bordeaux red would be fantastic here.

- 6 **tablespoons unsalted butter, softened**
- 3 **tablespoons chopped parsley**
- 2 **medium garlic cloves, minced**
- 1 **tablespoon Cognac or other brandy**
- **Salt and freshly ground pepper**
- 3 **tablespoons extra-virgin olive oil, plus more for brushing**
- 3 **large leeks, white and pale green parts only, sliced 1 inch thick**
- 2 **pounds trimmed hanger steaks**

1. In a bowl, mash the butter, parsley, garlic and Cognac; season with salt and pepper.

2. In a large skillet, heat the 3 tablespoons of olive oil. Add the leeks and season with salt. Cover and cook over moderately low heat, stirring occasionally, until tender, about 10 minutes.

3. Light a grill or heat a grill pan. Brush the steaks with olive oil and season with salt and pepper. Grill over high heat, turning once, until nicely charred outside and medium-rare within, 5 to 6 minutes per side. Transfer the steaks to a carving board and let rest for 5 minutes. Slice the steaks across the grain and spread the garlic-brandy butter all over the meat, letting it melt in. Serve with the leeks.

Index of Producers

A

Aalto Bodegas y Viñedos, 122
Abadía Retuerta, 122
Achaval Ferrer, 252
Adam, A. J., 139
Adelsheim Vineyard, 205
Alban Vineyards, 169
Almaviva, 260
Alpha Estate, 157
Alzinger, Weingut, 150
Andrew Will Winery, 212
Angélus, Château, 28
Ànima Negra, 118
Antica Napa Valley, 169
Antica Terra, 205
Antinori, 84
Argiolas, 99
Argyle Winery, 205, 286
Argyros, Estate, 159
Arnaldo Caprai, 95
Artadi, 109
Astrolabe Wines, 242
Au Bon Climat, 169
Aveleda, 131
Avignonesi, 84

B

Badenhorst Family Wines, A.A., 270
Badia a Coltibuono, 85
Banfi, Castello, 87
Barboursville Vineyards, 220
Barry Wines, Jim, 231
Bassermann-Jordan, Geheimer Rat
    Dr. von, 141
Baudry, Bernard, 48
Baumard, Domaine des, 49
Bea, Paolo, 96
Beaucastel, Château de, 59
Beaulieu Vineyard, 170
Bedrock Wine Co., 170
Bending Branch Winery, 220
Benton-Lane Winery, 206
Benziger Family Winery, 170
Bergström Wines, 206
Beringer Vineyards, 171
Bernardus Winery, 171
Bertrand, Gérard, 65
Bianchi, Valentín, 255
Big Table Farm, 206
Bindi Wines, 227
Biondi Santi, 85

Black Star Farms, 220
Blandy's Madeira, 299
Bodegas Franco-Españolas, 109
Bollinger, 278
Bonneau, Henri, 59
Bonterra Organic Vineyards, 171
Borgogno & Figli, Giacomo, 74
Boscarelli, Poderi, 91
Bouchard Père & Fils, 35
Boutari, 158
Bouvet-Ladubay, 283
Brancott Estate, 242
Breton, Catherine & Pierre, 48
Brewer-Clifton, 172
Brokenwood Wines, 227
Bründlmayer, Weingut, 150
Brusset, Domaine, 55
Buehler Vineyards, 172
Buena Vista Winery, 172
Buty Winery, 213

C

Cadence, 213
Calera Wine Company, 173
Canon la Gaffelière, Château, 28
Cape Mentelle, 227
Cape Point Vineyards, 270
Capezzana, 86
Carlisle Winery & Vineyards, 173
Carmen, 261
Casa de la Ermita, 118
Castellare di Castellina, 86
Castell'in Villa, 86
Castro, Álvaro, 130
Catena Zapata, Bodega, 252
Cavallotto, 71
Caymus Vineyards, 174
Cayuse Vineyards, 213
Cerbaiona, 87
Ceretto, 71
Chalk Hill, 174
Chambers Rosewood Winery, 300
Champalou, Domaine, 49
Chapoutier, M., 60
Chappellet Winery, 174
Charvin, Domaine, 56
Chateau Montelena Winery, 175
Chateau Ste. Michelle, 214
Chave, Domaine Jean-Louis, 57
Chehalem, 207
Cheval des Andes, 253
Chevalier, Domaine de, 32